ACADEMIA, INC.

*Tony, one more for your collection! Wishing you all the best,
Love Jamie*

ACADEMIA, INC.
HOW CORPORATIZATION IS TRANSFORMING CANADIAN UNIVERSITIES

JAMIE BROWNLEE

FERNWOOD PUBLISHING · HALIFAX & WINNIPEG

Copyright © 2015 Jamie Brownlee

All rights reserved. No part of this book may be reproduced or transmitted in any form by any means without permission in writing from the publisher, except by a reviewer, who may quote brief passages in a review.

Editing: Jessica Antony
Cover design: John van der Woude
Printed and bound in Canada

Published by Fernwood Publishing
32 Oceanvista Lane, Black Point, Nova Scotia, B0J 1B0
and 748 Broadway Avenue, Winnipeg, Manitoba, R3G 0X3

www.fernwoodpublishing.ca

Fernwood Publishing Company Limited gratefully acknowledges the financial support of the Government of Canada through the Canada Book Fund and the Canada Council for the Arts, the Nova Scotia Department of Communities, Culture and Heritage, the Manitoba Department of Culture, Heritage and Tourism under the Manitoba Publishers Marketing Assistance Program and the Province of Manitoba, through the Book Publishing Tax Credit, for our publishing program.

Library and Archives Canada Cataloguing in Publication

Brownlee, Jamie, author
Academia, Inc. : how corporatization is transforming Canadian Uuniversities / Jamie Brownlee.

Includes bibliographical references and index.
Issued in print and electronic formats.
ISBN 978-1-55266-735-4 (pbk.).--ISBN 978-1-55266-752-1 (epub)

1. Education, Higher--Economic aspects--Canada. 2. Education, Higher--Research--Economic aspects--Canada. 3. Universities and colleges--Economic aspects--Canada. 4. Academic-industrial collaboration--Canada. 5. Business and education--Canada. 6. Corporatization--Canada. I. Title.

LC1085.4.C3B76 2015   338.4'337871   C2015-900675-9
                        C2015-900676-7

CONTENTS

ACKNOWLEDGEMENTS — VIII

1. THE CORPORATE TAKEOVER OF THE UNIVERSITY — 1
CORPORATIZATION 2
WHY FOCUS ON UNIVERSITIES? 5
    Universities as Sites of Social Change 7
CONSTRUCTING A NATIONAL PICTURE 9

2. HIGHER EDUCATION AND CORPORATE POWER — 13
ELITE POWER AND THE ORIGINS OF CANADIAN UNIVERSITIES 14
EARLY CRITICS OF THE CORPORATE UNIVERSITY 16
BETWEEN CAPITALISM AND DEMOCRACY:
REFLECTIONS ON CANADA'S "GOLDEN AGE" 21
CORPORATIZATION AND ACADEMIC CAPITALISM 26
    Academic Capitalism in the Canadian Context 28
FORCES OF RESTRUCTURING: INSIDE-OUT OR OUTSIDE-IN? 29
    The New Corporate Ethos 30
    Globalization, Neoliberalism and the Corporate Offensive 32
    Retrenchment, Austerity and Corporatization 36

3. UNIVERSITY TEACHING AND THE CASUALIZATION OF ACADEMIC LABOUR — 44
CHANGING PRIORITIES: THE TEACHING–RESEARCH NEXUS 44
CASUALIZED ACADEMIC LABOUR 49
    Contract Faculty 50
    The Rise in Contract Faculty 52
    Management Strategy or Market Forces? 59
    The Conditions of Contract Faculty Work 61
    Impacts on Students and Student Learning 65
    The Role of Permanent Faculty 68
    A "Perfected System" 69
    From Tenure to "Just-In-Time": The Future of University Hiring 71

4. THE RISE OF THE STUDENT-CONSUMER — 75
LIBERAL EDUCATION OR VOCATIONAL TRAINING? 75
EDUCATING THE STUDENT-CONSUMER 78
Surveying the Surveys: The Growing Importance of Money and Jobs 79
University Enrolments 81
Learning as a Service Encounter 81
Academic Dishonesty as Market Response 83
The Student-Consumer Paradox 84
CUSTOMERS PAY: TUITION, DEBT AND THE HIGH COST OF LEARNING 84
Provincial Variation in Tuition Fees 87
Canada in Context 89
International Student Recruitment and Fees 91
Proponents and Critics of Tuition Increases 92
What Does the Public Think? 95
Student Debt and Student Aid 96
The Negative Consequences of Rising Tuition and Student Debt 99

5. MANAGING UNIVERSITIES LIKE A BUSINESS — 106
CHANGING OF THE GUARD: UNIVERSITY ADMINISTRATORS IN THE ERA OF CORPORATIZATION 107
The Impact of Fiscal Retrenchment 107
Expanding Ranks and Salaries 108
The New University CEOs 110
Boards of Governors and University-Corporate Board Interlocks 113
CORPORATE GOVERNANCE MODELS 116
The Discourse of Managerialism 117
Centralizing Power in the Academy 117
Performance Indicators 119
University Rankings 120
Marketing the Corporate University 122
Suppressing Academic Freedom 123
CURRICULUM REFORM, CAMPUS INFRASTRUCTURE AND CORPORATE CONTROL 126
Killing Liberal Arts 127
Structured Inequalities: Capital Funding and Public-Private Partnerships 130
Donor Agreements 134

6. THE CORPORATE CORRUPTION OF ACADEMIC RESEARCH — 139
A HISTORY OF FEDERAL RESEARCH POLICY IN CANADA 140
PRIVATIZING PUBLIC KNOWLEDGE: INTELLECTUAL PROPERTY AND COMMERCIALIZATION 147
   Creating the Commercial Infrastructure 148
   Public Subsidy, Private Profit: Universities as Patent Holding Companies 150
   Commercialization: The IP Payoff 151
CORRUPTING ACADEMIC RESEARCH 155
   Research Topics 156
   Research Secrecy 157
   Research Bias 160
   Big Pharma, Biotechnology and the Perversion of Academic Medicine 162
CORPORATIZATION AND SHIFTING RESEARCH AGENDAS 170

7. RESISTING THE CORPORATIZATION OF THE UNIVERSITY — 173
REGULATING CORPORATIZATION 174
IRRECONCILABLE DIFFERENCES 176
   Radical Reformation 177
STUDENT AND FACULTY ENGAGEMENT: BUILDING INTERSECTORAL ALLIANCES 182
   Recent Developments in the Student Movement 182
   Academic Intellectuals Opposing Corporatization 185
RELEVANCE REVISITED 190

APPENDIX A: CHARACTERIZATIONS OF MODERN UNIVERSITIES — 192

REFERENCES — 194

INDEX — 224

ACKNOWLEDGEMENTS

Writing about Canadian universities was a highly personal experience, as I have been part of the university system for my entire adult life. During this time, I have counted on a number of close friends and colleagues. Thanks to Chris, Kevin, Dale and Robyn for their intellectual support and companionship. And to my PhD supervisor, Wally — who has long been a source of academic inspiration — thanks for your guidance and your kindness.

It is, once again, an honour to work with the people at Fernwood. A huge thanks to Wayne Antony, whose insights greatly improved the book. Thanks also to Jessica Antony for skillfully editing the final draft; Beverley Rach and Debbie Mathers for production layout and design; and John van der Woude for cover design.

My family has always been a tremendous source of encouragement, especially my parents Dale and Rod. Thank you for everything you have done for me. And thanks to my uncle Doug, who, as a corporate CEO, has forced me to better defend my arguments through our regular debates. Thanks also to my partner's family, especially the Almdals for the good times and Rodney for always pushing me to "get 'er done." My most heartfelt thanks go to Salena. In addition to being my dance partner and a constant source of love and good humour, she is the most gifted editor I know. Her intellectual contributions were indispensable to improving the quality of this book.

I have always believed, and still do, that public universities are unique and irreplaceable institutions. They are amazing places. I want to thank the students and faculty of this generation, and the next, who are actively working to oppose the corporatization of universities in Canada and around the world.

CHAPTER ONE
THE CORPORATE TAKEOVER OF THE UNIVERSITY

In 2012, Quebec students undertook a series of protests opposing the provincial government's planned tuition increases. The 75 percent fee hike was included in the budget of the Liberal government of Premier Jean Charest. These protests quickly expanded into a broader popular movement and province-wide student strike. On May 22, 2012, the one-hundredth day of the strike, demonstrations took place across the province with students staging a massive rally in Montreal that brought hundreds of thousands of activists into the streets. CLASSÉ, the student federation leading the strike movement, described the march as "the single biggest act of civil disobedience in Canadian history" (Mennie et al. 2012). During the uprisings, Quebec students faced police repression, thousands of arrests and a new law aimed at criminalizing dissent. The provisions of the new law contravened the Quebec and Canadian charters of rights, and included unprecedented restrictions on public protest activity (Annis 2012).

Quebec's striking students received widespread support from parents, teachers, unions, public sector workers and university professors. One of the groups involved in the movement was "Angry Mothers in Solidarity," who launched frequent and spontaneous marches. High school students also staged solidarity walkouts and had a strong presence in the demonstrations. Nightly "casserole" protests (marked by the banging of pots and pans from apartment balconies and streets) and neighbourhood assemblies took place across the province, with solidarity rallies also being held across Canada and in other countries. This high level of support for the Quebec students resulted from the fact that the movement became, over time, a larger social and political struggle against educational commodification and a new social and economic vision of Canadian society (Camfield 2012).

Similar student movements have surfaced in other parts of the world. In 2009, for example, the most dramatic U.S. student mobilizations since the 1970s took place, with thousands of California university students taking part in a mass walk-out and a series of occupations across the entire University of California system (Wollan and Lewin 2009). These protests were in response to a decision to increase tuition fees and other cutbacks to universities, which followed a series of similar actions that had already compromised a post-secondary system once known as one of the finest in the world. Also in 2009, universities in France were disrupted by strikes and occupations in opposition to President Nicolas Sarkozy's proposed neoliberal "reforms," while student groups in Austria occupied university classrooms for an entire semester to contest university financing proposals. Two years later in Greece, hundreds of schools and university departments came under student occupation as the government faced mounting opposition to its higher education agenda (Marseilles 2011). Perhaps the most visible confrontations over university restructuring in Europe took place in 2010 in England, where citizens and activists aggressively challenged austerity measures, such as funding cuts to higher education and proposed tuition increases of nearly 300 percent (Coughlan 2010). These events are only a small sample of the wide range of education-based activism taking place around the world.

While the initial focus of many of these resistance movements — in Canada and elsewhere — was to prevent tuition hikes and government cutbacks to higher education, their attention has evolved to include broader educational and social challenges. Critiques of educational restructuring morphed into a wider critique of the capitalist system and the fate of the public sphere. Students and other activists are locating educational concerns within the context of declining public programs and services, austerity agendas, attacks on worker rights, structural unemployment, environmental destruction and the expansion of corporate power. All of these movements are also grounded in broader demands to rethink the governance of the public university and the restructuring or "corporatization" of higher education.

CORPORATIZATION

The ties between higher education and corporate interests have deep roots. The historical, evolving relationship between universities and the business world has been a contentious one for scholars across many generations. Writing in the U.S. in the early 1900s, Thorstein Veblen (1918) criticized the intrusion of business ideals and methods upon the true and professed values of the university. For Veblen, business principles were spreading throughout the institutional structure, including university governing boards, academic research practices and in the classroom. In 1946, Harold Innis, one of Canada's most renowned political economists, warned that universities would be severely compromised if business gained a more explicit hold over their operations. In Innis' words, "the descent of the university into the market place reflects the lie in the soul of modern society" (1946: 76). Some years later, E.P. Thompson (1970) criticized the process in England where public universities were developing a symbiotic relationship with the aims and ethos of industrial capitalism, while David Noble (1977) drew attention to how corporations in the U.S. were refashioning higher education to meet their needs as employers and to gain control of scientific invention.

Of course, not everyone has been critical of the growing relationship between corporations and universities. William Wickenden, one of the earliest and most prominent advocates of corporate-university linkages in the U.S., explained:

> The very word university comes from the Latin word for corporation and the college dormitory is simply a continuation of the plan of the guilds by which the master workmen not only trained their apprentices but took them into their households to live. That is where our circle began, but as it swung out on its wide arc, the world of education drew further and further away from the world of industry ... But the two circles went swinging on, bringing industry and education ever closer and closer, until tonight they are closing back once more at the point of origin where industry and education are one; where corporation and university again mean the same thing. (cited in Noble 1977: 167)

These early connections between universities and business interests that caught the attention of scholars are still evident today, though they have assumed new and more intimate forms.

"Corporatization" refers to the process and resulting outcomes of the ascendance of business interests, values and models in the university system. This term is not a new one; "corporatization" and the "corporatized" university are now commonplace. Corporatization cannot be viewed as merely the entanglement of universities with business interests because there has never been a period in modern history when universities have been completely free from or untouched by corporate practices. Universities have always functioned to serve the practical interests of businesses and their other stakeholders; however, this utilitarian approach in and of itself does not constitute corporatization. Henry Steck (2003: 74–75) sees the corporatized university as the following:

> An institution that is characterized by processes, decisional criteria, expectations, organizational culture, and operating practices that are taken from, and have their origins in, the modern business corporation. It is characterized by the entry of the university into marketplace relationships and by the use of market strategies in university decision making.

While corporatization reflects several long-standing trends in educational reform, what is changing over time is the nature and extent of the penetration of the university by the corporate economy. Universities have not totally abandoned their traditional functions of teaching, research and service, but the context in which this work takes place has undergone a significant shift. What is new about the current threat to higher education is the increasing pace of corporatization and the extent to which corporate values, policies and modes of governance are permeating universities.

Corporatization, it should be noted, is not the same as privatization. At a basic level, privatization involves the act or process of transferring ownership from the public to the private sector. Corporatization is more complex, with its various manifestations being associated with a number of key indicators and outcomes. One indicator is the enhanced integration between universities and corporate institutions through, for example, the expansion of public-private "partnerships" and donor agreements, and the acceptance of corporate control over university curriculum and infrastructure development. Other indicators are the increasing use of "business-like" practices and objectives by universities themselves. Business-like practices can be seen in new policies and incentives that direct research missions toward commercialization and private gain, the casualization of academic labour, new restrictions on academic freedom in both teaching and research, challenges to collegial self-governance and the adoption of corporate management models.

The outcomes or consequences of corporatization are equally complex. They include the more general transformation of higher education from a public to a private good. Advanced education as a private good is reflected in the growing reliance on student tuition fees and the redefinition of students as educational consumers, a shift in the university's mission away from the provision of liberal arts education, and growing inequality and stratification within and between universities. Corporatization in the university context involves providing businesses with the means to socialize the risks and costs of research while privatizing the benefits, and to accrue advantages through the transfer of technology to the private sector. It subsidizes the retraining of the corporate workforce through an increasingly vocational and technically oriented curriculum, at the same time as increasing marketing opportunities for corporate managers. It bolsters the perception of business legitimacy in higher education and provides the corporate sector with greater control over an institution that has, at times, directly challenged its power. Rather than being "sold off" to the private sector, the uses and benefits of university resources and knowledge production are being handed over to private interests at the public's expense.

In general terms, corporatization is based on efforts to transform the university's mission and modify its operations to better serve the private marketplace. In the words of William Carroll (2004: 181), today's university campus has been identified as "a site of capital accumulation, a place for creating or enhancing the profit-making capacity of individuals, businesses, or the country itself." Under corporatization, the public mission of the university — which has often emphasized democratic goals and service to the broader community — is being reduced in favour of private and commercial interests. The next question is how does this process unfold? Corporatization involves a combination of institutional changes that, taken together, form a comprehensive, tangible process. These shifts are not isolated or distinct from one another; they are closely related and mutually reinforcing. They should not be seen as simply a series of discrete changes. As Claire Polster (2004: 95) explains, the corporatization process is not "additive," it is "transformative." That is, corporate-university linkages "are not an 'add-on' to the university, such that after their establishment we have the old university plus these links." On the contrary, these relationships are changing the nature and function of the university through qualitative changes in its culture and its system of governance, as well as its approach to teaching and research. Put another way, the public university is shifting from "an institution whose practices emerge from its distinctively academic and educational character, to one whose practices emerge from its character as a business organization" (Newson 1994: 152).

The transformative aspects of corporatization — market infringements and institutional practices that systematically undercut the educational process and the free pursuit of knowledge — are the subject of this book. Corporatization has been underway for some time, but some aspects are simply more unpleasant than they are dangerous or transformative. Having more corporate branding (or Pepsi machines) on campuses may be irritating, but is relatively unimportant compared to the casualization of academic labour or research contracts that limit the ability of faculty members to share their findings. Other changes that have been connected to the corporatization process — for example, the growth of online education — are also not addressed in any detailed way because, in my view, they no longer pose the same threat they once did. In the chapters that follow, I focus on four key aspects to demonstrate the deepening of institutional transformation: teaching and academic labour, student life and learning, institutional governance and university research.

WHY FOCUS ON UNIVERSITIES?

Canadian post-secondary education encompasses many types of instructional programs offered by universities and colleges, as well as academic, technical, vocational and continuing professional education institutes. In Canada, there has been a large growth in the number and type of degrees and other credentials offered by a wider variety of institutions over the past thirty years. One of the consequences, according to Dave Marshall (2008: 5), has been the proliferation of "new 'degree' experiences that are delivered by private for-profit, private not-for-profit, non-secular, virtual and non-university institutions." The complexity of Canada's post-secondary system is of course amplified by the fact that education in Canada is a provincial responsibility, with each province and territory managing its own system of institutions, structures and policies. The Organization for Economic Cooperation and Development (OECD) considers Canada to be the only member country without a national system of post-secondary education.

While the corporate restructuring of higher education has implications for the entire post-secondary system, the focus in this book is on universities. Canadian universities range from small, undergraduate liberal arts schools to large, multi-campus research-centred institutions. I do not consider private universities for two primary reasons. First, unlike the U.S., Canada's university system remains a largely public one. A small number of private non-profit and private for-profit schools operate across the country, but otherwise Canadian universities are public. Second, the recent history of private for-profit universities suggests that, although the private education sector is expanding globally, the industry has declined in Canada with few of these institutions remaining operational.[1] Nevertheless, the existence of private universities in Canada should not be dismissed, especially in the context of international investment agreements like the General Agreement on Trade in Services (GATS) where there is the potential for foreign companies to at some point be granted the same rights and government supports as public institutions.

Focusing on public universities in Canada is also important given recent trends in enrolment and employment. Between 2000 and 2011, the number of full-time undergraduate students rose by 44 percent, while those enrolled in graduate degree programs grew by 82 percent (AUCC 2012). In 2011, the number of those enrolled in Canadian undergraduate programs surpassed one million students, setting a new enrolment record. University education is also increasingly important for securing stable and meaningful employment. In today's economy, higher education is no longer considered a luxury; it is a requirement for many fields of work. The Association of Universities and Colleges of Canada (AUCC) reports that from 1990 to 2009, the number of jobs occupied by people with a university degree more than doubled — from 1.9 to 4.2 million — whereas the number of jobs for individuals with a high school diploma or less declined by 1.1 million (AUCC 2010a). Statistics Canada notes that between 1991 and 2011, the proportion of employed persons aged 25 to 34 with a university degree rose from 17 to 27 percent among men, and from 19 to 40 percent among women (Uppal and LaRochelle-Côté 2014a). Of course, obtaining a university education does not guarantee stable employment. Young people in Canada are increasingly vulnerable to the current environment of precarious and insecure work, and record numbers are underemployed and working part-time once they leave school (Tal 2013). At the same time, many predict continued growth in employment opportunities for occupations requiring a university education (see, for example, Miner 2010). Thus, understanding the changing role and function of universities is imperative in a socio-economic context where large numbers of citizens are pursuing a university education, and where these skills and credentials are increasingly required to secure decent employment.

UNIVERSITIES AS SITES OF SOCIAL CHANGE

Universities play an important role in other areas of Canadian society and around the world. They are widely understood to have an unquantifiable impact on our individual and collective identities, our communities, our culture and our ability to perceive and resist other powerful institutions. They have also been implicated as sites of social change. In this sense, universities occupy a complicated and, in many ways, contradictory role in society. On the one hand, universities are institutions that function to preserve class privilege and protect and legitimate the social order. According to Pierre Bourdieu (1988) and other critical education scholars, universities legitimate structural inequalities by mystifying the capitalist production process, socializing students to accept existing distributions of power and wealth, and preparing them for work in occupational hierarchies. In fact, one reason why business leaders continue to support public higher education is because they recognize that universities are agencies of social control, promoting a strong identification with the values, attitudes and beliefs necessary for the maintenance of the capitalist system.

On the other hand, this understanding of the university's role in society is a partial one. Institutions of higher education have never simply reflected the imposition of elite rule nor are they the mere instruments of dominant social groups. Throughout history, universities have been expected to teach the "truth" and denounce deception, to liberate the mind from orthodoxy and conventional thought, and to advance democratic and egalitarian concerns, such as social justice and public service. Higher education is generally equated with a public service mission to prepare people to be citizens as well as to produce public knowledge. The university's role is understood to be so critical to informing public life and civic participation that it might even be considered "the paradigmatic institution of the public sphere" (Calhoun 2006: 10). As Henry Giroux (2008: 148–49) explains:

> While the university should equip people to enter the workplace, it should also educate them to contest workplace inequalities, imagine democratically organized forms of work, and identify and challenge those injustices that contradict and undercut the most fundamental principles of freedom, justice, and respect for all people who constitute the global public sphere. Higher education is about more than job preparation and consciousness-raising; it is also about imagining different futures and politics as a form

of intervention into public life. In contrast to the cynicism and political withdrawal fostered by media culture, education demands that citizens be able to negotiate the interface of private considerations and public issues, be able to recognize those undemocratic forces that deny social, economic, and political justice, and be willing to give some thought to the nature and meaning of their experiences in struggling for a better world.

Given these functions, the university has often been cast as the social critic or conscience of society. It also has a key role to play in transforming society, including, for example, through the rise of dedicated curricular programs like labour studies, urban studies and women's studies. Universities, writes David Noble (2001: 107–108), have never been the "autonomous, disinterested citadel of objective scholarship and social criticism that some lovers of learning imagine." However, universities, he continues, "have provided a living for moderate dissenters, a vantage point from which to observe critically what is going on outside (if not inside), and a platform from which to address with relative safety controversial social questions." The subversive role of the university should not be exaggerated, but it should also not be dismissed. So, while it is true that higher education functions to incorporate workers into the capitalist economy and legitimate inequalities, it is also true that workers, students and academics have used universities to pursue entirely different objectives.

The social and institutional roles of the university, most notably its public service mission, often place it in opposition to the values and objectives of the corporate sector. It is these functions of the university that are most threatened by corporate actors and institutions. And it is these sources of tension — between liberal education and corporate job training, critical research and commercial invention, public service and profit making — that have been the subject of sustained debate and opposition. Public universities have come under attack not just because of the services they perform but, at a more fundamental level, because of the values they do and could represent.

Again, it is important to stress that universities have a complex set of functions and goals — many of which do not align with freedom of inquiry or public service — and they function more to support the values of dominant social groups than to challenge them. Nevertheless, the university remains an institution in modern society that encourages the development of new social visions and modes of thought, and that explicitly claims, as part of its mission, to raise questions about the social order and offer challenges to society's most fundamental beliefs. While many public universities have already moved a considerable distance towards a corporate model of organization, they are still counted on to challenge established structures of power and to provide a reliable source of disinterested inquiry. Community colleges and other institutions of higher learning are experiencing many of the same kinds of pressures (such as financial stress and curriculum reform), but the consequences of the changes taking place are different because of the unique role that universities are supposed to play.

In short, there is something distinctive about the university that cannot be found elsewhere in society, and for this reason many contend that the university should be a centre for radical social inquiry, activism and social change. Today's critics look at whether universities are supporting this kind of thinking and activism to evaluate the extent to which they are fulfilling their public roles. In spite of what elites tell us, the greatest challenges facing universities today are not related to economic growth, "innovation" or national competitiveness. They centre on the willingness and capacity of these institutions to confront the myriad of global problems that produce needless human suffering, increasing social exclusion and inequality, chronic poverty and unemployment, a rapidly deteriorating natural environment and the potentially disastrous effects of climate change. In the years to come, universities will be relevant to the extent that they interrogate, and aim to solve, these pressing social problems.

CONSTRUCTING A NATIONAL PICTURE

Critical analysis of corporatization emerged relatively recently. Throughout the 1980s, for example, academics paid little attention to the increase in corporate-university linkages. The work of Janice Newson and Howard Buchbinder was particularly significant in this time period because they were among a small group of critics who offered a dissenting voice. In *The University Means Business* (1988: 9), they challenge the "almost unquestioned assumption that Canadian universities should overcome their recent misfortunes by building renewed links with the corporate sector." In the words of the authors, the "marriage between ivory tower and marketplace" — a process they likened to "an unfolding drama with few critics and perhaps no audience" — required an immediate and robust debate (p. 90). Central to their critique was that these changes should not be viewed as an aberration or as a short-term solution to underfunding, but as the "blueprint" for carrying universities forward into the twenty-first century. For the most part, Canada's academic community did not perceive the beginning of corporatization as a threat to the teaching, research or public service mission of the university. Few scholars took the threat seriously and most believed that the impact would be marginal. According to Newson (2010: 255, 1992: 228), early critics were accused of seeing "shadows in the bushes" and adopting an "anti-business" or "turgid Marxist" position (see, for example, Skolnik 1988).

In the 1990s, more critical attention was focused on the potential negative ramifications of corporatization (see Carroll et al. 1992; Nelsen 1997; Newson

1992, 1994, 1998). Around the same time, the Canadian Association of University Teachers (CAUT) emerged as an organized, vocal critic of corporatization, and sponsored a series of books on the growing impact of restructuring on teaching and research agendas, the erosion of collegial governance and academic freedom and the declining ability of universities to serve the public interest (see, for example, Bruneau and Savage 2002; Tudiver 1999; Turk 2000, 2008, 2014).

Others engaged more directly with the impact of restructuring on teaching and learning. Arguing that the quality of university education was in a state of decline, these critics raised important questions about a range of issues, including distance education and the commodification of instruction (Noble 2001); the emphasis on specialized research at the expense of undergraduate teaching (Pocklington and Tupper 2002); the transformation of students into educational "consumers" (Côté and Allahar 2007); the precarious employment of contract faculty (Rajagopal 2002); and how the pressures of the marketplace threatened the democratic values of liberal education (Axelrod 1998, 2002). Still others examined the unique experiences and challenges faced by women in a more corporatized academic setting (Reimer 2004); the changes in academic culture and its implications for university research (Chan and Fisher 2008a); and the ways in which academic freedom and university autonomy have been subordinated to corporate agendas (Woodhouse 2009). Claire Polster's work on the declining public service mission of universities and the changing social relations of research (for example, Polster 1998, 2000, 2002, 2007a) has been instrumental in the Canadian context, as has that of leading educational theorist Henry Giroux on the corporatization of higher education in Canada, the U.S. and elsewhere (for example, Giroux 2007, 2014; Giroux and Giroux 2004).

This expanding discussion and critique over a relatively short period reflects how quickly the academic terrain shifted from general ambivalence to widespread recognition and critical concern. Nonetheless, there has not been an analysis of corporatization that looks at Canada as a whole. The majority of the work on university restructuring has analyzed changes and trends at the provincial level. This is not surprising because, as noted above, Canada's approach to higher education policy is the most decentralized of any advanced industrialized country; Canada has never had a federal higher education policy framework or a federal ministry of education. While the federal government provides core funding support to universities and is involved in a range of policy-relevant research and student financial assistance, provinces have substantial autonomy and control over higher education. It is precisely because Canada has a decentralized system of higher education that developing a national picture is important. Nevertheless, constructing such a picture is not without challenges.

For one, there is significant variation between provinces with respect to the timing, breadth and intensity of corporatization. Following the large reductions in transfer payments associated with the federal budget cuts of the 1990s, the policy frameworks of provincial governments began to diverge. By the early 2000s, Canadian higher educational policy was "riding madly off in all directions" (Jones and Young 2004: 204). In each province, a unique intersection of federal and provincial market-based strategies has been layered onto more traditional public sector regulation and funding structures. Moreover, the process of university restructuring is not linear because the process expands and contracts depending on the provincial context, including the political party in power and the policies of the governments that preceded it. In many instances, the unique political history in each province is important to understand university restructuring in Canada.

In the same way as a national assessment of corporatization is complicated by differences across provinces, variation also exists across universities and subject areas between and within provinces. For example, faculty members in larger, research-oriented institutions and in commercially relevant fields experience corporate and commercial pressures more acutely. On the other hand, academics who are further removed from the market and less dependent on corporate funding may have greater autonomy to shape their research practices, but they also may be at a higher risk of being deemed "irrelevant" in the eyes of business, governments, university managers and even the public.

Another complicating factor is the tendency to treat mutually reinforcing processes discretely and in isolation. For example, writing about the commercialization of research often neglects how this trend is connected to rising tuition fees or reductions in collegial governance, while the exploitation of contract faculty is often not informed by an understanding of intellectual property regimes. Polster (2007b: 319) explains why these elements should be viewed as an integrated process:

> The centralization of power by academic administrators facilities the establishment of university/industry research alliances and the commercialization of academic research. In turn, the commercialization encourages — indeed, compels — administrators to run universities more as businesses by curbing collegialism, transparency, and other long-standing academic traditions and values ... These changes also contribute to and, in turn, are reinforced by changes in the social relations of Canadian university teaching.

In this book, I bring together topics that are usually considered separately — notably federal and provincial higher education policy, teaching and academic labour, university governance, curriculum reform, research commercialization and student life — illustrating the linkages between these elements.

Finally, analyzing corporatization is made more challenging by the fact that the number and size of universities varies within and between provinces, which affects the amount and quality of available information. For some aspects of corporatization, information and the corresponding analysis may be partial or limited to specific provinces/regions of the country. Thus, at times I focus mainly on Ontario, largely because more has been written about the nature and history of Ontario universities than of those in any other province and because nearly half of Canada's full-time university students are located there.

In spite of these challenges, providing this kind of national picture of public universities in Canada is timely. The idea that public universities have reached a critical juncture in their history, or that they are in the midst of or approaching a "crisis," has been a theme in the higher education literature for many years. Writing in the *Canadian Journal of Higher Education* over two decades ago, Glen Jones (1990) argued that convincing evidence that a crisis was imminent was missing from the literature. According to Jones (1990: 3), it is "not enough simply to identify a problem or demonstrate an element of decline … One must provide evidence that the problem is of such a magnitude that a failure to resolve the problem will lead to a decisive moment in which some characteristic of higher education will be threatened." In my view, there is a crisis. In this book, I will demonstrate that the transformation of higher education is of such a magnitude that it threatens many of the defining characteristics of Canadian higher education. Beyond its detrimental impacts on university teaching, learning, research and governance, corporatization also poses a serious threat to the health and well-being of the general population. It is critical to understand the full extent of this transformation and to identify strategies to reverse the "market makeover" of universities.

NOTE

1 In 2008, for example, the University of Phoenix — the largest for-profit educational provider in the world — closed all of its Canadian operations; its campuses in Burnaby and Calgary were officially shut down in 2010. Others also closed, including Meritus University, Lansbridge University and University Canada West. The problems facing these Canadian profit-oriented universities were connected to enrolment issues and faltering profits, as well as legal and ethical violations. For instance, the Vancouver branch of Lansbridge University was closed by the B.C. government in 2007 for violating the province's *Degree Authorization Act*; charges against the university included illegal advertising, exposing students to financial risk and providing misleading information to government. A few years later, the university lost its degree-granting status in its New Brunswick branch due to non-compliance with provincial regulations and the substandard quality of its academic programming (Chapin 2010).

CHAPTER TWO
HIGHER EDUCATION AND CORPORATE POWER

Universities have always been dependent on — and to a varying extent constrained and controlled by — external sources of power in society. Over time, the locus of this power has shifted from the church to the state and the market. At their outset, universities were closely tied to the church. The development of the first Western universities coincided with the administrative progression of the Roman Catholic Church through the twelfth and thirteenth centuries. Universities provided theological instruction and entrenched the supremacy of church authorities through the legitimation of religious doctrine. Beginning in the Renaissance era, universities gradually expanded their services to include the nation-state and the education of a more secular and bureaucratic elite. During this period, tensions emerged around the university's role in advancing theologically based higher learning and its support of nation building. In the eighteenth and nineteenth centuries, the terrain continued to shift as universities became more assimilated into the service of the market. Technical and managerial knowledge was viewed as essential for state bureaucracies and corporations, so universities were reorganized to produce the experts and the expert knowledge needed to support the emerging capitalist system.

Throughout this long transition period, the inherent contradictions between service to power and support for critical inquiry was a source of tension. Somewhat contradictorily, universities have been set up as institutions whose role it is to challenge established power relations. As Noam Chomsky (2003) explains, the social and intellectual role of the university is supposed to be a subversive one, regardless of the particular "relations of ruling" in a society. That is, the university should be a disruptive and liberating force that fosters the challenging of conventional thinking and of systems of illegitimate authority. But the university's close association with external power inhibits and, at times, prevents it from fulfilling this role. This association is complex. Universities are economically (and otherwise) dependent on outside institutions for their survival, and those who provide this support often have a vested interest in ensuring that the status quo of wealth and power remain unchanged. In Chomsky's words:

> Naturally, the reigning institutions, state and private, use their power to try to shape the social and intellectual world in their own interests. Universities are economically parasitic, relying on external support. To maintain this support while serving their proper liberating function poses problems that verge on contradiction. In practice, universities face a constant struggle to maintain their integrity, their fundamental social role in a healthy society, in the face of external pressures. The problems are heightened with the expansion of private power in every domain. (2003: 198)

By necessity and/or by choice, universities have had to offer some loyalty or service to power in order to maintain a measure of autonomy. This lack of independence from outside power limits the ability of universities (and teachers and students within them) to explore the full range of human capacities and knowledge. Immanual Wallerstein (1969) writes that universities have persevered in a state of "perpetual tension," where the institution is constantly reasserting itself, its own reality, as an "idea" at the same time as society seeks to constrain and harness it for its own purposes. While this has always been the case, I would argue that the heightened pressures of corporate and market forces are a growing challenge for universities; in no other historical period have universities assumed such a close relationship with an institution so incompatible with their defining values and principles.

ELITE POWER AND THE ORIGINS OF CANADIAN UNIVERSITIES

In Canada, the training of clergy and the general education of social leaders informed the establishment of the first English- and French-speaking colleges and universities. These universities existed, largely, to prepare a small proportion of the white male population for religious, and later managerial and professional life. Prior to 1850, Canadian universities (for example, Acadia, McGill, Queen's and Victoria) were largely imitations or "transplants" from other countries, including England, Scotland, Germany and the U.S. Tom Pocklington and Allan Tupper (2002) note, for example, that Canadian institutions were influenced by English ideals about higher education as a transmitter of culture, the Scottish emphasis on accessible undergraduate education, the German tradition of advanced research and the public service commitments of U.S. land grant universities. From approximately 1860 onwards, Canadian universities developed characteristics that differentiated them from foreign institutions, such as a distinctively Canadian curriculum. Although Pocklington and Tupper (2002) contend that a unique Canadian "idea" about the role and purpose of the university never really emerged, Glen Jones (1998) argues otherwise. According to Jones, the Canadian "idea" of a university is exemplified by a public, secular, autonomous, degree-granting institution, combined with more universal notions about the dissemination and advancement of public knowledge. While many of these features are common to universities around the world, Jones argues that there are facets or "first principles" associated with the Canadian conception of the university that cannot be found elsewhere.

Economic and political elites were closely involved in the development and expansion of Canada's university system. King's College, the first university established in Upper Canada, was founded in the late eighteenth century by John Strachan. Strachan was a prominent member of the "Family Compact," which was an organization of merchants, landowners and government officials from Upper Canada's ruling class. Members of the Family Compact dominated the first governing council at King's College (Barkans and Pupo 1978). Throughout the nineteenth century, financial and industrial elites increased their influence over universities in Canada through monetary contributions and by assuming positions of institutional management. For example, land and infrastructure for McMaster University was provided by Senator William McMaster, President of the Bank of Commerce. McGill University received "magnificent benefactions" from wealthy elites, placing it, alongside the University of Toronto, at the forefront of scientific research (Cameron 1991: 26). Through these kinds of channels, educational preparation for the privileged classes was extended to include managerial training for economic leadership.

In their formative years, Canadian universities also received support from foreign sponsors, both individual and institutional. Dalhousie University, for instance, was sponsored by George Munro, a New York publisher and brother-in-law of Dalhousie president John Forrest. Many large American foundations also provided money and expertise to new institutions. By the early 1900s, almost every Canadian university had received a grant from the Carnegie Foundation (Harris 1976), and it was well understood that this kind of support was not provided with purely philanthropic goals.[1] At the same time, business leaders began to channel large sums of money to programs, professors and graduate students whose work they influenced and/or approved of, and occasionally even paid for professors' salaries (Enros 1983). For example, "Tobacco King" William Macdonald financed agricultural programs at McGill; prominent distiller Colonel A.E. Gooderham provided research support for the study of fermentation at the University of Toronto; and leading Canadian bankers organized to influence business curriculums (Barkans and Pupo 1978).

In addition to exercising power through various paths of direct financial support, elites gained influence in Canadian universities through legislative mechanisms, as well as by encouraging public awareness efforts and programmatic changes. In 1906, Canada's economic elite formally increased its control over the country's university system with the passage of the *University Act*. The Act placed control and management of the University of Toronto in the hands of an appointed body, the Board of Governors, which consisted largely of wealthy business leaders. This move laid the ground for a new basic university governance model and strengthened business influence over higher education. Around the same time, elites in Canada were working to ensure that the timing and nature of university expansion aligned with corporate interests. Professional and vocational programs were expanded and tailored to reflect the growth of major resource industries. Queen's University, for example, established a school of mining in 1893 and an engineering faculty in 1905, while the University of Toronto opened a school of forestry in 1907 (Axelrod 1982a). Campaigns by business groups were also used to restructure higher education to meet corporate demands for technical and commercial training and industrial research facilities. The Canadian Manufacturers' Association (CMA), for instance, successfully lobbied for new programs in commerce, finance and business administration. The CMA also exerted an "extended propaganda campaign" to ensure the establishment of university-based industrial research facilities and to usher in the creation, in 1916, of the National Research Council of Canada (Enros 1991: 211).

In sum, universities have always had a close relationship with external power and Canadian universities are no exception. From the beginning, the structure and purpose of Canadian higher education was modified — at least in part — at the behest of powerful elite interests. Out of this transition, from religious/aristocratic power to industrial/capitalist power, emerged the "corporate university." The views of some of the earliest critics of the corporate university reveal the changing relationship between corporate power and higher education.

EARLY CRITICS OF THE CORPORATE UNIVERSITY

In the first half of the twentieth century, political debates over who "owned the universities" were commonplace in the U.S. (Barrow 1990: 32). These conflicts were understood as a battle over who should control the direction of university reform and, with it, economic development. For the U.S. business community, universities were viewed as a key industrial resource for corporate expansion. For others, however, the growing collaboration between universities and industry was a cause for deep concern. Writer and intellectual Randolph Bourne (cited in Chomsky 2003: 183), one of the earliest critics of business influence in higher education, likened the university's growing role in this period to:

A financial corporation, strictly analogous, in its motives and responses, to the corporation which is concerned in the production of industrial commodities ... The university produces learning instead of steel and rubber, but the nature of the academic commodity has become less and less potent in ensuring for the academic workman a status materially different from that of any other kind of employee.

Under the control of business-minded trustees, Bourne said, the American university had shifted "from its old, noble ideal of a community of scholarship" to a private commercial enterprise.

Other work substantiates Bourne's concern surrounding the role of trustees in reshaping U.S. higher education. Earl McGrath (1936), for example, reported that bankers and business leaders on governing boards increased from approximately one quarter of total membership in 1860 to one half in 1930. Scott Nearing's study of trustees in 1917 revealed a similar trend. To complement their control over boards of trustees, some corporate leaders, like those in the utility industry, actively participated in other campaigns to control higher education. In the early 1930s, for example, the U.S. Federal Trade Commission discovered that the utility companies were hiring professors, subsidizing utilities courses and research, designing textbooks and curriculums and even conducting summer school programs for faculty members (Noble 1977). Journalist Upton Sinclair (1923) also challenged the growing relationship between U.S. universities and corporations. Sinclair's critique drew attention to business influence through trustee control and the suppression of academic freedom, but he also called into question the fact that universities were actively embracing a corporate service role. To publicize the corporate affiliations of many of the nation's top schools, he used labels like "Chicago as the University of Standard Oil" and "Columbia as the University of J.P. Morgan."

Writing in the early 1900s, Thorstein Veblen, one of the most well-known critics of business power in higher education, condemned the expansion of professional/vocational training in universities, and equated this shift with a "cult of business principles" and a betrayal of the university's mission (see Veblen 2004: 137). For him, "practicality" in education was not only a contradiction in terms, but a euphemism for private gain, where business proficiency was exhibited as enlightenment, "value" was synonymous with economic value and citizenship was reduced to a form of barbarism. Veblen was particularly concerned that universities were expanding vocational programs, to the detriment of the liberal arts, at the behest of purposeful business campaigns and with the support of business-friendly administrators. He explained the purpose of this approach as twofold: to dispense with courses of study deemed "useless" or obsolete, and to acquire trained employees at low wages. Although liberal education remained "the enduring purpose and substantial interest of the university establishment," Veblen argued that business values and practices were systematically destroying it (43).

At the core of business leaders' interventions was an opposition to liberal learning. As Frank Donoghue (2008: 2) explains, corporate dissatisfaction with higher education began when "the great capitalists of the early twentieth century saw in America's universities a set of core values and a management style antithetical to their own." This antagonism reflected their belief that universities were not conducive to wealth creation. However, this particular concern did not account for the "intensity, bordering on outrage, of their critiques," which were more fundamentally rooted in "distrust of the ideal of intellectual inquiry for its own sake" and the principles of collegial governance (3). As business criteria began to assert a greater influence over social and intellectual life, the term "academic" was increasingly associated with useless or impractical pursuits. Some academics held equally potent critiques of business leaders. As Robert Nisbet (1971: 53) puts it, the academy has always held a "certain, noticeable, disdain for the businessman ... nothing would have so offended a bona fide prince of learning as to have been mistaken somewhere for a mere man of trade and commerce."

Early critics focused their critiques on the influence of business leaders on university governing boards. According to Veblen, "they have ceased to exercise any function other than a bootless meddling with academic matters which they do not understand. The sole ground of their retention appears to be an unreflecting deferential concession to the usages of corporate organization and control" (2004: 46). But Veblen's critique went deeper. From his perspective, the encroachment of business principles compromised higher education completely. He saw a fundamental incompatibility between business enterprise and higher learning, such that they should be considered polar opposites or "two extremes." As Veblen explained it, "within the ordinary range of lawful occupations these two lines of endeavour, and the animus that belongs to each, are as wildly out of touch as may be. They are the two extreme terms of the modern cultural scheme" (50). For Veblen, academic governance, research and teaching were all among the casualties of this relationship between universities and corporations. He claimed that administrators were fixated on fundraising at the expense of academic priorities, research had become an adjunct of the industrial system, and teaching had been infected by the elevation of impersonal, mechanical relations in the place of personal guidance. The consequences of this new relationship were so far reaching that it left its mark on the "ideals, aims, methods and standards" of scholars and scholarship (7).

Following the early critiques of Veblen and others about the changes in U.S. higher education, critics of corporate-university ties also emerged in Canada. For instance, Harold Innis, one of Canada's most respected economists, warned in 1946 that universities would be severely compromised if business gained more influence over their operations. In fact, Innis argued that many Canadian universities had already abandoned their commitment to the impartial search for truth and that, in their place, administrators were beholden to departments and lines of inquiry that generated external funding. Innis was especially concerned about the impact on the social sciences, which he believed needed to be independent of outside influence. In Innis' words:

> The impression that universities can be bought and sold, held by businessmen and fostered by university administrators trained in playing for the highest bid, is a reflection of the deterioration of western civilization. To buy universities is to destroy them ... The descent of the university into the market place reflects the lie in the soul of modern society. (75-76)

Traces of early criticism also emerged in the writings of prominent Canadian university administrators, such as President Claude Bissell at the University of Toronto. Bissell (1968: 208–209) did not believe that universities should reject business prerogatives, arguing that "isolation from the world of corporate enterprise would condemn the university to a twilight world of self-bemused impotence." Yet, Bissell was concerned about the influence of corporations in many areas of university life, especially the curriculum. Speaking of the U.S., he claimed that corporate-university linkages could be seen "most disastrously in the increasing domination of American universities by the undergraduate school of business, which is frankly and unabashedly a training ground for the large corporation" (170–71). The danger, according to Bissell, was that business and management studies were "usurping a central and dominating position in the undergraduate curriculum" at the expense of basic arts and sciences. More broadly, Bissell was troubled by the idea that universities should function as "a sort of production line," turning out "well-packaged products for the corporation super-market (171–72).

In the 1960s, students in the U.S., Canada and elsewhere began to organize efforts to increase their influence over university affairs, including by calling for reforms to the content and organization of university education. In particular, students demanded to be involved in, some even demanded veto power over, university decisions that involved corporations. In Canada, these decisions included the solicitation of private grants and research funding, the practice of corporate recruiting on campus and the university's role in the military-industrial complex (Reid and Reid 1969). As part of this struggle, students rejected the notion that the university should function as an isolated ivory tower that was detached from social and political affairs. They demanded that the university take its critical function seriously and address social justice issues, problems related to racial, class and gender inequalities, as well as civil rights, war and militarism. As a result, university "relevance" became a sort of watchword for the movement. For these students, relevance meant immediate practical engagement with pressing social issues; in contrast, university "relevance" from the perspective of corporate and government representatives was typically synonymous with a form of education that emphasized narrow, specialized training and research in the service of private interests.

Student concerns about university relevance went hand-in-hand with a rejection of the "corporate university" — euphemistically referred to as the "knowledge factory" — where campus relations resembled those of a business establishment. Embracing the work of critical scholars like Herbert Marcuse (1964) and Paul Goodman (1959), students argued that higher education had been subverted by narrow and instrumental concerns. As Robert Nisbet (1971: 111) explains, large numbers of students in the 1960s were disillusioned by campuses that were "not community but corporation, led not by aristocrats but businessmen of the mind." Who, they asked, gave wealthy corporate leaders the right to remake universities in their own image?

In the U.S., the 1964 "Machine" speech by Mario Savio — a prominent member of the Berkeley free speech movement — exemplified growing discontent with the encroachment of the knowledge factory. Savio's speech likened the university to an industrial machine, its governing board to a corporate board of directors and students to raw materials that were packaged and sold to external clients. Interestingly, the talk took place in the administration building of Clark Kerr, then President of the University of California. In *The Uses of the University*, first published in 1963, Kerr famously argued that the traditional university had evolved into a "multiversity." He characterized the multiversity as actively embracing multiple constituencies, assuming a more practical and commercial role. In Kerr's eyes, the multiversity was being called upon to merge its activities with industry, which he looked upon in generally favourable terms. Just as critiques arose in response to corporate influence in the university, the specific concept of the multiversity also came into question. Robert Wolff (1969), for example, contended that a key problem with the multiversity — a problem that was also recognized and critiqued by the student movement — was its failure to distinguish between social need and market demand. The multiversity "must" adjust higher education to meet the needs of external power, rather than the social needs of the population. It is worth noting that Kerr modified his views in later years. In his most recent edition of *The Uses of the University* (2001), Kerr acknowledges that greater corporate influence over the goals and practices of universities has had a detrimental impact on higher learning. In his words:

> Education for its own sake is being replaced by education for the sake of employment ... The ivory tower of old has become an arm of the state

and an arm of industry ... What are perceived by some as the injustices in the external labor market penetrate the system of economic rewards on campus, replacing policies of internal justice. (2001: 214–15)

This notion of the multiversity — and the critiques it has generated — is important for many reasons, including that it foreshadowed the current, more complete reorganization of universities under corporatization. It is also important to note that this and other early critiques of the corporate university focus on the fundamental incongruity between the competing and, in some instances, contradictory goals and principles of corporate and academic institutions. Corporate influence over higher education has existed for some time and the tensions between the role and interests of universities and corporations have not abated. In fact, they have increased and are at the heart of the current crisis.

In order to better understand the role of the university and its relationship to business, and to further illustrate some of the contradictions between the economic and democratic functions of higher education, it is useful to examine the 1960s period in Canada in more detail.

BETWEEN CAPITALISM AND DEMOCRACY: REFLECTIONS ON CANADA'S "GOLDEN AGE"

In Canada, the major period of university growth and expansion in the 1960s is often referred to as the "golden age" of higher education. In the "golden age," university reform was influenced both by democratic and public service commitments as well as by economic considerations. On the one hand, university reform was shaped by popular movements inside and outside of the academy as well as the values and goals of a burgeoning public sector. On the other, it was influenced by the economic interests of corporations and the interventions of political and economic elites.

According to Janice Newson (1998), universities in the 1960s were cautious about being tied too closely to the market. In other words, their democratic commitments were considered as — if not more — important than their economic role. During this period, the expansion of higher education was viewed as a means to promote social and economic mobility, extend the rights of democratic citizenship and advance public knowledge. There was also some momentum to move beyond equality of opportunity to promote the principle of universal access to higher education. For example, the 1972 Commission on Post-Secondary Education in Ontario stated:

[The] guiding principle of the Province's policy of financing post-secondary education should continue to be *universal access* to appropriate educational services for all who wish and are able to benefit from them. All financial barriers to accessibility should be progressively abolished ... When faced with the imperative need of education for survival, universal access should seem not a benevolent dream but a categorical necessity. (cited in Porter, Porter and Blishen 1982: 22, emphasis in original)

This approach to reshaping the educational sphere was set within the broader context of new social movements, welfare state expansion, the growth of public sector employment and the prominence of Canadian left nationalism.

Prior to and during this period of reform, there was also a growing, somewhat competing, tendency (particularly among government and business leaders) to see the expansion of university education as a primary means of enhancing economic growth and development. In part, this view reflected the increasing dependence of Canadian corporations on scientific and engineering research as well as business management training. Working through organizations like the Canadian Chamber of Commerce, the Canadian Manufacturers' Association and the Industrial Foundation on Education, corporate leaders organized to advance their own vision of university reform. These organizing efforts were evident in 1955 when the A.V. Roe Company sponsored a conference of Canadian industrialists to discuss the university's role in providing scientific and technical "manpower" (Cameron 1991). Given that the corporate vision of higher education reform was predicated on system expansion, it aligned with the perspectives of liberal and even radical reformers.

The power of business in influencing educational reform during the golden age was evident in three main areas. First, corporate elites increased their presence on university governing boards as a way to exert influence over university governance, infrastructure and program development (see Barkans and Pupo 1974; Clement 1975; Ornstein 1988). Second, the funding relationships between business and education became more significant. As an example, business raised its funding for higher education by 450 percent in just one year in the 1950s, with most of the money coming from dominant industrial and commercial sectors (Axelrod 1982a). Third, recognizing that their own financial contributions were insufficient to achieve the desired reforms, business leaders called upon government to meet the national "crisis." They did so by using an extensive lobbying campaign to sell the message that only a massive influx of public education dollars would ensure Canada's competitive position in the global economy. Canada's advertising industry, as a result, launched a coast-to-coast media campaign to inform Canadians that the country faced significant dangers if higher education was not expanded.

The business community also engaged in a number of activities to force the alignment between higher education and their economic interests. In 1956, partly at the behest of big business, the National Conference of Canadian Universities sponsored the "Canada's Crisis in Higher Education" conference for representatives from academia, business, government and the labour movement to discuss the financial difficulties facing universities. Building on these business-led efforts, it was declared that there was a major crisis in higher education. In Axelrod's (1986: 46) words, "the very survival of the country was pinned to the expansion of educational facilities." One year later, the Royal Commission on Canada's Economic Prospects issued a powerful statement about the economic value of universities, and placed system expansion at the heart of the country's economic development strategy. The Economic Council of Canada, which was established in 1963, also promoted this line of argument. In its influential series of annual reviews, the Council argued that universities were not producing the professional, business or technical skills required in the new economy (see, for example, Economic Council of Canada 1964, 1965). The Council also maintained that a greater supply of post-secondary education was needed to facilitate economic growth. Its overriding message was that education should be viewed primarily as a form of economic investment.

The increased public spending on higher education elicited near unanimous support from the private sector, whose extensive lobbying played a key role in bringing it to fruition. There were also a number of examples of direct corporate involvement in system expansion, especially for newer institutions with large capital expenditures. For example, in some areas of the country, business leaders were involved in preparing proposals for new campuses, overseeing their implementation and influencing university policies. Over this time period, national and local business interests played a pivotal role in the creation and expansion of virtually every university in Ontario (Axelrod 1982a). Other universities bypassed the development of full or expanded curriculums built around basic arts and sciences in favour of more specialized programming, such as Université du Quebec and Waterloo. As James MacAulay (1984: 68) explains, as interactions with business became more commonplace within these specialized institutions, they "readily adopted industry as their clientele for an expanding range of services." One of the best illustrations of how university expansion came to reflect economic interests was the establishment of Athabasca University in 1970. Upon its creation, Athabasca developed a "radical" mandate that merged the demands of education and vocational training to support corporate industry (Adria 2000). It also developed a distinctly consumerist orientation spearheaded by distance education programs with little academic control over planning.

For the business community, a healthy supply of skilled workers in engineering, business management and the applied sciences had obvious benefits. But Axelrod (1986: 52–53) notes:

Those who viewed the importance of higher education in primarily economic terms included arts programs in their prescriptions. In virtually every major industrial and commercial enterprise, businessmen were firm in their conviction that a student's study of the liberal arts was as vital to the well-being of the economy as was specific professional training.

In other words, the requirements of a flexible and adaptable white-collar workforce necessitated the expansion of business and science as well as liberal arts education. Here, the position of business leaders again coincided with those of many academics and the public who argued that these programs should be expanded. The arts benefited, according to Axelrod, "on the coattails of a university system designed primarily to serve economic ends" (1986: 53).

University curriculums were expanded to reflect more flexibility in undergraduate studies and an increase in student choice over courses and programs. Universities increased the provision of general liberal arts education; the proportion of undergraduate degrees in the arts and social sciences rose from 46.8 percent in 1960–61 to over 60 percent in 1968–69. According to Alan Sears (2003: 53), this shift "reflected the need for a flexible white-collar workforce but it also reflected a conception of citizenship and character-development in which jobs skills were not the only consideration." Echoing the principle of broad accessibility, student assistance plans were improved to support increased enrolment. Total government loans for full-time undergraduates increased from $1 million in 1957–58 to nearly $60 million 1969–70. The Canada Student Loan program created in 1964 played a significant role in this expansion.

Not surprisingly, and reflecting both economic and democratic visions of higher education, the country's university system expanded in multiple directions during this era. Undergraduate enrolment increased fivefold between 1955 and 1975, while graduate enrolment grew twelvefold (Hardy 1984). Eighteen new universities were founded between 1959 and 1969 alone. To accommodate campus growth and the large influx of new students, the number of full-time university teachers increased from approximately 6,500 in 1960 to nearly 25,000 in 1970 (Fisher et al. 2006). In terms of funding, universities' share of provincial education budgets increased from 16 percent in 1960 to 25 percent in 1967–68. At the national level, university expenditures in Canada rose from 0.36 percent of GNP in 1956 to 2.09 percent in 1970 (Ornstein 1988). Overall, Canada was spending over 7 percent of its GNP on education in 1973, more than most other Western nations. By 1970–71, government grants accounted for 76 percent of university operating revenues. In comparison, private donations comprised less than 10 percent.

Under the growing leadership of the Canadian Association of University Teachers, faculty also gained more control over university governance. Academics expanded their representation in senate bodies and new systems of peer review offered more input into hiring, tenure and promotion decisions. In many universities, faculty associations were created or strengthened to advance the professional interests and the organizational capacity of academic labour. Partly as a result of these changes, faculty salaries doubled, working conditions improved and the idea of collegial self-governance assumed a concrete (albeit relatively weak) institutional form. Students also gained some power within universities by acquiring representation on departmental committees, faculty councils, senates and, in some cases, boards of governors. All of these advances were achieved within a broader political framework that emphasized the need for universities to be more independent of external power. This need was exemplified by the importance attached to institutional autonomy, collegial self-governance and academic freedom.

To summarize, university expansion over this time period was driven by three main factors. First, there was a growing corporate interest in creating a skilled labour force and a university system that would support capitalist growth and development. Second, governments supported university expansion and instituted other changes — including improved salaries and working conditions for academics — on the expectation that these would correspond with sizeable economic returns. And third, broader social movements and democratic forces improved educational opportunities and strengthened the university's public service role. While these three forces, combined, brought about significant expansion, the narrative that this was a "golden age" of Canadian higher education is somewhat misleading. Significant challenges remained within the university during this period. For example, there were major constraints on academic freedom and the free pursuit of knowledge, larger social inequities based on race and gender were reproduced in the university context and harmful linkages existed between academic research and agendas supporting war and imperialism (much like today).

By the early 1970s, the expansion phase of universities in Canada came to an end. A confluence of forces combined to transform the conventional wisdom about higher education. These included shrinking employment opportunities, the "fiscal crisis of the state" that called into question the legitimacy of generous public funding and an ideological shift touting the inefficiencies of the public sector in general, including universal programs (in education, this meant an attack on universal accessibility and comprehensive curriculums). At the same time, liberal arts education was largely decoupled from having any economic "relevance" as business began to focus on targeted funding and more specialized programming. By the end of the decade, per capita education spending had fallen significantly in all provinces such that universities started to transform their operations in an effort to cope with these losses. The choices made by universities and governments in response to these changes — along with the emergence of more direct and active corporate involvement in higher education — would precipitate a new era of economic rationality, "accountability" and market-based restructuring. In essence, this was the beginning of the corporatization of Canadian universities. Long-time critic of the corporate university, David Noble (2007: 6), summarizes the far-reaching impact of the transformation in this way:

> [Corporatization] left chaos in its wake ... class sizes swelled, academic programs were cut and 'restructured,' course offerings were reduced, tuition and fees were substantially increased while student financial support was slashed, staff salaries were frozen, faculty hirings and tenure tracks were minimized and full-time faculty were increasingly replaced by cheaper contract instructors and graduate students ... a new emphasis on non-disclosure, confidentiality and secrecy subverted open and free intellectual interchange, and intensified the suppression of dissent ... the selfless pursuit of contributions to human knowledge gave way to proprietary and pecuniary interest as the mark and measure of academic achievement, fatally eroding the integrity of the institution as a unique and invaluable repository of disinterested expertise. Censorship, heightened competition, delays in publication, scientific fraud and theft, greed, corruption, conflict of interest, and commercial litigation became the hallmarks of the new university, as the ethos of academia came ever more to resemble that of the so-called private sector which administrators strove so hard to emulate.

CORPORATIZATION AND ACADEMIC CAPITALISM

While the public interest commitment of Canadian universities was relatively strong in the 1960s — represented by the importance placed on institutional autonomy, collegial governance and academic freedom — this commitment has been steadily eroding. Both supporters and critics of corporatization acknowledge that the values that have historically framed the role of the public university are changing. Others go further, arguing that the mixing of commercial objectives with academic norms and values has evolved from the irregular to the customary state of affairs. There are many consequences of this institutional transformation. University presidents have been recast as "CEOs," students as "customers," graduates as "products" and professors as "service providers." Contractual business relationships and measures of fiscal viability have been elevated in relation to social commitments. Profit has become a leading goal of academic inquiry and a guiding principal for deciding what products and services to offer. Decisions about course offerings, research funding and hiring and enrolment practices are assessed less in terms of academic criteria and more on whether they represent good business decisions.

Increasingly, then, university education is regarded as a private rather than a public good, where higher learning is viewed less as a right of citizenship and more as a purchasable commodity. Under corporatization, the public interest — once defined as shielding public entities from the market — is assumed to be enhanced by embracing commercial values and practices. From an institutional standpoint, serving the needs of the global economy and preparing young people for corporate employment has become the university's primary mission. As Stanley Aronowitz (2000: 81) observes, "what was once the hidden curriculum — the subordination of higher education to the needs of capital — has become an open, frank policy ... today leaders of higher education wear the badge of corporate servants proudly."

A variety of frameworks have been used to explain and critique the corporatization process. Commonly, these frameworks theorize the emergence of a "new" type of university that more closely resembles corporations and is more heavily integrated with the market. They range from the corporate university to the service university and the McUniversity (the Appendix includes brief descriptions of these institutional configurations). Arguably, the leading theoretical models on university restructuring revolve around the concept of "academic capitalism."

While commonly attributed to the work of Sheila Slaughter and Larry Leslie (1997) and Sheila Slaughter and Gary Rhoades (2004), the term "academic capitalism" was actually coined several decades ago by Robert Nisbet (1971). In his work, Nisbet claimed that the billions of dollars made available to U.S. universities after World War II (much of it from private sources) had an immediate and profound impact on the academy. "For the first time in Western history," he writes, "professors and scholars were thrust into the unwonted position of entrepreneurs in incessant search" of capital, revenue and profit (1971: 73). "Whereas for centuries the forces of commerce, trade, and industrialization outside the university" had little impact upon the academic community, a new force — "academic capitalism" — was transforming scholarship and the role of the professoriate. The introduction of new financing models also had a deep impact on university governance. Managers were hired not because they were respected members of the academic community but because they had an administrative ability to attract external revenues and market their institutions.

Like Nisbet, Slaughter and Leslie (1997) conceptualize academic capitalism as the encroachment of the profit motive into the academy; however, they highlight different reasons to explain this change. Drawing on case studies in Canada, the U.S., Australia and Britain, they argue that government spending cuts in the 1980s and 1990s compelled universities to engage in additional market activities. These activities included direct, for-profit ventures, such as patenting, licensing and the formation of spin-off companies, but also "market-like behaviours" in the form of enhanced competition for external research grants, increasing student fees and aggressively seeking corporate donations. At the same time, industrial research collaborations and high technology programs were prioritized over more established academic programs and practices. According to Slaughter and Leslie, this new entrepreneurial environment altered the purpose, reward systems and decision-making structures of higher education, so much so that the centre of the academy "shifted from a liberal arts core to an entrepreneurial periphery" (1997: 207).

Slaughter and Leslie's (1997) work focuses on research funding and commercialization as the key components of academic capitalism. Looking specifically at the U.S., Slaughter and Rhoades (2004) construct a broader vision of academic capitalism where market forces are ingrained in all facets of university life. The authors conceptualize higher education as shifting from a "public good knowledge/learning regime" to an ascendant "academic capitalist knowledge/learning regime" (2004: 28). This latter regime is characterized by new "circuits of knowledge" where corporations and university administrators play a more prominent role in the creation and transmission of knowledge emanating from the university (for example, through intellectual property agreements and distance education centres). Under this regime, knowledge is redefined as a private good and the principal goal of knowledge production is the creation of high-technology products for the global marketplace. The new regime is also typified by shifting boundaries between the public and the private. New networks of actors and structures mediate and blur the boundaries between universities, the state and corporate world (for example, offices of technology transfer and the Canadian Foundation for Innovation).

Slaughter and Rhoades (2004) also show how profit-oriented activities have become internally embedded in the academy under academic capitalism. For example, many universities have developed an expanded institutional capacity to commercialize research products outside of traditional academic structures. This is evidenced, in Canada and elsewhere, by growing university involvement in patenting and licensing activities. Moreover, academic units that are "closer to the market" are more and more likely to be prioritized within the institutional hierarchy. In Canada, this trend is taking shape through a decrease in funding for the social sciences and humanities and an increase in support for professional and applied programs. In the areas of teaching and learning, greater emphasis is placed on marketing educational services while fewer resources are devoted to undergraduate instruction. As a consequence, contract faculty have been taking on much of the teaching responsibilities once performed by tenure stream faculty in Canada and elsewhere.

ACADEMIC CAPITALISM IN THE CANADIAN CONTEXT

When did Canada's transition to corporatization or academic capitalism begin and how does it compare to university restructuring elsewhere? According to Slaughter and Leslie (1997) Canadian universities began to turn to academic capitalism in the 1980s and 1990s. This shift was marked by the growing preference for curricula with market relevance, an increase in applied and entrepreneurial research, and greater reliance on tuition fees and other sources of private funding. It was also facilitated by corporate lobbying and government policies that encouraged commercial research and development, vocational programs and a more competitive institutional environment. Slaughter and Leslie point out, however, that Canadian universities succumbed to market pressures somewhat later than other countries and that they underwent a lesser degree of structural reform. The reasons behind this difference include the fact that Canada has a less centralized system of higher education, which means it is more difficult to bring about rapid, systemic change. Moreover, in Canada, there was stronger state support for core university operations and a strong, decentralized unionization of the faculties, which insulated Canadian universities from market forces.

In my view, arguing that Canada was an exception to the trend toward academic capitalism is, in some ways, inaccurate. As noted in the opening chapter, Canadian scholarship (Buchbinder and Newson 1990; Newson and Buchbinder 1988) suggests that corporatization and academic capitalism had taken root by the middle of the 1980s. Furthermore, Slaughter and Leslie acknowledge that their analysis was limited by a lack of data on Canadian higher education (such as data on post-secondary revenues and expenditures in the 1990s), something that continues to plague national research efforts. Writing in the *Journal of Higher Education*, Amy Scott Metcalfe (2010: 490) revisits Slaughter and Leslie's claims and asserts that "Canada is certainly no longer, and perhaps never was, the 'exception' to academic capitalism." In any event, according to Metcalfe (2010: 503), Canada has since moved "swiftly into the realm of academic capitalism," erasing any notion of Canadian exceptionalism. As I will demonstrate, a more comprehensive model of academic capitalism — where market forces permeate all facets of academic life — has come to characterize many Canadian universities today.

FORCES OF RESTRUCTURING: INSIDE-OUT OR OUTSIDE-IN?

Analysts and policy makers generally agree that a new, market-based vision for university education has taken shape in recent years. There is also agreement on the changing direction and priorities of higher educational policy in Canada. The fact that corporatization is occurring is not in question. Prior to turning to a more detailed discussion of the corporatization process and its impacts on teachers, researchers, students and the public, it is important to first consider debates around the sources of this restructuring; that is, whether the determinants of change are inside or outside of the university.

THE NEW CORPORATE ETHOS

There are some who attribute the corporatization of higher education to internal factors, such as the modern university's "lack of purpose." For proponents of this perspective, the university's role is no longer clearly defined; they have lost sight of any clear mission beyond a general commitment to "excellence" and are operating in a policy vacuum that is easily exploited by outside interests (see, for example, Readings 1996). Others highlight different internal factors by arguing that restructuring is largely an expression of the autonomous initiatives and commitments of academic actors. Put another way, the logic of the private marketplace has shaped the consciousness and practices of professors and administrative professionals so that they pursue the commercial potential of academic and non-academic products and support the restructuring of their institutions in the corporate image.

Slaughter and Leslie (1997) provide a nuanced position of the role academics play in shaping the direction of higher education in relation to market influences. They note the contradictory position that professors and academic managers find themselves in within the context of corporatization. Operating in a competitive market environment, these workers are employed by the public sector but are increasingly autonomous from it, so, they "act as capitalists from within the public sector; they are state-subsidized entrepreneurs" (1997: 9). In other words, academic capitalists are actively engaged with the market at the same time as they are cushioned by public money and institutional resources (much like their counterparts in other state-supported industries). In the 1990s, Slaughter and Leslie viewed academic entrepreneurship as a reaction to external pressures and resource dependency, where individuals were "pushed" and "pulled" in particular directions by corporations and other resource providers (211). Yet, it may be that the academy should no longer be considered a passive entity that is acted upon by external forces. In their more recent work, Slaughter and Rhoades (2004) point to the active, sometimes leading, role that professors and administrators play in corporatizing higher education. In their words, these individuals are "actors initiating academic capitalism, not just players being 'corporatized'" (2004: 12).

The "inside-out" perspective is supported by Canadian university vice presidents. These administrators were asked about the culture and practice of "innovation" — defined as the competition for external dollars, knowledge transfer and the promotion of commercial research opportunities — at their institutions (Crocker and Usher 2006). Overwhelmingly, those administrators who considered their innovation climates to be positive maintained that its key drivers came from within. Very few believed that innovation on their campuses was driven by external forces. This was especially true for schools with a preponderance of younger faculty members, which speaks to the growing generational divide with respect to the culture and expectations of university research.

It would appear that many universities have become willing co-capitalists, with some enthusiastically embracing market values. But why have so many academics and academic managers assumed this role? Is it simply that they "sold out" to corporate interests, or are they reacting to funding shortfalls? To be sure, both of these explanations hold some merit. For example, the growing division between commercial and non-commercial research has allowed academic entrepreneurs to acquire a greater and greater share of available resources. This means, in practical terms, that many have a vested interest in corporatization. And in a more competitive educational environment, academic workers are understandably more aware of and concerned about their own security (and that of their institutions). For this reason, entrepreneurialism is often viewed as both an individual and an institutional necessity.

Some of the other reasons why academics have assumed this role are more complex. For one, the context of academic work is highly competitive, both in the appointment, tenure and promotion processes, as well in as the ways in which research and research reward structures are tied to the production of an academy hierarchy. Academic work is also highly individualistic. Intellectuals tend to view themselves as independent entrepreneurs who enjoy considerable autonomy and control over their labour. As a result, they have a social identity and a set of working conditions similar to that of semi-autonomous craft workers. As Mike Burke and Joanne Naiman (2003) explain, the entrepreneurial identity linked to the nature of academic work can and has been exploited by those who want to encourage competitiveness among faculty. The strong emphasis on competition and private procurement under corporatization twists the professoriate's entrepreneurial orientation (centred on independent scholarship) into one based more on profit-making and performance-based rewards. Indeed, the idea of independent scholarship today often serves as a mask for commercial activities.

However, to fully appreciate the new entrepreneurial culture, I think we also need to recognize that academic capitalism has become part of a new set of core values within the university. Polster (2010: 15) refers to the "progressive normalization of a corporate ethos within Canadian universities," where a new "common sense" has emerged in which corporate values and practices are taken for granted as the only legitimate way to function within a university setting. Elsewhere, Polster (2007a: 615–16) likens this ethos to a creeping "instrumentalism," or the incorporation of instrumental rationality into all aspects of university life:

> Canadian universities and those within them are becoming ever more frantic and calculating as they seek new opportunities and "edges" that allow them to maintain and advance their positions in an increasingly insecure and unstable environment. And from institutions where the

intrinsic worth of ideas, values, and people was recognized and respected, Canada's universities are becoming places where worth is progressively determined in relation to financial costs and benefits, at the expense of people's dignity, integrity, solidarity, and security.

What Polster is referring to here implies that a deeper process is at work than simply the replacement of public values with private ones. Within the academy, altruism and public service are becoming synonymous with market engagement and are increasingly mediated by the university's service to the economy. Likewise, conceptions of the public good are becoming aligned with individualism and private gain, as opposed to notions of collective benefits for society as a whole. Under corporatization, this is more and more the case. The freedom to maximize material wealth for business entrepreneurs is similar to the notion of "freedom" championed by today's academic entrepreneur. And for many academic capitalists it is entrepreneurial freedom — not academic freedom — that is taking precedence. These individuals are not abandoning their public commitments so much as they are redefining their means according to market logic.

GLOBALIZATION, NEOLIBERALISM AND THE CORPORATE OFFENSIVE

Contrary to those who emphasize internal factors, many analysts argue that the main sources of educational reform are external to the university, particularly the pressures associated with economic globalization. According to the dominant globalization discourse, the nature of a nation's higher educational institutions has become a marker of its competitive position in the global economy, and of its capacity to attract and retain both a skilled workforce and corporate investment. The focus here is on the importance of higher education to economic growth, science and technology and (often vague) conceptions of innovation and prosperity. From this standpoint, national policy makers look to global market pressures to inform their decisions. Universities, in turn, have modified their managerial practices and institutional arrangements to be consistent with changing policy priorities.

Proponents of this perspective see the practice of linking universities with the corporate sector to enhance national economic competitiveness as crucial to drawing universities into the process of globalization. Among these proponents, there is some debate about who or what is responsible for this shift and its key consequences. The political right tends to view the changes associated with globalization as positive and resulting from impersonal market forces. Educational restructuring is seen as a rational and necessary response to the inevitabilities of a changing market, and the process of corporatization is presented in technocratic rather than political or ideological terms. In short, universities should serve domestic corporate interests with the goal of strengthening Canada's economic position. In contrast, those coming from a left political view often locate educational restructuring within the wider political or neoliberal context of globalization. Neoliberalism, they contend, is a carefully crafted political project involving broad economic and political transformations. And a key part of this project has involved changing the function of universities from institutions that serve the public good to those that provide a more profitable ground for capitalist expansion.

In my view, there is significant evidence to support the contention that outside influences, ushered by agents of neoliberalism, have played a key role in shaping educational reform in Canada and elsewhere. Neoliberal restructuring in the area of higher education began in conjunction with the well-recognized "corporate offensive" that accelerated throughout the developed capitalist world in the early-mid 1970s (Brownlee 2005). During this period, falling profits and stagnating economic growth led corporate leaders to mobilize their collective resources to increase their power and control over the global economic system. This offensive was a response to the widespread political upheaval of the 1960s, when marginalized groups, such as workers, women and ethnic minorities, began to organize, with universities being a key site of "subversive" activities and student radicalism.

Some elite groups, like those in the Trilateral Commission, viewed the prospect of normally passive and marginalized sectors of the population organizing themselves into the political arena as a "crisis of democracy" (see Crozier, Huntington and Watanuki 1975). In part, they saw this "crisis" as resulting from a failure on the part of schools and universities, or those institutions responsible for "the indoctrination of the young" (1975: 162). They also pointed to the threat of "value-oriented intellectuals," who devoted themselves to "the derogation of leadership, the challenging of authority, and the unmasking and delegitimation of established institutions" (7). Similar concerns were expressed by the Carnegie Commission on Higher Education. The Commission argued that the culture of the university was undermining the legitimacy of the capitalist system by increasing expectations among the general population — expectations of meaningful work, a decent standard of living and political participation. In its Final Report in 1973, the Commission stated that professors and students were "disrupting" society by operating outside of normally prescribed democratic channels. In their words, campus activism in the 1960s went "far beyond the historic limits of dissent" as faculties took "institutionalized positions on political issues of an off-campus nature and abandoned the traditional position of political neutrality by the institution" (1973: 25).

Campaigns by conservative groups to reassert control over and monitor universities started in the U.S. Supreme Court Justice Lewis Powell (1971) developed a comprehensive political strategy that involved monitoring textbooks, curriculums and campus lectures; financing the work of conservative intellectuals via think-tanks and foundations; lobbying boards of trustees; and establishing a new conservative network of university academics (see Messer 1993; Schrecker 2010). This kind of general campaign also extended to Canada in the 1980s and was led by a new network of conservative speakers and writers. They launched a multifaceted campaign to protest against courses and programs devoted to race, gender and class inequality — representing the so-called politicization or "anti-intellectualism" of the curriculum — and to portray academics as hostile to Western values and interests.[2] These attacks succeeded in not only shifting intellectual discourse to the right, but in opening up political space for corporatization.

Also as part of the neoliberal corporate offensive, the university was portrayed as an institution that was unresponsive to market demands and where a great deal of "useless" learning takes place. The university's supposed inefficiencies placed it alongside other "failing" public programs and entitlements, such as health care and social security. In this way, higher education became a target of corporate/political efforts to change the culture of the public sphere. David Noble (2001: 27) explains:

> Corporate and political leaders of the major industrialized countries of the world recognized that they were losing their monopoly over the world's heavy industries and that, in the future, their supremacy would depend upon their monopoly over the knowledge that had become the lifeblood of the new so-called knowledge-based industries (space, electronics, computers, materials, telecommunications, and bioengineering). This focus upon 'intellectual capital' turned their attention to the universities as its chief source, implicating the universities as never before in the economic machinery. In the view of capital, the universities had become too important to be left to the universities.

To respond to these concerns and assert even greater control over higher education, business leaders propagated an ideology that defined the university as merely another business organization. The emphasis was on bringing universities to focus more on technical innovation, marketable skills and, at a broader level, to serving social and economic "needs" as defined by these same leaders.

More concretely, intellectual trade agreements and global intellectual property arrangements — created and enforced by organizations like the World Trade Organization (WTO), the General Agreement on Trade in Services (GATS) and the Trade Related Aspects of Intellectual Property Rights Agreement (TRIPS) — led to greater corporate involvement in higher education by unleashing new competitive pressures and a new business culture in the global economy and within universities themselves. A central premise behind the GATS and TRIPS agreements is that knowledge is a commodity like any other. One of their goals is to facilitate open markets and protections for the owners (sellers) of knowledge-based products. The GATS rules are also designed to promote "free trade" in higher educational services by guaranteeing market access for all providers, including foreign-owned for-profit companies (in the WTO's view, barriers to trade include public "subsidies" to higher education that restrict the ability of private providers to compete for students). Put simply, "trade in services" is a euphemism for handing over governmental functions, including education, to private power. Troubling questions have been raised about the potential impact of the GATS on public education in Canada (Kachur 2003; Robinson 2006).

The goals of Canadian business leaders were consistent with this larger neoliberal project. In the 1980s and 1990s, the Business Council on National Issues (BCNI), now the Canadian Council of Chief Executives, played a lead role in advancing an elite consensus on educational issues. In the area of higher education, the Council called for public-private research partnerships, vocational training and increasing the share of private funding to universities (see BCNI 1993).[3] During this period, the Corporate-Higher Education Forum (CHEF) — an alliance of twenty-five CEOs of major corporations and twenty-five university presidents — acted as chief spokesperson for the BCNI on issues of university reform. Many other organizations were also on board, including the Canadian Chamber of Commerce, the Canadian Manufacturers' Association, the National Council on Education, the Canadian Association of University Business Officers, the Fraser and C.D. Howe Institutes and the Conference Board of Canada. The power and consensus-building capacity of this alliance helps to explain why early restructuring efforts had near unanimous (if tacit) support from most sectors. As Norman Bowie (1994: 42) explains, the initial expansion of university-business partnerships in Canada "had solid support from all the affected constituencies — government officials, business executives, and university faculty and administrators," which meant that it was rarely called into question. Of course, the public, arguably the most important "affected constituency," had little or no input into this process.

The consequences of this growing elite consensus were almost immediate. For example, writing in *Report on Business Magazine*, Pat Ohlendorf (1985) documented the "astonishing number of companies" that turned to universities for leading-edge technology and commercial product development in the 1980s. University-corporate linkages, according to Ohlendorf, increased at an unprecedented rate in Canada and surpassed that of any other country outside of the U.S. Universities welcomed the infusion of new monies after a "decade of crippling budget cuts," while the goal of Canadian corporations was simple: "hitting the jackpot." These consequences are, of course, still evident today. John Valleau and Paul Hamel (2010: 57), two scientists at the University of Toronto, argue that Canada remains entrenched in a "highly orchestrated campaign by financial and industrial interests, in co-operation with our governments, to shift university activity away from scholarship toward bolstering the economic and social status quo and especially to assisting Canadian industries to increase short-term profits." While the extent to which corporate Canada's involvement in university affairs has been entirely deliberate or represents a convergence of mutual interests is open to debate, university restructuring needs to be understood within its wider political and economic context. The fact that universities reflect the impact of broader social forces is nothing new. As discussed at the outset of this chapter, universities have always been a product of their social milieu and closely linked to larger external sources of power in society.

In sum, university restructuring has been shaped by forces inside and outside of the university, with corporatization being a two-way process involving many different agents and institutional actors. On the one hand, some internal features of university life — including commercial preoccupations, heightened competition and reduced collegial governance — have supported the introduction of market methods and values. Here, institutional change should not be seen as an inevitable adaptation to external pressures, as it masks how the university community is implicated in the very political and economic forces to which it "must" then accommodate. At the same time, external forces have played an important role in reshaping higher education. Some of these forces operate primarily at the national level, including organized business campaigns and government policies. Perhaps the most pivotal "external" factor in shaping educational restructuring was the sharp and prolonged reduction in public funding that began in the 1970s.

RETRENCHMENT, AUSTERITY AND CORPORATIZATION

There are important linkages between public funding and processes of corporatization. The logic is simple: once underfunding has undermined the integrity and functionality of a public system, corporations can arrive and reinvigorate the "failing" institutions through restructuring or privatization. In some cases, these motivations have been articulated quite clearly by political and other leaders. In 1995, for example, Conservative Education Minister of Ontario, John Snobelen, remarked:

> If we really want to fundamentally change the issue in training and ... education we'll have to first make sure we've communicated brilliantly the breakdown in the process we currently experience. That's not easy. We need to invent a crisis. That's not just an act of courage. There's some skill involved. (cited in Sears 2003: 4)

In Canada, such a process began in the 1970s with two, interrelated objectives:

to convince the public that the system is "broken" and to ensure that it is broken through fiscal austerity. The pattern of reduced government expenditures for higher education ostensibly propelled Canadian universities from the so-called "golden age" into the era of corporatization.

A series of key events and decisions shaped the educational restructuring process in Canada. At the federal level, a key policy change was the creation of Established Programs Financing (EPF) in 1977. The EPF replaced the 50/50 cost-sharing program with the provinces — where federal contributions were matched dollar for dollar by provincial contributions — with a new funding arrangement based on tax points and cash transfers. Another feature of this new formula was that provinces were no longer accountable for how federal contributions would be spent, so there was no guarantee that federal funds for post-secondary education would be allocated to universities and colleges. From the late 1970s to the early 1990s, Liberal and Conservative governments reduced the monetary commitment to post-secondary education through repeated amendments to this funding formula; the billions of dollars cut by the Conservatives under Prime Minister Mulroney was especially noteworthy. Overall, between 1983–84 and 1994–95, the federal contribution to post-secondary education was reduced by nearly $13.5 billion (Tudiver 1999).

Partly a result of changes at the federal level, every province imposed funding cuts to universities in the 1970s, with different provinces reducing expenditures at different times. From 1976–77 to 1986–87, provincial grants in constant dollars per full-time student were reduced by an average of more than 20 percent nationwide. Tudiver (1999: 81) describes the impact:

> Universities eliminated frills, held back on salary increases, suspended hiring, replaced full-time faculty with limited-term and part-time appointees, laid off support staff, cut back on library operations and acquisitions, put off maintenance of buildings and equipment, and sought greater efficiencies wherever possible in the use of people, plant, and equipment. Short of major surgery to academic programs, universities did everything feasible to stay the course in the most trying fiscal setback since the Great Depression.

Tudiver (1999: 78) also notes that austerity led to governance conflicts between academic and corporate models, where "relations between faculty and administrators started to resemble worker-manager conflict in industry." Administrators were seemingly operating in a "Hobbesian environment" of recurrent budget crises, where they made decisions to cut budgets and control costs in line with a corporate management approach. A survey of Canadian academic vice presidents and deans in the early 1990s found that underfunding continued to be the most important external influence compelling university reform (Small 1994).

From the mid-1970s through the 1980s, the proportion of Canadian university revenues drawn from private donations and non-governmental grants increased considerably (Cameron 1991). The austerity programs over this period, and the resulting impacts nationally and at the provincial level, reflected resource scarcity on the part of governments to some extent, but they also reflected a deliberate plan to link universities more closely with the market and to lay the foundation for corporatization. The desire, on the part of social leaders, to facilitate this shift was evident in the work of the Task Force on Labour Market Development, headed by economist David Dodge (1981). The Task Force suggested a number of concrete ways that universities could be "induced" into a restructuring mandate. These included more reliance on private funding, redirecting federal funds to support sponsored research, market-based programs and skills-based training, and reallocating money away from arts-based disciplines. This series of recommendations implied that basic funding for core university operations and liberal arts education was a lesser priority, and necessitated a stronger focus on forging university-business partnerships. Other key actors, including the BCNI and the CHEF, also played leading roles in articulating an elite consensus on educational issues during this period. The BCNI launched a sustained assault to undermine public confidence in public education and called for government cutbacks to universities, while the CHEF explicitly advocated government underfunding to make universities more responsive to private interests (Barlow and Robertson 1994).[4]

Retrenchment continued in the 1990s. In 1995, the federal Liberals brought the EPF and the Canada Assistance Plan together under a single financing mechanism: the Canada Health and Social Transfer (CHST). The CHST further reduced federal transfers to the provinces and gave them more discretion over how funds were to be divided among health care, education and other social programs. As a result, the proportion of the federal transfer going to post-secondary education was reduced. According to Tudiver (1999), the percentage of university operating income paid for by students, which had been increasing since the early 1980s, accelerated from 24.3 percent in 1994–95 to 31.6 percent just three years later. Over the same three-year period, the percentage of operating income paid for by governments declined from 72.2 percent to 63.4 percent. In fact, when student enrolment is taken into account, the amount of federal transfer money spent per student declined by almost 50 percent between 1994–95 and 2004–05 (Fisher et al. 2006). Most provinces passed on these cuts to students and their families through increasing tuition and student debt. Over this time period, tuition at Canadian universities more than doubled.

Also in the 1990s, provincial governments added their own unique brands of restructuring and austerity. For example, as part of its broader plan to shrink the public sector and redirect higher education toward prescribed economic goals, in 1996–97 the Harris Conservatives in Ontario reduced the overall operating grant to universities by nearly 15 percent, about $1.55 billion (Axelrod 2008). This cut was part of a decade-long trend that saw the percentage of Ontario university funding covered by provincial grants fall from 55.1 percent in 1991–92 to 39.6 percent in 1999–2000. In the case of Alberta, beginning in 1994, the government reduced its spending on higher education by 21 percent over a three-year period (Barnetson and Boberg 2000). Perhaps more than any other province, the reallocation of post-secondary resources by the Alberta government was designed to achieve a specific set of policy objectives. These included increasing higher education's role as a source of vocational training as well as augmenting the amount of knowledge and technology transferred by universities to the private sector.

Over the 1990s, universities increasingly turned to the private sector for funding as a way to compensate for public funding shortfalls. In Ontario, for example, university revenues from all private sources increased, with corporate contributions outpacing the others with the exception of tuition fees (Robertson, McGrane and Shaker 2003). In British Columbia, private funding (excluding tuition) grew from 5.8 percent of university revenues in 1990–91 to 9.2 percent in 2002–03 (Malcolmson and Lee 2004). At the national level, private revenues increased by 167 percent between 1986–87 and 2001–02. Most of this increase was a product of rising tuition fees, but a considerable proportion came from corporate donations, non-governmental grants, contracts and investments (Tandem Social Research Consulting 2007). As corporatization accelerated in Canada, business leaders also became much more insistent about how their donations would be spent. Unlike most public funding, the donations of private benefactors — once celebrated as evidence of corporate "soulfulness" — were provided with clear expectations of direct economic returns. This change has been reflected in the growing business preference for "partnerships," as opposed to general donations.

In the late 1990s, Canada started to see some reinvestments in the post-secondary system, but in very targeted ways and to support a specific policy direction. After balancing the budget in 1997, the federal Liberals increased public expenditures to universities at the national level, even though the percentage increase in private funding continued to outpace the public contribution (Metcalfe 2010). Consistent with academic capitalism, university financing in this period (and continuing to the present day) has involved shifts, not necessarily reductions, in public subsidy. Some of these new "spending" initiatives came in the form of tax credits and personal education savings schemes. Others involved targeted investments in university research — such as the Canadian Foundation for Innovation and the Canada Research Chairs program — and selective grants aimed at supporting the private sector and university-industry ties. Although the budgets of the federal research granting councils increased, their priorities were reoriented in the same direction. James Turk, former long-time head of the CAUT, likens the process of channelling money through special targeted programs rather than reinvesting in core funding to "putting a fancy porch on a crumbling building" (cited in Grant 2002: 262). It should also be noted that of the billions of dollars in research spending that the Liberals added between 1997–98 and 2004–05, most was allocated to a small group of research-intensive institutions; only 12 percent of the funding went to the social sciences and humanities (Slaughter and Rhoades 2008).

By the time the Liberal's thirteen-year reign was over in 2006, Canada's university system was a shell of its former self. According to the AUCC (2008a), overall federal and provincial government funding for university teaching and non-sponsored research fell from more than $17,900 per student in 1980–81 to $9,900 in 2006–07. In 1980, governments contributed 84 percent of the funds available for these core activities, while student fees covered around 10 percent. By 2006, these shares were 66 and 24 percent respectively.

Impacts of corporatization have been different across provinces, illustrating the political nature of funding decisions through two key markers: (i) the substantial variation between provinces in their mix of public and private revenue streams, and (ii) the lack of a discernible relationship between the portion of university revenue that comes from provincial governments and the size and wealth of the province. In 2008–09, the government of Ontario provided just 37 percent of total university revenues — the second lowest in the country, while tuition fees accounted for 26 percent. In comparison to Ontario, Nova Scotia was the only province where the government paid a smaller proportion of total revenues and students paid a larger share, at 30 and 34 percent respectively. At the other end of the spectrum, the government of Newfoundland provided 56 percent of total revenues, with its students contributing 14 percent in fees. In Quebec, the provincial government provided 59 percent of funding, whereas tuition accounted for just 10 percent (OCUFA 2010a).

When the federal Conservatives took power in 2006, they increased core funding to universities. For 2008–09, the share of federal transfers earmarked for post-secondary education was increased by $800 million — the largest increase in core transfer payments in fifteen years — yet it was still $1.2 billion short of what was needed to restore funding to 1992–93 levels. However, the government failed to set any binding conditions or legislated guidelines for the new investment, which meant that while some provinces, like Saskatchewan, increased their grants to universities, others did not and some, like British Columbia, even reduced it. The Conservatives have also maintained the Liberal agenda of targeted research investments, in large part to support commercialization. This kind of focus has encouraged a process of institutional differentiation, both within and between universities.

Pressures in this direction are also coming from university leaders. Shifting priorities are evident in a 2008 proposal put forward by Canadian university presidents. Frustrated with the egalitarian pattern or "one size fits all" approach to higher education, the presidents of five of the country's top research institutions — Toronto, Alberta, British Columbia, Montreal and McGill — came together to propose changes to the way that Canada's university system is organized and funded. Under the "Big 5" proposal, federal funds would be differentially allocated to those universities that specialize in research and graduate training, and the rest who specialize in teaching and undergraduate education. Not surprisingly, the Big 5 wanted a greater share of research money and to be absolved, at least in part, of their undergraduate commitments. Critics of the proposal were quick to note that there is already growing institutional differentiation in Canada. By the mid-2000s, for example, a clear branch of research-intensive universities had emerged, with the Big 5 alone accounting for approximately 40 percent of available research funding (Turk 2009).

At the national level, public funding made up 84 percent of university operating revenues in 1979; by 2009 this figure was reduced to just 58 percent. Over this same period, tuition fees rose from 12 to 35 percent of operating revenues, and corporate and other private fundraising has also continued to rise (CAUT 2012). Private funding through donations, grants and bequests alone grew from approximately $54 million in 1972 to $2.9 billion in 2008, or from 3 percent to 10.8 percent of total university revenues. In 2008, almost 40 percent of this total came from corporations (CAUT 2009a). More business funding along with increased tuition fees has meant that Canada now has one of the highest proportions of private university funding in the world (CCL 2010b; Metcalfe 2010). Even Quebec, which has resisted the corporatization agenda relative to other provinces, has seen substantial increases in private funding.[5]

The period of fiscal retrenchment that began in the 1970s continues today, as evidenced by the current state of funding for education nationally and how this translates across provinces. Although the federal Conservatives have maintained education transfer payments to the provinces, they remain too low to cover inflation and enrolment increases. The government has also ignored skyrocketing student debt levels and tuition fees in recent budgets, investing instead in fighter jets, prisons and subsidies to the oil industry. As well, many of the recent policy and budgetary choices of provincial governments have reinforced the federal austerity agenda in higher education.[6] Financial cutbacks and other austerity measures have been a driving external force of university restructuring in Canada. Commenting on the long-term consequences of this underfunding, Erika Shaker (2006: 11, emphasis in original) notes that unless or until an adequate base of public funding is restored, we will "forever be scrambling to find less effective, less accountable, less equitable, less efficient, less *public* methods of compensating" for inadequate public support.

This chapter provided a historical backdrop in which to situate the university's relationship to external sources of power. While business influence in higher education began with the onset of capitalism, it has taken shape as a transforming force primarily over the past four decades. Moreover, both internal and external factors have created a more corporate university environment, with cuts in public financing being one major driving force. The impact of this transformative process in Canada can be seen in teaching and academic labour, the political economy of student life, the rise of corporate management models and the commercialization of university research.

NOTES

1   In 1954, a U.S. congressional commission investigated the goals and influence of large corporate foundations in the area of higher education (particularly their impact on the social sciences). Its conclusions are worth quoting at length: "The power of the individual large foundation is enormous. Its various forms of patronage carry with them elements of thought control. It exerts immense influence on educator, educational processes, and educational institutions. It is capable of invisible coercion. It can materially predetermine the development of social and political concepts, academic opinion, thought leadership, public opinion ... There is such a concentration of foundation power in the United States, operating in education and the social sciences, with a gigantic aggregate of capital and income. This Interlock has some of the characteristics of an intellectual cartel ... It has come to exercise very extensive practical control over social science and education ... [Social science research] is now almost wholly in the control of professional employees of the large foundations" (cited in Gatto 2003: 254–255).

2   In the U.S., see Bennett 1984, Bloom 1987, D'Souza 1991, Kimball 1990, Horowitz 2006, Horowitz and Laksin 2009 and Shapiro 2004. In Canada, the backlash against "political correctness" and democracy in the university can be found in works such as John Fekete's *Moral Panic* (1994), as well as David Bercuson, Robert Bothwell and J.L. Granatstein's *The Great Brain Robbery* (1984) and *Petrified Campus* (1997). Self-described "intellectual elitists," Bercuson, Bothwell and Granatstein (1997: 5) have openly called for less democracy in university governance, less faculty unionism, less student participation in academic decision-making, the elimination of tenure, large increases in tuition fees, and the elimination of courses and programs they deem "useless" or overtly political.

3   At the First National Conference on Business-Education Partnerships in 1990, corporate leaders were explicit about the way they understood the relationship between universities and the business community and identified future ways to capitalize on this relationship (Bloom 1990). At the conference, Norman Kissick, CEO of Union Carbide Canada, stressed the need for a "permanent commitment by business and education leaders to develop a closer partnership," and added that "excellence must be chosen over

breadth of curricula" so that students could be trained to "create, produce and market high-technology, value-added products" for the corporate economy (6). Similarly, Vice-President of IBM Canada, Anita Ross, argued that the entire educational system required "radical change" to shift it to an economic rather than a social enterprise (13).

4   Randle Nelsen (2002) argues that by the mid-1980s, the efforts of these groups had a noticeable impact, with university presidents starting to act more and more like corporate CEOs. Nelsen quotes University of Regina president Lloyd Barber, who responded to a 1985 media inquiry concerning the influence of the CHEF by saying that: "If you sat around the table and listened to the discussion and didn't know, you'd be hard-pressed to know who was a university president and who was a corporate president" (133). For a good illustration of CHEF's position on corporate-university relations in the 1980s, see Maxwell and Currie (1984).

5   Between 1988 and 2009, the proportion of university income from the private sector increased from 7.5 to 21.2 percent in the province. During this period, the proportion of university income from individuals rose from 5.4 to 12.2 percent, while income from the public sector fell from 87 to 65.8 percent (Martin and Tremblay-Pepin 2011). In 2012, the Quebec government launched the "Placements Universités" program, with the goal of encouraging philanthropy from individuals and corporations by providing matching grants equal to the amount of money universities raised in private donations (Beeston 2012).

6   In 2013, for example, the Alberta government imposed a seven percent reduction ($147 million) in base operating grants to the province's universities, colleges and technical institutes. British Columbia's budget included a $46 million cut to post-secondary education. In Quebec, the government imposed cuts of $250 million on universities. Post-secondary institutions in Manitoba, Ontario and several Atlantic provinces have also faced austerity measures.

CHAPTER THREE

UNIVERSITY TEACHING AND THE CASUALIZATION OF ACADEMIC LABOUR

The changing nature of university teaching and academic labour is one of the most visible manifestations of corporatization. Corporate restructuring has had a significant impact on university teaching and, with it, the nature of academic work. The focus of university teaching has been dramatically altered, and it is seen to have little value relative to university research. Under corporatization, the esteem attached to teaching for the sake of learning and fostering critical thinking has declined along with the associated resources and institutional supports. One of most marked shifts within academic work has been the casualization of academic labour.

CHANGING PRIORITIES: THE TEACHING–RESEARCH NEXUS

For most of its history, teaching was the primary obligation of the public university. The overriding importance of teaching to the university's mission is evident, for example, in the views of prominent Canadian scholars and administrators in the post-World War II period (Neatby 1985). Over time, research also assumed a central place in institutions of higher learning. Moreover, the obligations of teaching and research are often seen as closely tied to one another or even interdependent, where research is seen to be improved by an active commitment to student learning, and teaching is most effective when combined with an active involvement in research. The interdependence, or unity, of teaching and research has come to define an important ideal about what the university — and university scholarship — should be. Building on this assumption, what presumably distinguishes university teachers from other educators is that they are actively engaged in knowledge production, not simply knowledge transmission. As Ian Angus (2009: 85) explains, underlying the unity of teaching and research is the belief that a field of knowledge "is seen very differently by a person who is in the process of contributing to its current state than by someone who simply accepts the current state as given." It is also necessary for students, as future knowledge producers, to "experience through the university researcher/teacher an *active* organization of a field such that currently interesting questions could be advanced by further research" (2009: 86, emphasis in original).

In principle, the unity of teaching and research remains a foundational concept in Canadian universities. I would emphasize, however, that there are growing tensions in this relationship, especially as corporatization has advanced. For one, research has overcome teaching in many respects. In 1990, the president of the Carnegie Foundation for the Advancement of Education, Ernest Boyer, famously denounced the university's overemphasis on research at the expense of undergraduate teaching. Boyer called for a redefinition of scholarship that would restore teaching and service to their central position in academia. Around the same time, a study commissioned by the AUCC argued that the growing primacy of research in the Canadian academy had detrimental effects on undergraduate education (Smith 1991). The report also noted that the nominal distribution of effort in faculty work — which assumes 40 percent for research, 40 percent for teaching and 20 percent for service — was being challenged to support a stronger emphasis on research.

Related to this, research has come to be defined as more prestigious and is more valued than teaching. As a result, an institution's status and reputation is now generally defined more by the name recognition of its researchers than by quality teaching or student learning. A recent study of thirty-four universities found that, regardless of a university's policies on teaching, most faculty indicated that research was the key priority of their institutions (Jaschik 2011). Others studies have had similar results. A survey by the Ontario government's Higher Education Quality Council, for instance, found that only 61 percent of professors believed that teaching was important to their institutions, while 70 percent believed that research was more valuable than teaching in enhancing one's academic reputation and access to funds (Serebrin 2010). In another survey, the proportion of Ontario faculty who said that research was their institution's top priority was more than double the proportion who believed that their institution valued teaching above other aspects of academic work (OCUFA 2012a).

It follows that research productivity is now the strongest indicator of faculty compensation in Canada. According to one study, high quality instruction — including measures such as the amount of time spent in the classroom — was found to be either unrelated or negatively related to rates of pay (Usher and Potter 2006). Moreover, Phaneuf et al. (2007) have shown that research is clearly favoured over both teaching and service in promotion reviews at Canadian universities. As it stands now, an established record of published research can easily override a poor teaching record in hiring, tenure and promotion decisions. In some cases, having fewer teaching commitments has actually come to be associated with higher professorial status in the academy; the most renowned scholars usually teach the least, often as a reward for research productivity or success in obtaining external grants. The result is a "strange and perverse" system whereby "experienced professors, who have had time to reflect on the nature, problems, and prospects of their subject and its relationship to other subjects, generally teach specialized courses to small classes, while inexperienced sessional lecturers deal with basic questions in large classes" (Pocklington and Tupper 2002: 56). Sessional or contract faculty are under no obligation to conduct research as part of their jobs and are not compensated for doing so. Noting the reliance of universities on contract staff, Pocklington and Tupper (2002: 112) contend that only two conclusions are possible:

> First, either research is not required to be an effective teacher and university practice contradicts university ideology about teaching and research. Or second, if mutual enrichment is true, universities' practice of employing part-time, nonresearching professors is an admission that undergraduates receive an inferior education. Universities cannot logically claim that teaching and research are intertwined to the benefit of students when they employ professors who are not required to do research.

Not surprisingly, shifting perspectives on the value of teaching and research have had an impact on how resources are allocated within university institutions. In the context of corporatization, one of the most significant differences is that universities are devoting a greater proportion of their resources to research. This attention includes concerted efforts to attract "star" researchers to their campuses. These celebrated professors, who often teach very little, can have a significant impact on university prestige and the (market) value of academic programs. As a result, alternative investments in areas such as curriculum or professional development are often pushed to the bottom of the agenda. A good illustration of this reorienting of priorities can be found in the 2010 *Report of the Steering Committee on Resource Optimization* for the University of Ottawa, which notes that the university recently made a "strategic decision to become more research intensive," yet the "progressive reduction in teaching loads necessary to enable professors more time to dedicate to research activities" has led to financial strain (2010: 5). To free up money for its research mandate and achieve the desired teaching reductions, the Committee recommended: reducing course offerings; increasing class sizes; cutting bursaries, scholarships and teaching assistants by nearly $5 million; downgrading library collections; and reducing support services for both students and teachers. It also suggests that additional revenues to offset the recommended cuts might be generated by inviting corporate sponsors to attend teaching events on campus and "charging a fee for the booths where they can display their products or services" (40). Similar "resource optimization" reviews have been conducted at other Canadian universities. At the University of Manitoba, the process led to the closure of its Learning Technology Centre, while at the University of Calgary, it resulted in significant staff reductions (CUPE 2010).

At the same time as changes have taken place at the institutional level, there have also been changes in the nature of the day-to-day work lives and responsibilities of faculty members. In Canada and elsewhere, there has been a substantial rise in research-related expectations and tasks for a range of faculty. Competition for grants has intensified and more time is required to prepare funding applications and manage other "accountability" requirements, especially for projects involving external partnerships. According to the AUCC (2007a), a survey of 6,000 U.S. researchers found that 42 percent of the time professors allocated for research was actually taken up by research-related administrative work. In some disciplines, greater expectations also exist for faculty to advance research with commercial applications. On this point, evidence suggests a negative relationship between faculty entrepreneurialism and commitment to teaching (Lee and Rhoads 2004). Not only can a preoccupation with research detract from teaching and pedagogical commitments, it has been associated with a steady decline in "academic citizenship" — defined as participation in and commitment to institutional governance and administrative service — in most major North American universities (Thompson, Constantineau and Fallis 2006).

The seemed unity between teaching and research has also been challenged by the differentiation of the full-time faculty role through the creation of teaching-only streams. Some teaching stream positions currently exist in most Ontario universities, and they are becoming more common in other parts of the country (Sanders 2011; Vajoczki et al. 2011). The University of Toronto, for example, employs hundreds of these workers, and York University recently announced plans to bring in two hundred such faculty over the next few years. Moreover, several universities in Canada now explicitly restrict research activity and are considered "teaching-first" institutions. Examples include Fraser Valley, Kwantlen and Vancouver Island universities, all of which are located in British Columbia and received their university status in 2008. For Ian Clark and his colleagues (2009: 108), these changes signify that the "teacher-researcher is in retreat, and the vision of a university system where almost all students are taught by teacher-researchers is no longer with us." Ontario has also been considering proposals to construct three entirely teaching-oriented universities, where the "distractions" of research activities would be reduced (see Clark, Trick and Van Loon 2011). While these proposals are often framed in terms of the need to improve access and the quality of education, the ultimate goal appears to be cost reduction. And, like the use of contract labour and teaching-stream positions, the proposals are based on the assumption that it does not undermine teaching and learning to decouple them from academic research. At the same time, the proposals tend to ignore, or at least not be concerned with, how institutional differentiation might facilitate a two-tier system of university education, or the fact that many are opposed to the separation of teaching and research. A recent survey of over 2,000 Ontario faculty and academic librarians found that 91 percent of respondents agreed (64 percent "strongly agreed") that teaching by faculty who are active in research is an important part of a university education (OCUFA 2012b). Moreover, a recent public survey found that more than two thirds of Ontarians believe that universities must combine research with teaching in order to fulfill their mandate (OCUFA 2013).

Of course, it is not only a shift in the relative value of teaching and research that has changed institutional arrangements and priorities. Under corporatization, funding mandates are also heavily influenced by external — and especially corporate — research alliances. To participate in corporate research partnerships, universities must "spend significant funds developing proposals, attracting partners, building labs, and purchasing equipment. They also need to support a growing cadre of administrators and other specialists to help broker and negotiate complex agreements, monitor them, and resolve inevitable conflicts" (Polster 2007b: 320). These observations are supported by considerable evidence, some of which has been reported in the mainstream press. For example, relying on data from Statistics Canada and the Canadian Association of University Business Officers, W.D. Smith (2010) found that sponsored research in Canada's 25 largest universities accounted for 14.9 percent of university expenditures in 1988; by 2008, this figure had grown to 24.7 percent. This increase in sponsored research related expenditures coincided with parallel declines in general operating expenditures — including in areas central to undergraduate teaching — and academic salaries. Smith (2010) concludes that "teaching has not just fallen down the priority list; it has been pushed there by conscious resource allocation decisions. Less money is reaching the classroom."

Some critics have challenged the assumption that the relationship between teaching and research is or ever could be a harmonious one. Alex Usher and Andrew Potter (2006: 47), for example, liken excellence/productivity in teaching and research to a "zero-sum game," where any relationship that exists between them is likely to be antagonistic rather than mutually reinforcing. Similarly, Clark et al. (2009) argue that there is little relation between excellence in teaching and excellence in research; instructors who are not active researchers are no more or less effective in the classroom than tenured professors. Tom Pocklington and Allan Tupper (2002) perhaps go even further, arguing that in the current era of research specialization and the preoccupation with commercial concerns, a lot of university research detracts from teaching and is removed from the needs of undergraduate students. They maintain that instructing students who have not yet achieved a mastery of their disciplines requires teachers who are adept at "reflective inquiry" — an intellectual process aimed at largeness or breadth of vision — not those who are consumed by specialized "frontier" research or a "publish or perish" mentality. It is worth noting that some high-level university administrators have also questioned the viability of the relationship between teaching and research. In a 2011 report on undergraduate education produced by the AUCC (2011c: 4), one university president expressed frustration that institutional status is no longer "built on teaching. The things that really determine the reputation of our institutions right now are research and attracting high-profile talent and big infrastructure. What doesn't count is teaching, the local interests, engaging in civil society."

Whatever the legitimacy of these arguments, the trends make clear that the logic of the corporatized university holds that knowledge production should be reserved for a minority of well-compensated, research-driven scholars with few teaching commitments, while knowledge transmission should be relegated to lesser valued, and lesser paid, instructors. And regardless of what one believes about the interdependence of teaching and research, corporatization has reduced the capacity for these two activities to be mutually reinforcing. Put simply, corporatization has been a key driving force behind the apparent "decline" of the integrated teacher-researcher model. Although Canadian universities continue to position teaching as an important ideal — or at least as equal to research — the reality is very different. For educational administrators, liberal education is too often seen as costly, time consuming and irrelevant. It is for these reasons that they increasingly rely on contract faculty to assume a greater proportion of teaching responsibilities.

CASUALIZED ACADEMIC LABOUR

In 2008, the longest university strike in English-speaking Canada took place at York University when 3,400 contract faculty and research and teaching assistants walked off the job for 85 days. While the main issues were wages and working conditions for contract academic staff, the strike was viewed by many students and teachers as a broader political struggle against neoliberal restructuring in the university. The strike ended only after the provincial government imposed back-to-work legislation, effectively allowing the university to continue to save millions of dollars each year by relying on contract instructors rather than renewing its tenured workforce. It also thwarted the possibility that the strike would be used as a precedent-setting event for improving the job security and working conditions of contract faculty across Canada. The victory for the administration was as much political as it was economic. Incorporating principles of greater job security for contract staff into the collective agreement would have interfered with the broader process of educational restructuring at York, just as it would have set a "bad example" for the government to allow gains for public sector workers in a time of austerity. At York and elsewhere, the casualization of academic labour — marked by the increasing use of contract faculty in university teaching — is one of the most important aspects of the corporatization of the university. It is a process that Benjamin Johnson (2003: 62) has characterized as the "rot at the heart of the new corporate university system."

CONTRACT FACULTY

Many different terms have been used to describe the growing segment of academics who work off the tenure track, including contract instructors, adjuncts, part-timers, sessionals, limited-term employees, lecturers, stipendiaries, migrant workers, contingent workers, "hidden" or invisible academics, the precariat, the academic "underclass" and intellectual proletariat. Some have even used the phrases "freeway flyers" and "road scholars" to refer to workers who string together several positions at multiple institutions. There are also several different kinds of contract appointments. Most contracts fall within the category of part-time work; however, they can also include full-time, limited-term positions. Regardless of these nuances, there are some commonalities about contract work that distinguish it from permanent full-time employment. Whereas tenured and tenure track academics are expected to perform the full range of academic activities — including teaching, research and service — contract instructors are hired solely to teach. This limited job description means that, unlike their tenured counterparts, contract faculty are typically excluded from participating in university governance. Moreover, their salaries are usually a fraction of those earned per course by tenured professors, and their benefits — including sick leave, parental leave, health and disability insurance, vision and dental care — are often limited or non-existent, despite the fact that they may be employed by the same institution for long periods of time.

Contract faculty differ from one another in many ways, including their life circumstances, level of education, career aspirations, motivations for teaching, and employment status outside the university. Indhu Rajagopal (2002) distinguishes between two main groups of contract faculty: "classics" and "contemporaries." Classics typically have full-time careers outside of academia, in areas such as education, social work, business, dentistry, law or medicine. For this reason, they may find the conditions of part-time academic work acceptable or even desirable. These hires have been important to universities since their inception, as they provide specialized expertise and connections to new advances in professional fields. Sometimes "classic" hires have a high social standing. In 2010, for example, former head of the Canadian Council of Chief Executives, Tom D'Aquino, assumed an academic appointment in the Norman Patterson School of International Affairs at Carleton University. Classics, however, are the exception rather than the rule. Most contract academics are not well-paid professionals, but are contemporaries

— individuals who usually teach core courses rather than narrow specialties and whose livelihoods are dependent on part-time teaching. Contemporaries comprise a greater proportion of teaching staff in Canadian universities and, relative to their numbers, provide a higher proportion of the courses taught. This group also contains a higher proportion of scholars who desire a full-time academic career. Although both groups of contract faculty may value teaching, the practicing professional who teaches courses as part of their personal or professional life is very different than the aspiring academic who teaches multiple courses at substandard wages as a means of earning a living. Overall, classics can generally be thought of as "willing" part-timers, while contemporaries are the "real" part-time faculty within the university.

The increasing use of contract workers in Canadian universities also has distinct gender and racial dimensions. Contract employees are disproportionally women and persons from ethno-racial minority groups (Muzzin 2008). Women are over-represented among contingent faculty, particularly in relation to the proportion of women in higher academic ranks (Bauder 2006; CAUT 2006). Moreover, women part-timers make less money, are more likely to derive a greater share of their income from contract work, and are less likely to have outside employment than men (Rajagopal 2002). In part, these inequities can be attributed to the fact that women are more likely to be contemporary contract workers. More recently, a 2012 report by the Council of Canadian Academies (2012a) found that, despite significant improvements in recent years,[1] women remain significantly under-represented within Canada's highest academic ranks and women occupy a much higher proportion of contract faculty.

In addition to differences amongst contract labourers, there are also differences between faculties and departments in their use of contract labour. Narrow professional disciplines such as law or business are often in a better position to hire practice-based specialists from the community (classics) to mitigate budget cuts or fill gaps left by permanent faculty on leave. However, this option is not as readily available for the humanities and social sciences, which rely on contemporaries to a greater extent. In Ontario, for example, 65 percent of all doctoral graduates pursued their degree with the intention of becoming university professors. In the humanities, this figure was 86 percent (Desjardins 2012).

Despite the diverse characteristics of contract employees, including who they are and where they are most likely to be employed, their defining characteristic is their limited-term contract. As I mentioned, there is a large and growing number of contemporaries who do not have careers outside of academia, who desire full-time academic employment, and who rely on contract teaching as their chief source of income. When we talk about contract faculty, we are really talking about contemporaries.

THE RISE IN CONTRACT FACULTY

Contract teaching is not a new phenomenon. The increase in these kinds of academic appointments is the result of a longstanding transformation of academic labour that began in the 1970s. But these appointments generally served a different purpose in the past than they do today. During the expansion phase of higher education in the 1960s, limited-term appointments usually functioned as stepping-stones to permanent academic jobs. Furthermore, contract appointments were generally beneficial for both the university and instructor. They allowed academic departments the opportunity to evaluate new recruits before offering them a tenure track position, and they offered young scholars teaching and other valuable academic experience prior to assuming a full-time job. This situation changed with the onset of fiscal restraint in the 1970s. During this period, the academic job market shifted in the direction of intermittent, part-time positions. Rather than replace vacated spots previously held by tenured faculty, large numbers of contract academics were hired on a course-by-course basis in order to reduce costs. Universities justified substandard wages and meager benefits by limiting employment responsibilities to instruction, with no "requirements" (and therefore no support) to conduct research or provide service to the institution.

The number of part-timers hired and their ratio to permanent faculty increased significantly in Ontario, for example, from the mid-1970s through the 1980s (Rajagopal 2002). Similarly, in Quebec, there were almost as many contract instructors (or chargés de cours) as there were permanent faculty by the end of the 1980s, although a significant number were of the "classic" variety (Cameron 1991). This transformation of academic work did not go unnoticed. As early as 1976, the Ontario Confederation of University Faculty Associations and the Council of Ontario Universities were criticizing their memberships for using more term appointments in an effort to reduce costs. In the opinion of both organizations, the increasing reliance on contract faculty was creating "second-class citizens of the university community [who are] unable to participate fully in various aspects of its life and work or to plan their lives and careers with reasonable hope" (Axelrod 1982a: 187).

Today, there is much more detailed information on the nature and extent of this transformation at the national level in the U.S. than there is in Canada. According to a 2010 report by the American Association of University Professors (AAUP), between 1976 and 2007, the number of part-time faculty in the U.S. increased by 264 percent, while the number of full-time non-tenure track faculty rose by 211 percent. In contrast, the increase in tenured and tenure track faculty was just 28 percent and 7 percent respectively. A more recent study by the AAUP shows that contract employees now constitute over three quarters of U.S. faculty across all institutional types, from community and liberal arts colleges to large research universities (Curtis 2014). Joe Berry (2005: 4) comments that the casualization of the faculty workforce in the U.S. "represents one of the few instances in the U.S. economy (another is taxi driving) where an entire occupation has been converted from permanent career status to temporary, often part-time, status in the space of a single generation of workers." Indeed, a "two-tiered" professoriate has emerged in the U.S., where a minority of professors in the top tier are well compensated, enjoy considerable job security, control their own work and occupy what Stanley Aronowitz (2001) once described as "the last good job in America." In contrast, the more than three quarters of academics in the bottom tier are poorly paid, lack benefits and pensions, have little or no say in academic governance, and are denied the opportunity or support to do research or service.

Documenting the increasing use of contract faculty in Canada is more difficult. There continues to be no reliable data on the number of contract faculty working in Canadian universities. There are three key reasons for this scarcity in data. First, there have been few academic studies on the topic, with the most detailed research to date — Indhu Rajagopal's *Hidden Academics* (2002) — being limited to the early 1990s. Indicative of the lack of research is that the most recent empirical work comes from an unpublished Master's of Arts thesis (Bauer 2011) and U.S. scholars (Dobbie and Robinson 2008).[2] Second, government cuts to organizations involved in generating educational statistics and analysis, including Statistics Canada, have compounded challenges in collecting and releasing these kinds of data. Third, and most importantly, universities have directly caused and contributed to the problem as many have been reluctant to release this information.

Exposing Administrative Secrecy and Hidden Academics
Obtaining employment data on contract faculty in Canada is not a new challenge. Three decades ago, Helen Breslauer (1985: 86) observed that university administrators were "unwilling or unable" to provide information on their contract instructors, even though Statistics Canada was prepared to conduct the necessary research. In fact, Statistics Canada has attempted, repeatedly, to assemble these data through its surveys on part-time faculty. Unfortunately, this research was compromised because a number of major universities chose not to complete the surveys. Another attempt was made in 2004 by the Ontario Confederation of University Faculty Associations (OCUFA). The OCUFA submitted access to information (ATI) requests on faculty hiring to Ontario universities asking for the number of full-time tenure stream faculty, full-time contract appointments, and part-time contract appointments hired each year from 1999 to 2004. The response of the universities was revealing. Over a three-month period, four universities ignored the OCUFA's requests entirely while nine acknowledged receipt of the request but did not provide any data. In fact, only seven institutions made an effort to provide any information and, within this group,

four supplied data that did not conform to the request or was of partial/limited use. In short, universities have been "unwilling or unable" to supply employment data on contract faculty for decades. But, which is it?

I was able to shed some light on this question by doing research using Ontario's Freedom of Information and Protection of Privacy Act (FIPPA). Ontario expanded its freedom of information laws in 2006 to include public universities, which meant that they were now included under the FIPPA legislation. In 2010, I sent ATI requests to eighteen Ontario universities. Similar to the OCUFA, I asked for longitudinal data on the number of full-time tenured or tenure track faculty, full-time contract faculty, and part-time contract faculty hired each year from 2000 to 2010. By analyzing responses to similar ATI requests before and after the new FIPPA laws came into effect, it is apparent that universities had been reluctant to release this information. While thirteen institutions provided no data whatsoever to the OCUFA, I received complete datasets from fifteen institutions (and partial datasets from the remaining three). Needless to say, the differential response of universities to the two sets of requests is striking. It suggests that universities are not now, nor have they likely ever been, unable to provide data on contract faculty, and that the problems encountered by past researchers resided in political self-interest and "unwilling" administrators who were not compelled to provide the data under the FIPPA.

This conclusion about the reluctance to release this information was also supported by some of the informal information I gathered during the data collection process. Research on the ATI process in Canada has shown that ATI coordinators occupy a role somewhere between "neutral mediator," or an honest broker between two parties, and "information gatekeeper," where a coordinator seeks to preserve informational secrecy on the part of an agency, organization or institution (Larsen and Walby 2012). Some common gatekeeper strategies include the use of broad exemption clauses in ATI laws, lengthy extensions/delays and prohibitive fee estimates. Although these strategies were used on occasion in an effort to thwart my requests, most of the information coordinators I worked with assumed the role of mediator. The same cannot be said, however, about several of the senior administrators I worked with on a more informal basis. These managers tended to assume a gatekeeper role.

At one institution, for example, I was informed by the access coordinator that no decision had been made about releasing the data, even though a fee estimate had been produced and data collection was nearly complete. After an additional two month delay, the coordinator conceded that certain "interested parties" within the administration wanted to see what the data showed before making it public, and one of them spoke with me directly to inquire about how the information would be used. At another institution that relies heavily on contract faculty, a high level administrator provided me with a number of justifications (without evidence) as to why so many contract faculty were employed at the institution. For these reasons, he said, the information I was requesting could be misleading or "contentious," and I should consider dropping the request. When I eventually received the contentious data, this same administrator warned me (on three separate occasions) to interpret the figures with "caution" and "care." Another case of note involved a university president intervening to delay my request twice under section 27 (1) of the FIPPA, which states that an institution head is permitted to extend the time limit (for a "reasonable" period) in those circumstances where processing the request would "unreasonably interfere with the operations of the institution." Critics have noted that this kind of broad language can be interpreted is such a way as to delay most information requests indefinitely. In sum, the issue of contract hiring has clear political overtones and I experienced this firsthand in my encounters with multiple institutions.

I should also note, however, that an explanation that reduces the problem to "unwilling" administrators is probably too simplistic. I would contend that the longstanding inability of researchers to gain access to these data also resides in the nature of university data management, which has been made more problematic by the precarious relationship between universities and their contract employees. For example, part of the difficulty in generating statistics on contract faculty has to do with the way they are defined, categorized and prioritized within the academy. Some universities maintain records of full-time faculty but not part-time faculty. As well, part-time faculty are variously defined by the number of courses they teach, the length of their contract, how they are appointed and by reference to a union bargaining unit. These categorical ambiguities also extend to the tenuous hold these workers have over their status as faculty. The tenuous employment status of sessionals — in that they are not defined as "real" faculty in the institutional hierarchy — generally means that less care is taken in institutional record keeping and information management, which has a range of implications for data collection.[3] At a few Ontario institutions, data management was so shoddy that the ATI coordinators speculated it must be somehow deliberate on the part of the university. Poor data management and data extraction difficulties suggest that some administrators may have sincerely believed that they were "unable" to supply this information to researchers.

Contract Faculty in Ontario Universities
Despite challenges in obtaining the information, the employment data I received from my ATI requests confirmed a growing reliance on contract faculty in Ontario universities. My requests focused primarily on faculties and departments within the social sciences and humanities, as previous research has shown that contract

faculty (and especially part-time faculty) are over-represented in these fields.[4] For a more detailed overview and analysis of my data, see Brownlee (2015a, 2015b). Here I provide a summary as well as some specific examples to illustrate how the casualization process has taken shape in Ontario.

At several Ontario universities, the increase in contract faculty hiring has been dramatic. For example, in those departments that are now part of the Faculty of Liberal Arts and Professional Studies at York, the number of part-time contract appointments increased from 531 to 1253 (136 percent) between 2000–01 and 2009–10, while the number of tenure stream faculty grew from 493 to 593 (18.3 percent). Interestingly, my data indicate that there were far more part-time sessionals hired during the 2000s than the "official" figures in the York University (2012) Factbook suggest.[5] The growth in part-time positions was especially prominent in certain departments, such as English (563.6 percent); Languages, Literatures and Linguistics (179.5 percent); Administrative Studies (174.1 percent); and Philosophy (168.8 percent).

For Carleton, I was able to obtain data for the university as a whole. Across all departments, the number of part-time appointments increased from 475 to 821 (72.8 percent) between 2001–02 and 2011–12, while those in the tenure stream rose from 608 to 745 (22.5 percent) over roughly the same period. In the Arts and Social Sciences, these figures were 93.4 percent and 17.5 percent respectively. As well, between 2003–04 and 2011–12, the number of undergraduate courses taught by part-time sessionals at Carleton increased from 705 to 1327. This change represented an increase of 88.2 percent (or 122.8 percent in the Faculty of Arts and Social Sciences). Over the same period, the total number of undergraduate courses offered in the university grew by just 15.9 percent (from 3444 to 3993). So, not only are part-timers being hired in greater numbers, they are performing a larger and larger share of university teaching. In 2003–04, part-timers were responsible for teaching one out of every five undergraduate courses at Carleton; eight years later, they were teaching one in three.[6]

Trent also stands out in terms of its growing dependence on part-time appointments. In the 16 departments I reviewed, the number of part-time positions increased from 66 to 200 (203 percent). At the same time, the number of tenured/tenure track positions increased from 138 to 156 (13 percent). In the Faculty of Arts and Science at Canada's largest university — the University of Toronto — the reliance on part-time contract faculty increased dramatically over the decade. According to the data I received, the number of part-time appointments climbed from 85 to 285 between 2001–02 and 2007–08 (a 235 percent increase), while the number of tenure stream faculty rose from 665 to 711, or by just 6.9 percent. However, it must be noted that these data do not account for the large number of graduate students working as contract instructors. In the latter half of the 2000s, there was an average of 169 teaching appointments held by graduate students in the Faculty of Arts and Science. This means that the faculty's use of contract instructors is significantly greater than the official numbers suggest.

Across all 15 institutions for which comparative headcount data were available, the number of part-time appointments increased by 68.5 percent between 2001–02 and 2009–10. Over the same period, the number of tenure stream positions increased by 30.4 percent. Put another way, in 2001–02 tenure stream appointments outnumbered part-time appointments by 637 (3113 versus 2476); by 2009–10, there were fewer tenure stream appointments than part-time appointments (4060 versus 4173) in the faculties and departments under review.

It is also interesting to note that most of the growth in part-time hiring occurred between 2001–02 and 2007–08 (a 60.2 percent increase). From 2007–08 to 2009–10, part-time appointments increased by just 5.2 percent. And if York is excluded from the analysis (that is, if part-time appointments at York remained constant), the number of part-time positions would have remained the same over this two-year period. Indeed, with a few notable exceptions, part-time hiring at most universities declined somewhat late in the decade. Based on my research and discussions with various university personnel throughout the process, I would contend that one of the key contributing factors was the global economic crisis that took place over this timeframe. Unlike the situation in the U.S., the financial impact of the crisis on higher education in Canada was relatively small (OCUFA 2010a). That is not to say, however, that it did not have an impact. For Canadian universities, the impact was primarily political in nature. That is, many institutions used the crisis to justify a series of austerity measures, such as hiring freezes, course/program reductions, layoffs and service cuts. In fact, by early 2010, two thirds of Ontario universities had announced hiring freezes or slow-downs (OCUFA 2010b). In turn, these measures contributed to declining employment opportunities for part-time faculty late in the decade.

What about full-time contract faculty hiring? Full-time hires are defined differently depending on the university, but generally speaking these are contract instructors who either teach a full course load, or whose position has been "regularized" in some way, and therefore may be eligible for full-time or "semi-permanent" employment status, greater job security and/or access to pensions and benefits. Most of these regularized appointments are teaching-only positions. According to the AUCC (2007a), the number of full-time faculty in Canada declined in the 1990s. These reductions were achieved through a combination of retirement incentive programs and constraints on replacing retired professors with similar full-time positions. In contrast, the number of full-time faculty increased by over 20 percent between 1998 and 2006, largely as a result of additional tenure stream hiring. In fact, the AUCC claims that the number of full-time contract faculty in Canada has

58 ACADEMIA, INC.

Table 3.1: Part-Time Contract Faculty Appointments (Fifteen Institutions)

University	2000	2001	2002	2003	2004	2005	2006	2007	2008	2009	2010
Ottawa	304	295	327	382	378	395	408	410	418	396	425
Windsor	118	116	123	136	136	146	144	158	169	160	160
Trent	66	69	94	123	141	170	183	153	197	189	200
UOIT*	-	-	-	19	33	47	83	105	120	117	153
Waterloo	141	133	153	146	150	169	168	164	153	152	181
Queen's	56	67	59	74	63	65	98	103	84	70	n/a
Brock	51	50	62	37	38	59	78	71	75	69	n/a
Ryerson	39	45	40	33	49	52	71	73	79	53	47

Academic Year	2000/01	2001/02	2002/03	2003/04	2004/05	2005/06	2006/07	2007/08	2008/09	2009/10	2010/11
York	531	681	758	675	882	746	883	1047	1027	1253	n/a
Carleton*	n/a	475	520	521	519	628	671	700	761	794	815
Western	n/a	263	320	351	334	340	353	363	347	315	n/a
Nipissing	42	37	56	56	44	70	88	82	83	89	72
Guelph	104	123	109	92	125	145	174	177	219	204	n/a
Laurentian	40	37	42	50	45	61	75	76	66	68	n/a
Toronto	n/a	85	149	153	187	265	261	285	256	244	n/a
Total Contract Faculty	n/a	2476	2812	2848	3124	3358	3738	3967	4054	4173	n/a
Total Tenure Stream Faculty	n/a	3113	3189	3337	3513	3522	3696	3943	4019	4060	n/a

* Includes totals for entire university

remained proportionally small and relatively unchanged since the mid-1970s and that "there is no indication that Canadian universities typically use these contractual arrangements to meet hiring requirements" (24).

Generally speaking, these claims are not supported by my data. At some universities, the number of full-time contract faculty did remain relatively stable. Overall, however, there was a large increase in the number and proportion of full-time contract faculty in the faculties and departments under review. At most institutions, I was able to identify two overarching trends: (i) the percentage increases in full-time contract hires were greater — often much greater — than those observed for tenure stream faculty; and (ii) the ratio of tenure stream faculty to contract faculty declined. Across all 18 institutions, the number of full-time contract faculty increased by 59 percent between 2002–03 and 2008–09, while the number of tenured/tenure track faculty increased by 25 percent (like part-time contract hiring, there was a noticeable decline in full-time contract hiring toward the end of the decade). These figures suggest that contrary to the AUCC's claims, universities *are* using these contractual arrangements to meet hiring requirements. My findings align with those of Louise Desjardins (2012), who reports that the proportion of tenured/tenure track positions for doctorate holders working full-time in Canadian universities declined significantly between 1981 and 2007. Similarly, Jones et al. (2012) note that the rate of growth for full-time contract positions in Canada was significantly higher than that of tenure stream positions between 2000 and 2008.

My data suggest that a distinct "third tier" of academic labour made up largely of these full-time contract positions has taken shape in Ontario. This middle tier represents a parallel alternative to the tenure system, where a growing number of limited-term academics occupy a stratum just above that of part-timers in the academic hierarchy. While data for the rest of Canada is limited, anecdotal evidence suggests that similar trends are taking shape across the country.

MANAGEMENT STRATEGY OR MARKET FORCES?

Administrators have played a significant role in the transformation of academic labour. In the early years, administrators were seen to be leading the charge largely because of the cost-cutting benefits associated with an increasing reliance on contract staff. For one, the salaries of these workers represent a fraction of the money earned per course by tenure stream professors. By 1987–88, the salaries of part-timers amounted to just 7.6 percent of Ontario university salary expenditures, even though they comprised 32.4 percent of all faculty and performed one fifth of the teaching (Rajagopal and Farr 1992). Little has changed in this regard. At Wilfrid Laurier, over half of the university's students were taught by contract faculty in 2012, while less than four cents out of every dollar spent by the university went to contract faculty salaries. This means that the university spends less than four percent of its budget to teach over 50 percent of its students (Basen 2014). Other cost savings accrue as a result of the fact that these workers are generally not eligible for benefits and there is little obligation on the part of employers to provide them with the support services typically provided for permanent faculty.

While the motivation to cut costs is uncontested, there is less consensus about the extent to which the accelerated use of contract employment represents a deliberate management strategy to impose labour "flexibility" and increase the power of administrators. In my estimation, these trends are connected to a conscious, longer-term strategy to transform the nature of academic work. Writing about the current period, Harald Bauder (2006) argues that casualization has become a fixed and deliberate strategy of reducing wages and working conditions in the academic labour market. This change has taken hold because contract positions are increasingly being created where tenure stream positions can and should exist. In other words, labour market segmentation in the academy "no longer serves to stabilize the positions of tenured faculty; rather, the secondary segment threatens to replace the primary segment" (231). This shift runs parallel to developments in the larger economy, where neoliberal campaigns have led to more labour flexibility and a situation where the number of part-time and temporary workers is growing beyond what is necessary to fill temporary labour needs. Like Bauder, Marc Bousquet (2008) sees little evidence that the transformation of academic labour is driven by the "invisible hand" of the market. For example, while market theory assumes that universities *want* to hire more permanent faculty and that they *will* hire these faculty when they can afford to do so, the reality is that permanent positions are being systematically reduced. Again, this is evidenced by the fact that the jobs of retiring professors are often not replaced by tenure track appointments. At the same time, the low pay and lack of benefits that come with these jobs are usually justified by the claim that it is ultimately market forces — not management decisions — that determine compensation rates. So, like the wider process of labour market restructuring, the transformation of academic labour has come to embody the erosion of key rights obtained by workers through decades of labour organizing.

Just as the practice of relying on contract faculty has been challenged, so too has the claim that this change is an inevitable result of market forces. Universities are not over-producing PhDs, they are under-producing quality jobs. For decades, Bousquet (2008: 205–206) writes, free market ideology has "proceeded to do the corporate university the enormous service of covering up the processes of corporatization, managerialism, and casualization." Although they rarely say so publicly, administrators cannot fail to recognize that an insecure reserve army of part-time workers performs many of the same functions in the academy that it does in the broader workforce, namely, to divide workers, to reduce their power relative to management and to make workplace organizing more difficult. Considering its central importance to the ongoing restructuring process, maintaining a large segment of highly skilled, "just-in-time" workers is a key priority for the corporatizing university.

THE CONDITIONS OF CONTRACT FACULTY WORK

Several years ago, the Association of Universities and Colleges of Canada produced a report on university faculty in Canada, including past and present hiring practices, changes in demographics and salaries, and key "drivers of change" (AUCC 2007a). Remarkably, the document lacks any real attention to contract faculty. Further, there is no acknowledgement in the report of the diverse challenges and hardships experienced by these employees. In fact, according to the AUCC, part-time academic work benefits employees, students and universities alike. The document states, for example, that part-time positions "provide both the employer and the employee with an opportunity to determine if each is suited to the other" (24). In other words, these positions offer a testing ground for institutional fit or as precursors to tenure track jobs. While this may have been true half a century ago, it bears little reality in the corporatized academy. The preponderance of errors and omissions in the AUCC's discussion of part-time faculty is notable, but is not surprising given that the organization's thirteen-member board of directors includes twelve university presidents. Canadian senior administrators have every interest in downplaying the precarious nature of contract employment.

Integrated Scholarship

Most contract faculty desire a full academic career. A survey of contingent faculty in the U.S., for example, found that over three quarters of part-time instructors said they "have sought, are now seeking, or will be seeking a full-time tenure-track position," and a similar proportion indicated they would definitely or probably accept such a position if it were offered (Coalition on the Academic Workforce 2012). As previously noted, however, whereas tenure stream faculty are expected to perform the full range of academic activities, contract instructors are hired solely to carry out teaching duties. Limited-term contracts rarely recognize the research and service components of academic work, or provide employees with appropriate resources and protections to participate in a full academic career. As a result, contract workers often do not have the time or the financial security to engage in sustained research and other collegial responsibilities, which diminishes their ability to obtain permanent positions in the future. It is also difficult for these workers to engage is integrated scholarship when their work appointments vary from year to year, or even term to term. "Freeway fliers," who combine two or more part-time jobs at different institutions, are especially vulnerable in this regard. The use of contract appointments undermines the research and service components of academic work and amounts to a process of academic deskilling.

Academic Governance
Contract faculty are generally not required, and usually not encouraged, to participate in university governance. In fact, they are often excluded from even the most basic decision-making bodies, such as departmental committees. In contrast to permanent faculty in Canada, who report having a substantial degree of input and influence over academic decisions at the department level, contract faculty have little or no input into teaching/curriculum priorities and other aspects of workplace management (Jones et al. 2012). The lack of participation of contract staff in academic governance impacts the entire professoriate. It decreases faculty control over the curriculum by allowing administrators more power over its design and priorities. It can also adversely affect the teaching and research commitments of permanent staff because they are assigned all or most of the responsibilities of academic service (for example, program reviews, accreditation exercises, student supervision and committee work). In short, most contract instructors have little say in how their departments are run. Even if they do, faculty governance is weakened by constant employee turnover.

Salaries and Benefits
Full-time tenured faculty in Canada are, on average, the highest paid in the world (Altbach et al. 2012; Brown 2012). This is in spite of the fact that expenditures on academic rank salaries have fallen in the last three decades, from over 30 percent of university expenditures in 1980 to 20 percent in 2009 (CAUT 2012). Of course, Canada's international ranking could be different if the large number of under-paid, part-time instructors were taken into account. Given their level of education and despite significant provincial variation, contract faculty are generally paid very poorly.[7] Even removing non-teaching work from faculty salaries and considering only teaching, the pay of most contract staff remains well below other professors. In some instances, these salary levels are shocking. In 2014 at the University of Winnipeg, for example, a contract instructor teaching five single term courses would make approximately $20,000, which is right around the city's low-income cut-off (Canada's version of the poverty line). While salary structures in Canada ensure that most contact faculty are not actually impoverished (as many are south of the border[8]), one can expect that the number of faculty relying on social assistance will increase as Canadian universities progress towards a U.S.-style two-tiered academic workforce. Presumably, the low wages of contract faculty is one reason why Statistics Canada's 2007 *National Graduates Survey* found that earning a PhD does little to boost earnings compared with master's degree graduates (Fine 2009).

These matters are made worse by a lack of pensions and benefits, which are often not available to contract faculty even though they may be employed by the same institution(s) for a considerable period of time. The lack of benefits is especially unjust for those who work at multiple institutions, as each university considers them to be "part-time" even though they are full-time employees in the university system. Contract faculty in Canada are also ineligible for employment insurance (EI) benefits if they have not accumulated enough hours to qualify, and the actual number of hours worked by contract faculty (for example, course preparation, grading, consultation with students) is normally far greater than can be leveraged for EI compensation or eligibility. These incompatibilities mean that it can be especially difficult for contract faculty to apply for and receive the benefits that many of them should be able to rely on during the non-teaching months.

Working Conditions and Institutional Support
While most universities provide some institutional supports for contract faculty, they are not obligated to provide these workers with the basic services that permanent faculty take for granted. These include access to library resources, photocopying, computers, email, clerical support, telephones, mailboxes and office space. Even when contract faculty do acquire office space, it is often shared and overcrowded and therefore insufficiently private to meet with or mentor students. Indeed, some universities appear reluctant to grant anything that would suggest that contract workers are part of the university community, or have the right to expect reappointment. For example, in a recent round of contract negotiations between Dalhousie University and CUPE Local 3912, the university asserted that it was not appropriate for part-timers to claim affiliation with Dalhousie when seeking publication (Kennedy 2010).

Another consequence of this lack of support is that contract instructors are routinely denied access to faculty development programs, including training in pedagogy. Limiting professional enrichment activities to permanent faculty is not only unjust but it threatens the quality of academic programs in which part-timers do most of the teaching. Substandard working conditions and a lack of professional support reduces the status of contract workers to second-class citizens within the university. As well, the "just-in-time" approach to contract hiring means that instructors often receive their course assignments just days or weeks before courses begin. They therefore suffer the double contingency of either "using their own unpaid time to prepare for classes they may not be assigned or accepting the reality of teaching a course for which they have been unable to adequately prepare" (Street et al. 2012: iii).

Academic Freedom and Job Security

Although not a guarantee against censor or dismissal, the protections of tenure continue to provide a substantial degree of academic freedom for permanent faculty. In fact, the widespread adoption of collective bargaining by faculty associations has resulted in Canada having some of the best protections for academic freedom in the world. While it remains difficult to dismiss tenured faculty for their teaching, research or political views, the same cannot be said for the large number of contract faculty currently working in Canadian universities.

Contract employees have little to no job security. Most of these employees must apply for their jobs as often as every few months, and they have no guarantee of reappointment. Those who are fortunate enough to be assigned courses for multiple terms are vulnerable to changes in enrolment trends. In the absence of job security, controversial positions or provocative statements can easily result in a contract not being renewed. And for the growing cadre of mostly part-time workers, there continues to be limited protections from colleagues, administrators, politicians, parents and even students who may be offended by what they say or write. Indeed, there are numerous examples of contract faculty being terminated simply for unpopular utterances. In 2010, for instance, Daniel Peterson, a philosophy lecturer at the University of Hawaii, was suspended from his position for using the phrase "shit happens" during one of his lectures (Jaschik 2010). Evidently, Mr. Peterson was attempting to illustrate concepts such as free will and determinism to his philosophy students.

Many contract staff can be dismissed from their positions without the right to appeal or due process and without administrators even having to provide a reason. This creates a powerful disincentive to refrain from engaging with controversial material inside and outside of the classroom. Any university in which the fear of taking risks hampers the free exchange of ideas or the exploration of experimental pedagogies is a diminished institution. The silent self-censorship of thousands of professors holding insecure appointments has had a detrimental impact on the academy. More generally, the vulnerability of contract faculty has contributed to "a large pool of crippling fear, insecurity, and resentment that makes it difficult for teachers to take risks, forge bonds of solidarity, engage in social criticism, and perform as public intellectuals rather than as technicians in the service of corporate largesse" (Giroux 2003). This reality represents a significant victory for those who want to silence dissent and activism emanating from the university. The precarious position of contract faculty also highlights a critical (and often overlooked) dimension of academic freedom that is threatened by corporatization, which is the right of faculty as a collectivity to exercise sovereignty over the educational process and govern their institutions in a manner that accords with academic values.

Rank, Status and Power
Even though they may accumulate years — or even decades — of teaching service, many universities will not consider contract faculty for promotion to higher academic ranks (let alone tenure). The nature of contract work also makes organizing difficult so these workers are often in a poor position to bargain for increased wages, benefits and job security. Once again, the precarious nature of contract employment even extends to the tenuous hold these workers have over their status as "faculty," which is often questioned by administrators and, in some instances, their tenured colleagues. It should be noted that these kinds of vulnerabilities are not restricted to part-timers. In her work, Rajagopal (2004) found that three quarters of full-time contract staff represented by a union or faculty association believed that these organizations were powerless in voicing their concerns and half felt unprotected against arbitrary treatment by administrators.

Contingent employment also limits professional opportunities. According to Berry (2005: 10), longtime contract instructors are seen as "damaged goods" by hiring committees. In other words, their teaching experience and commitment to the profession act as a detriment, increasing with the number of years on the job. Given their lack of power and diminished academic status, it is not surprising that "contract academic staff are paying a heavy price with health issues and stress" (Stewart 2010). In contrast, permanent faculty in Canada report some of the highest levels of job satisfaction in the world (Jones at al. 2012; Tamburri 2012).

One final indication of the marginal status of contract faculty is their invisibility. In my research on contract faculty in Ontario, I discovered that many universities do not keep systematic records of their contract employees, further devaluing this segment of the academic workforce. Indeed, "hidden academics" and "invisible faculty" are not simply catchphrases — they often describe their employment situations in literal terms.

IMPACTS ON STUDENTS AND STUDENT LEARNING

Contract instructors are not inherently bad teachers. Their enthusiasm and ability to facilitate student learning, and their knowledge of the subject matter, often exceeds that of permanent professors. Nevertheless, academic casualization negatively impacts students. The reasons for this have to do with the precarious nature of contract employment, which results in barriers and disincentives to quality teaching on the part of contract faculty. Put another way, poor teaching conditions lead to poor learning conditions. If contract faculty do excel at teaching, it is usually in spite of their employment circumstances.

Academic casualization has both direct and indirect impacts on students. The direct impacts stem largely from the fact that substandard pay often forces casual employees to teach multiple courses at a time, sometimes at different institutions.

As a result, many are overburdened by heavy teaching loads, and have little time for the writing and research necessary to keep up with their disciplines. Such a system offers little room for professional growth and development, which means that students of contract instructors are not always exposed to new advances in the field. Likewise, many contract instructors have less time for class preparation and student evaluation than full-time faculty with lesser teaching loads. For this reason, they may be more likely to use standardized methods of assessment, such as multiple-choice exams. The American Association of University Professors (2003) found that full-time faculty in the U.S. spend between 50 to 100 percent more time per credit hour on instruction than do part-time teachers. Moreover, a recent study by the Center for the Future of Higher Education (2012) confirms that the "just-in-time" approach to contract hiring is detrimental for students because it is associated with "insufficient preparation time, insufficient time to incorporate and update meaningful material for students, and insufficient time to explore pedagogical methods and materials" (Street et al. 2012: 7).

The job insecurity and lack of academic freedom inherent in contract work often translates, indirectly, into impediments to student learning. Contract instructors are evaluated solely in terms of their teaching, which means that student evaluations can make the difference between being renewed or being unemployed. In this context, teachers are under pressure to "keep their customers happy" (Puplampu 2004: 177). There are also incentives to refrain from teaching in a critical or challenging manner and experimenting with innovative forms of pedagogy. Michelle Webber (2008: 48) has shown, for instance, that contingent faculty in Canada experience pressure to water down the feminist content of their courses and "pander to the perceived conservatism" of their students in order to remain uncontroversial.

Casual employment also impacts the student-professor relationship in other ways. Patrick Deane, president of McMaster University, attributes today's "crisis in higher education" to the inability of universities to provide "meaningful contact with accessible professors" (cited in Bradshaw 2011). Although Deane does not explicitly connect this observation to contract work, this lack of contact is rooted — at least in part — in the casualization of academic employment. The demanding schedules of contract faculty often do not permit them to hold office hours; one study in the U.S. found an 11:1 disparity between full-time and part-time faculty in their probability of keeping no office hours (Benjamin 2003). This study also found that contract faculty are less able to provide prompt feedback on assigned work, and discuss course materials and ideas outside the classroom. Similarly, Paul Umbach (2007) found that compared with their tenure stream colleagues, part-time faculty spend less time preparing for class, use active or collaborative teaching techniques less often, have lower academic expectations and interact with students less frequently. This lack of interaction is especially significant, given the positive outcomes associated with contact between professors and students, such as improved academic performance, increased cognitive and affective development and a greater degree of satisfaction with the educational experience (Jaeger 2008).

It should be noted that a student's ability to interact with his/her professor has already been compromised by growing class size. In fact, large classes are now the norm in most Canadian universities, especially in the largest institutions. According to the AUCC (2007a), in the late 1970s there were twelve full-time students for every full-time faculty member. By 2003, this ratio had climbed to 20:1. The most dramatic increases in student-faculty ratios have occurred in Ontario, where they rose from 16:1 in 1987 to 27:1 in 2007 (OCUFA 2010c). While some organizations, like the Council of Ontario Universities (2011a), view "reduced teaching costs through larger class sizes" as enhancing educational efficiency, most are more critical. In a recent Ontario faculty survey, 62 percent of respondents said they were facing larger classes than just a few years ago, and this was cited as the most pressing example of declining educational quality (OCUFA 2009; see also OCUFA 2012a). Because contract faculty are increasingly relied upon to teach large classes, the problem of student-faculty interaction has become more acute.

Contract employment can also impact student persistence and degree completion. Audrey Jaeger (2008) discovered that attrition rates increase for students who take courses with contract faculty. First-year students, for example, were far less likely to persist into their second year after being exposed to part-time faculty in introductory "gatekeeper" courses. Jaeger also found that exposure to contract faculty reduced the likelihood of student graduation. She argues that the negative effects on student persistence are attributable to the pressures and challenges of contract work, especially reduced student-professor interaction. It is important to point out, however, that many contract instructors are doing what they can to mitigate these challenges. In spite of structural obstacles, contract faculty report doing additional unpaid work to meet their students' needs and protect them from the effects of academic contingency. As Street et al. (2012: 13) note:

> While intensely aware of their own "second-class" status and its potential negative effects on students, many ... expressed a desire to protect their students from the effects of their employment situations even when doing so entailed considerable personal cost. A surprisingly large number ... spoke of "living in poverty" and identified terrible pay as a significant problem. Nevertheless, [they] also reported spending their own money — on copies, on personal computers, software, and more — to provide and ensure their students receive a quality educational experience.

In the context of broader university ideas and principles, contract instructors occupy a highly contradictory location. The reliance on contract faculty suggests to students that teaching and learning are activities unworthy of public and institutional support. It also suggests that universities merely pay lip service to equality, fairness and other high ideals. As Barbara Ehrenreich (1997: xi) puts it, the casualization of academic labour encourages students to believe that "some lives are valued a lot more than others ... this is what students learn in a place that purports to teach the world's most noble philosophical traditions, that teaches the humanities while ignoring the humanity of its own employees and part of its teaching staff."

THE ROLE OF PERMANENT FACULTY

What of the relationship of tenured and tenure track professors to the scope and significance of the casualization process? Are they largely oblivious or are they a primary cause of the problem? In the 1980s, Rajagopal and Farr (1989: 268, 276) argued that senior professors functioned as "gatekeepers" in the academy, and adopted a "decidedly non-collegial, managerial stance toward part-time academic employees." This authority role accentuated the academic hierarchy and reduced the potential for solidarity between academic ranks. In *Hidden Academics* (2002), Rajagopal showed that most full professors favour a separate teaching stream for part-timers, believe that collegial decision-making should be an exclusive tenure track right, and that universities are under no obligation to offer permanent positions to long serving, part-time employees. In short, according to Rajagopal, most permanent faculty (especially full professors) do not regard contract workers as full members of the academy. These attitudes are apparently not lost on contract workers themselves. A large number of them recognize — or at least believe — that full-timers view them as subordinates with a limited academic role (Rajagopal 2002, 2004). Many also think that the abolition of tenure would improve the quality of higher education, likely because the tenure system is seen by many lower-tier academics as a "pernicious hierarchy within the profession itself, one that gives inordinate power to senior professors" (Johnson 2003: 79).

In Canada, this separation between permanent and contract faculty may be compounded by the fact that contract workers are often represented by different unions. Some even suggest that unionization has had a counter-intuitive effect of increasing casualization. Dobbie and Robinson (2008) note a positive correlation across provinces between faculty unionization and reliance on part-time workers. They suggest that this trend could be a result of union preoccupation with the needs of permanent staff, which has its roots in the fact that most unions were founded in the 1970s when the majority of members had tenure. At a more general level, Bousquet (2008) argues that academic unionization movements across North America have been inattentive to the casualization process, while in Canada, Alison Hearn (2010: 208) describes a "deafening silence on the part of the tenured and tenure-streamed faculty about the segmentation of academic labour and the fate of contingent academic workers."

It is true that the response of many permanent faculty to the issue of casualization has been less than admirable, but it would be a mistake to hold permanent faculty responsible for academic contingency. First, it is administrators, not professors, that primarily control the kinds of positions that are allocated and budgeted for, and this type of managerial control has increased under corporatization. Second, these divisions between full-time and contract staff do not translate into significant opportunities or benefits for tenured faculty. The growing reliance on contract academics is not necessary to protect tenure or the salaries of tenured professors, just as the wages and job security of tenured positions are not the cause of casualization. Again, these views reflect market myths. The market is not stratifying academic labour or pitting different streams of workers against each other. On the contrary, permanent positions are being systematically eliminated through deliberate management decisions facilitated by government funding cuts. Casualization reflects the failure on the part of governments and universities to provide *all* university employees with a decent living. It is the systematic bifurcation into a two-tiered labour force — not tenure or the attitudes of senior faculty — that is the root of the problem.

A "PERFECTED SYSTEM"

In principle, teaching is a rewarding occupation that offers a high level of intrinsic satisfaction. Given that most contract faculty are engaged in something they value and enjoy, some wonder why the casualization of academic labour should warrant so much concern. After all, contingent workers are found in other sectors of the economy, where working conditions are often significantly worse. What does it matter, then, if privileged young people are having some trouble finding permanent jobs? To be sure, the level of exploitation is greater in other precarious occupations, and the inherent rewards of teaching may partly compensate for the otherwise poor conditions of contract work. That being said, there are a number of reasons why the situation of contract faculty is unique and, therefore, warrants specific attention. For one, in no other occupation is there such a wide disparity between groups whose jobs and training are so similar. For another, contract faculty in Canada have normally obtained — or are in the process of obtaining — a PhD. While the opportunity to pursue graduate education is a privilege in itself, these individuals are also delaying their earnings for years, if not decades, possibly in addition to accumulating high levels of student debt. Added to this is the fact that a considerable number of contingent academics have foregone the material rewards of state and corporate positions in the pursuit of social ideals. William Deresiewicz (2011) addressed this issue in *The Nation*. He writes:

Academia may once have been a cushy gig, but now we're talking about highly talented young people who are willing to spend their 20s living on subsistence wages when they could be getting rich (and their friends *are* getting rich), simply because they believe in knowledge, ideas, inquiry; in teaching, in following their passion. To leave more than half of them holding the bag at the end of it all, over 30 and having to scrounge for a new career, is a human tragedy.

Academics may also be uniquely suited to "tolerate" exploitation in the workplace. The time, effort and money invested in a lengthy PhD program means that contract academics, in spite of the unjust nature of their appointments, are less likely to turn their backs on these investments and pursue different occupations. Further, Andrew Ross (2000) has suggested that like other creative professions, many academics willingly accept low wages in return for the opportunity to do what they love. For Ross, their readiness to accept the tradeoff of job satisfaction instead of a decent salary and job security is reflective of the sacrifices intellectual workers are conditioned to make. Following Ross' work, Bousquet (2008: 63) contends that universities and governments have succeeded in associating academic work "with the 'bohemian' ideology that previously was reserved for artistic occupations," whereby intellectuals accept not simply poor compensation but the "superexploitation of the artist, in part because the characteristics of casual employment ... can so easily be associated with the popular understanding of normative rewards for 'creative' endeavor."

Compounding these problems is the fact that few professional sectors believe more strongly in meritocracy than intellectuals. For contract workers who are unable to find permanent positions, the idea that one's talent is the ultimate determinant of one's place in the occupational hierarchy has an especially demoralizing effect. Not only can it lead to feelings of inferiority but it reduces their ability to locate their precarious position within the context of broader structural forces. The supposed academic meritocracy thus prolongs their exploitation by creating "a state of mind in which giving up hope signifies something far worse psychologically than a sensible change of careers" (Donoghue 2008: 63). All of these factors help to maintain the large supply of cheap labour and limit resistance. For these reasons, Bousquet (2008: 71–72) describes the transformation of the academic work process as "a perfected system for recruiting, delivering, and ideologically reproducing an all-but-self-funding cadre of low-cost but highly trained 'just-in-time' labor power." Little wonder, he says, that "every other transnational corporation wants to emulate the campus."

Supporters of corporatization maintain that the greater utilization of contract faculty produces educational efficiencies because it contains costs in tough economic times and offers managerial flexibility in the face of changing enrolment and student demand. Cost cutting and institutional flexibility are not, in and of themselves, unreasonable objectives. Both of these practices have the potential to enhance "efficiency" in higher education. However, the claim that efficiency is produced through labour flexibility in the academy is unjustified. The displacement of secure, full-time professors with contract faculty may be highly efficient from an economic point of view, but it does not take into account the human, social and educational costs. For the instructors, this practice is consistent with job insecurity and a more precarious working environment. For students, it often means reduced faculty-student interaction time and other impediments to learning. For tenured faculty, there are costs associated with increased demand for administrative service and, for the faculty as a whole, a weakening of collegial governance. The same logic can be used to counter the supposed efficiencies associated with practices like for-profit online education and larger class sizes. In sum, there are huge ancillary costs associated with the growing reliance on contract appointments, so much so that the practice should be viewed as a "false economy" (Benjamin 2003: 93).

FROM TENURE TO "JUST-IN-TIME": THE FUTURE OF UNIVERSITY HIRING

Several years ago, I sent access to information requests to eleven Ontario universities requesting information on their future hiring plans. With respect to contract hiring, not one institution responded with any kind of detailed plan, and most stipulated that contract instructors were hired on a "just-in-time" basis in response to enrolment trends or to maintain institutional flexibility. For this reason, contract hiring was deemed by the respondents to be "impossible to forecast," to borrow from the remarks of one administrator. Despite these claims, the 2007 Multi-Year Accountability Agreement signed between the Ontario government and Ontario universities indicates that this kind of planning does exist (see OCUFA 2010b). The agreement states that almost one quarter of planned university hiring involves "contract, part-time or sessional" academic staff, a significant increase over previous years.

Most universities also stated that they had no definitive plans for tenure stream hiring. For example, the information coordinator at Windsor was informed by the university's Provost that the official policy was to no longer forecast faculty hiring because of budgetary cutbacks and financial uncertainty. At Trent, a senior administrator told me that the university had no current hiring plan but would "hopefully" be developing one soon. UOIT refused even to respond to this portion of the request and invoked an exemption under section 18.01 of the FIPPA, which allows the university to withhold information for "plans relating to the management of personnel or the administration of an institution that have not yet been put into operation or made public." On the other hand, a few universities did provide hiring information. The coordinator at Waterloo stated that the Faculty of Arts was "interested" in hiring twenty tenure track faculty over the next three years. At McMaster, I was instructed that the Faculty of Humanities was planning to hire twenty-four tenure stream positions over the next three years, which was interesting given that the number of tenure stream appointments in this faculty had remained virtually unchanged over the 2000s. In the end, Nipissing was the only university to provide a detailed list of planned hires in each department within the Faculty of Arts and Science. To its credit, a key component of Nipissing's plan was to convert limited-term appointments into tenure stream positions.

This lack of institutional planning around — or willingness to share information about — faculty hiring is troublesome for several reasons. For one, according to the Ontario Confederation of University Faculty Associations (2010b), the Ontario student body is expected to increase by 27 percent between 2008 and 2021, and this change is already fueling demand for new courses, programs and faculty. Moreover, even with the abolition of mandatory retirement in Canada, retirements in the university sector will continue to intensify hiring demands in the next decade(s). The lack of priority afforded to tenure stream hiring also runs counter to the stated interests of Ontario faculty, 63 percent of which assert that the *first* priority for any new funding should be to hire and retain full-time tenure track faculty (OCUFA 2012a). Currently, however, full-time faculty are being replaced with a similar full-time hire in less than 60 percent of all cases (OCUFA 2009). To be sure, thousands of new faculty positions will be created in the coming decades, in Ontario and across Canada. The question is whether these positions will include a high proportion of stable, full-time tenure stream positions, or whether they will consist primarily of contract appointments and precarious, part-time positions.

Just as teaching has become less valued in the corporate university, so too has student learning. As this chapter made clear, the declining resources and institutional supports available for university teaching have led to a similar devaluation of and support for students. Likewise, the precariousness nature of contract employment has resulted in structural barriers and disincentives to quality education. The changing composition of academic labour is connected to another aspect of corporatization: the rise of the student consumer.

NOTES

1 There has been some improvement in women's representation within the academy. For example, the proportion of full-time female teachers holding tenured positions more than doubled between 1989 and 2009, to over 30 percent (CAUT 2012). However, women remain under-paid and under-represented in relation to their male colleagues. Male professors earn higher salaries on average and this discrepancy is over $20,000 at some universities (Cross 2010). In terms of representation, women account for

approximately one out of five full professors and one out of three professors at the associate level (AUCC 2007a; CAUT 2010a).

2   Rajagopal (2002) conducted national surveys on contract faculty as well as interviews with faculty and university administrators. Her data showed that part-time faculty constituted more than one third of all faculty in the early 1990s. Focusing exclusively on Quebec, Louise Bauer (2011) found that the number of sessional academics — or chargés de cours — increased significantly in relation to permanent faculty between 1998 and 2008. Looking at all provinces outside of Quebec, David Dobbie and Ian Robinson (2008) argue that Canadian universities may now be relying on contingent academics as extensively as their U.S. counterparts. According to their research, the proportion of contract faculty in universities across the country range from 39 percent in British Columbia to 50 percent in Saskatchewan. However, these data are compromised by unreliable information on part-time contract faculty. For additional information on contract faculty working in Ontario universities, see Field et al. (2014).

3   At one university, I raised questions about the appropriate definition of "faculty" and received a patronizing lecture from human resources personnel about how universities work and the importance of accurate terminology in social science research.

4   Rajagopal (2002), for instance, found that two thirds of part-time faculty were employed in arts-related disciplines. The limitations of its data notwithstanding, Statistics Canada's surveys also support this conclusion (see, for example, Omiecinski 2003) as does U.S. research (see, for example, Cox 2000).

5   For example, my data show that the total number of part-time positions in the Faculty of Liberal Arts and Professional Studies was over 1,000 each year between 2007–08 and 2009–10. Yet, the 2011–12 edition of the Factbook (the only year for which headcount data was provided by faculty) claims that the total number of contract faculty (headcount by contract) in the faculty was just 773. I contacted the administration on more than one occasion about this discrepancy but did not receive a satisfactory explanation.

6   Anecdotal evidence suggests that contract faculty are teaching a greater percentage of courses at other Ontario universities. For example, it has been reported that part-time faculty at York are responsible for between 50 and 60 percent of all university teaching (Ghabrial 2009; Lafrance 2010). The Association of Part-Time Professors of the University of Ottawa (2011) asserts that its members are responsible for teaching nearly 60 percent of all courses. According to Alison Hearn (2010), over 50 percent of undergraduate teaching at Western is performed by contract faculty.

7   For example, chargés de cours in Quebec appear to be paid considerably more than contract faculty in most other Canadian provinces and universities. At the University of Sherbrooke, instructors are paid between $15,452 and $19,206 for two three-credit courses. At the University of Montreal, they are paid $16,776 per two-term course. In contrast, instructors at the University of Prince Edward Island receive between $10,248 and $10,778 for two half-year courses; at Dalhousie they receive between $9,131 and $11,166 per full-year course; while those at the University of Winnipeg receive just $7,556 for a full-year course (MacDonald 2013). Generally speaking, employee benefits for contract faculty in Quebec are also more generous.

8   There are growing connections between contract work and poverty in the U.S. Between 2007 and 2010, the number of people with master's degrees who received food stamps

and/or other federal aid increased from 101,682 to 293,029. For those with a PhD, these numbers grew from 9,776 to 33,655 (Patton 2012). Representatives of U.S. contract faculty contend that these figures underestimate the actual numbers because many academics do not report their reliance on federal aid. Other studies confirm that a surprisingly large number of U.S. instructors live in poverty and that low pay is a major cause of the problem (Street et al. 2012; U.S. House of Representatives 2014).

CHAPTER FOUR
THE RISE OF THE STUDENT-CONSUMER

There is a longstanding debate about whether the goals for students in higher education should focus on providing a liberal education or vocational training. The terms of this debate have shifted under corporatization. Today, the ideals of a liberal education are no longer considered sufficient to prepare graduates for the workforce or for life, and practical, applied or vocational pursuits are increasingly seen as the only "relevant" options. The shift to a more narrow vocational set of criteria to define the public university's role has been associated with a range of negative implications for students and for society. Most notably, it has helped to transform students into educational consumers — or as customers purchasing a service or private good — who are encouraged to extract maximum "value" for their tuition dollars. While students have always, in a sense, consumed knowledge, the new "student-consumer" model of higher education is impacting students' values and educational choices, learning experiences, finances, career prospects and relationship with the university. Contained within this model of higher learning is a shifting political economy of student life, including rising tuition fees and student debt, changing student aid and employment trends, access to university education and differences in national and provincial higher education policies and programs.

LIBERAL EDUCATION OR VOCATIONAL TRAINING?

John Henry Newman (1852) is often credited for drawing the classic distinction between liberal education and vocational training in the university. Newman argued that the ideals of liberal education were opposed to the principles of practicality and utility. The proper object of university study, therefore, was not "useful" knowledge but the unity of knowledge, or the creation of an intellectual culture. In addition to nurturing a range of mental capacities — intellectual curiosity and engagement, creativity, wisdom and sound judgment — Newman claimed that the pursuit of knowledge carried its own intrinsic importance, or that the process of "coming to know" was valuable in and of itself. This seminal idea has since been a cornerstone of liberal education philosophy.

For Newman, liberal education trained a person in such a way that he or she would be prepared for any professional, vocational or practical activity (in this sense, at least, he viewed liberal education as "useful"). Around the same time, John Stuart Mill argued that university education should not impart individuals with professional knowledge, "but that which should direct the use of their professional knowledge, and bring the light of general culture to illuminate the technicalities of a special pursuit" (cited in Fulton 1986: 240). Following this, Mill insisted that professional training should remain separate from the university. A related perspective is found in the writings of Wilhelm von Humboldt, one of the founders of the modern research university, who argued that universities must remain separate from other institutions of learning and "particularly from the various practical ones" (see von Humboldt 1963: 133). Much of this thinking was also echoed by Thorstein Veblen in the early twentieth century, who insisted that practical education was a contradiction in terms and a euphemism for private gain. He equated the expansion of vocational programs in U.S. universities with deliberate business campaigns to dispense with courses of study that were not conducive to wealth creation. Concerning the differences between liberal and professional education, Veblen (2004: 20) argued that "the divergent lines of interest to be taken care of by the professional schools and the university, respectively, are as widely out of touch as may well be within the general field of human knowledge." To varying degrees, each of these writers sought to keep vocational interests separate from the university's mission.

Others have argued otherwise, stating that the integration of liberal education and vocational training, including within a university setting, provides educational and social benefits. Former Harvard professor Alfred North Whitehead (1967: 51), for one, claimed that higher learning required "first-hand knowledge," or an explicit connection between the mind and "material creative activity." For Whitehead, sound thinking and practical or manual competencies were not merely complimentary but mutually necessary. In a similar vein, Bertrand Russell (1932: 156–57) criticized liberal education's over-emphasis on "book learning" and its tendency to equate "idleness" with elegance or virtue. Although pure learning had a place in the university, Russell contended that most people were better served by an education that supplemented liberal learning with some form of "practical utility." C. Wright Mills (1956) also advocated an integrated form of higher education. While Mills recognized that practical skills training was very different from liberal education's emphasis on values and self-development, he saw skills and values operating on a continuum. The middle range of this continuum — what he called "sensibilities" — was particularly vital to the educational mission. For Mills, sensibilities emerged through the integration of liberal learning and practical training, and could be a source of intellectual and social liberation for the general population.

The advantages of synthesizing liberal and vocational education were also articulated by legendary philosopher and educational reformer John Dewey. Although he was critical of capitalism, Dewey argued that universities should not operate in absentia of the outside world, including the world of business. In his words, "while there is no guarantee that an education which uses science and employs the controlled process of industry ... will succeed, there is every assurance that an educational practice which sets science and industry in opposition to its ideal of culture will fail" (Dewey 1964: 293). Dewey further claimed that many common educational distinctions (for example, between theory and practice, culture and utility, fine and industrial art) were false dichotomies that existed, in part, because of social inequality, especially the separation of people into "leisure" and "labouring" classes. It was unjust social conditions that accounted for the following:

> The narrowly disciplinary or cultural character of most higher education ... the tendency to isolate intellectual matters till knowledge is scholastic, academic, and professionally technical, and for the widespread conviction that liberal education is opposed to the requirements of an education which shall count in the vocations of life. (Dewey 1966: 136)

For Dewey, then, a key task for educators was to break down these dualisms. Like Mills, Dewey saw potential in integrating liberal education and practical training to reduce social inequalities and produce free and self-educating publics. Their arguments were informed by the belief that universities can and should be involved in contemporary issues and struggles, including struggles in the workplace. As Dewey explained it, education that acknowledges the "full intellectual and social meaning" of technical vocations can help workers to become "masters of their industrial fate" (318).

This distinction between liberal education and vocational training centres around two different — though not necessarily competing — visions of higher education: one that prioritizes intellectual self-development and one that focuses on the virtues of practical skills training. Today, the terrain of this debate has shifted, so that arguments in favour of vocational training in higher education are increasingly divorced from Mills' notion of "sensibilities," or Dewey's goal of empowering workers. As universities are transformed in the interests of corporate power, calls for practical and vocational "relevance" have become virtually synonymous with efforts to streamline programs and downplay the university's emphasis on liberal learning. Related to this, a growing chorus of criticism holds that the ideals of a liberal education are no longer sufficient to prepare graduates for the workforce.

According to Patrick Keeney (2011), liberal education in Canada is "being eroded and undermined, if not deliberately bulldozed, in the name of a reckless, unrelenting economic pragmatism." In its place, Canadian universities are adopting "industrial utilitarianism" as their chief operating principle, where the only learning that is considered worthwhile is professional, applied or vocational.

Supporters of these restructuring efforts — such as the Harper Conservatives, as well as many Canadian corporations and their advocacy think-tanks — point to a number of perceived benefits for employers and students alike. They argue that market-oriented curriculum reform has led to a greater symmetry between university education and the needs of employers, where industry sponsored courses, work placement programs, business internships and corporate-funded research projects provide students with hands-on technical training to expand the relevance of their skills and competitiveness in the job market. Corporations, in turn, profit from these arrangements through an increase in the quality and stock of their "human capital." Consistent with this ethos, recent federal policy changes in Canada have provided support to enhance university-business alliances through student placements. As part of the 2012 federal budget, for example, $14 million was earmarked to help graduate students obtain internships in the private sector, with the goal of doubling the number of students in the existing work placement program. Under corporatization more generally, governments and university administrators have shifted university resources away from arts-related disciplines toward business, engineering and the applied sciences to support business-minded objectives.

These shifting institutional priorities are part of a larger effort to rationalize the benefits of higher education according to economic criteria. Under corporatization, the division between liberal and vocational education has widened. The first is framed as useless and impractical and the latter as a prized educational ideal. Moreover, positioning higher education as labour market training serves to justify many of the changes that are occurring under corporatization, such as cutbacks in public funding, and rising tuition and student debt. In my view, the shift to rely on narrow, vocational criteria to define the public university's role has been associated with a range of negative implications for students. Redefining students as educational consumers — with similar roles, rights and obligations to customers in the private marketplace — has changed the way that universities relate to their "students," as well as the ways in which students view learning, knowledge production and their relationship to the university.

EDUCATING THE STUDENT-CONSUMER

University students are increasingly being targeted by corporations who lease space on university campuses to advertise their goods and services. Many aspects of public space in higher education are now based on the premise that students are "consumers and shoppers" (Giroux and Giroux 2004: 233). As public universities are transformed into "hyper-commercialized spaces," students encounter a "marketplace of logos rather than ideas" and are inundated with the message that the most important identity available to them is that of the good consumer. Put another way, today's colleges and universities are offering students a "hidden extracurricular course of instruction in consumption capitalism" (Slaughter and Rhoades 2004: 19). One of the striking examples of this new student-consumer identity was when two U.S. high school graduates — Chris Barrett and Luke McCabe — offered themselves up as "walking billboards" for any corporation willing to pay their tuition. The students advertised that they would "put corporate logos on their clothes, wear a company's sunglasses, use their golf clubs, eat their pizza, drink their soda, listen to their music or drive their cars" (Giroux 2002: 426). First USA, a subsidiary of Bank One Corporation, eventually agreed to sponsor them.

While it is not surprising that corporate leaders tend to view students as workers and consumers in training, the extent to which public universities have embraced this same logic is surprising. Reduced public funding and a greater reliance on tuition revenues have led many institutions to fixate on customer service, consumer satisfaction and "product quality." This service orientation is often explicit in university planning documents. For example, the *Report of the Steering Committee on Resource Optimization* at the University of Ottawa (2010: 51, 53) recommends that the university should "develop a strategic approach to monitoring and improving student satisfaction" in both "academic and non-academic services." It goes on to say that measurement strategies to gauge student (customer) satisfaction should include both "Phantom Shopper style assessments" and the use of social networking sites such as Facebook and Twitter. Developing a service culture within the university also necessitates the incorporation of customer service performance measures into staff evaluations and the use of "client satisfaction data." As universities employ marketing narratives to guide their relationship with students, it is only logical that students would also incorporate a consumerist model in their relationship with the university. In fact, cross-national research has shown that students who participate in heavily corporatized education systems manifest consumerist attitudes to a greater extent than those who do not (see Pritchard 2005). The corporatization of Canadian universities, in concert with broader changes in Canada's political culture, has likewise produced a more narrow, consumerist orientation on the part of university students. At least, that is one conclusion to be drawn from student surveys.

SURVEYING THE SURVEYS: THE GROWING IMPORTANCE OF MONEY AND JOBS

In the 1980s, student motivations for attending university were remarkably consistent. Their responses routinely reflected a dual motivation — intellectual development and job preparation — and there was no clear priority given to either objective. At Dalhousie, for example, 82 percent of first-year students reported that they were attending university to become a more educated person, while an equal percentage were motivated by occupational considerations. Likewise, York students gave equal weight to enhancing career prospects and furthering their own intellectual development. At the University of Toronto, four out of five incoming students said that "getting a good job" was an important reason for attending university, a figure matched by the number who mentioned personal or intellectual interests (Gilbert et al. 1997). In British Columbia, the proportion of the population citing better job opportunities as their main reason for valuing university education was only marginally higher than the proportion that prioritized the acquisition of knowledge for its own sake (Shrimpton 1987).

In more recent years, student values have begun to change. A 2010 study found that 63 percent of students at a mid-sized Canadian university reported that the most important reason for attending university was to obtain a good job or achieve a particular career goal, while only 10 percent indicated that they wanted to obtain an education to "better themselves" (Singleton-Jackson, Jackson and Reinhardt 2010). According to the Canadian University Survey Consortium, 67 percent of first-year students in 2010 chose "preparing for a specific job or career" or "getting a good job" as the most important reason for attending university; 9 percent indicated that "getting a good general education" was the most important reason; and 8 percent chose "increasing my knowledge in an academic field" (Prairie Research Associates 2010). Similarly, a study by the Maritime Provinces Higher Education Commission (2008) found that 45 percent of students cited the acquisition of relevant job skills as the most important reason for attending university. In contrast, higher order goals such as increased knowledge and broadening one's understanding of the world received just 13 and 12 percent respectively. Although not indifferent to the economic value of higher learning, students in earlier generations were more willing to endorse values of social engagement and self-development in education.

Similar survey results have been found in the U.S. One specific indicator of this shift is the change associated with two contrasting values: (i) "developing a meaningful philosophy of life," and (ii) "being very well off financially." In the late 1960s, the first value was endorsed as an important goal by over 80 percent of first year students, with the second lagging behind at 45 percent. By the early 1990s, however, the importance attached to these values had essentially traded places, with financial motivations assuming the top rank (Astin 1998, 2000). In 2011, the proportion of first year students who reported that being well off financially was an important life goal was the highest since the survey began in 1966 (Pryor et al. 2011).

UNIVERSITY ENROLMENTS

Not surprisingly, the growing importance students attach to career and monetary advancement has changed the way they view different academic programs. Students who are primarily concerned with money or job-related skills are less likely to be interested in courses that prioritize critical thinking or self-development. Good value for one's tuition dollars means purchasing courses labelled as relevant in market terms.

Student values and attitudes both reflect and have reinforced changing enrolment trends. A shift in university enrolments from basic arts and sciences to more practical fields of study was evident by the late 1970s. Between 1967–68 and 1977–78, the proportion of Canadian undergraduates registered in basic arts and science programs fell from 58 to 47 percent, while enrolment in business administration nearly doubled. Likewise, from 1976 to 1981, the number of bachelor degrees awarded in commerce, engineering and computer science increased by 39 percent, at the same time as "public sector-oriented degrees" in fields like education, the humanities and social sciences declined from 72 to 64 percent (Novek 1985). These changes continued in subsequent years. The number of students enrolled in "liberal arts and sciences, the social sciences, English and history" all declined significantly in the mid-1990s (AUCC 2011a: 8).

Although enrolment growth in arts-related disciplines rebounded somewhat in the late 1990s and 2000s, it did not match the expansion of business and management fields. According to Statistics Canada (2005), between 1997–98 and 2003–04, humanities enrolment increased by 14 percent while enrolment in business, management and public administration increased by 37 percent. Between 2005–06 and 2008–09, growth in these same disciplines increased by 4 percent and 12 percent respectively (Statistics Canada 2010a). From 1997 to 2007, the largest proportional increase in university graduates was in business, management and public administration; by the end of this ten-year period, the most popular program for full-time undergraduate students in Canada was business and management (AUCC 2011a; Statistics Canada 2009b).

LEARNING AS A SERVICE ENCOUNTER

Changes in student motivations and their enrolment patterns correspond to broader changes that have taken place in line with corporatization. Intentionally or otherwise, student-consumers have helped to transform broader pedagogical relationships to comply with market frameworks. That is, higher education becomes a passive commercial transaction, rather than an active process of mutual engagement between student and professor. In the corporatized university, learning has been refashioned as a service encounter. Many students have adopted a sort of "degree-purchasing" orientation, where educational credentials are viewed as purchasable commodities and learning is evaluated according to external motivations and rewards. There are a number of negative impacts that result from this orientation to student learning, including professor disengagement and the rise of a more adversarial classroom environment (Côté and Allahar 2011). Céleste Brotheridge and Raymond Lee (2005: 71) also note "poor study habits ... and poor course performance."

Consistent with the notion of purchasing a degree, students also tend to have a new and specific set of entitlements. In a just society, everyone should be entitled to a university education. Under corporatization, however, student entitlement has taken on pejorative connotations associated with consumer privilege. Many students now believe that their status as educational consumers affords them the right to demand precisely what their education should entail. For example, students increasingly expect the same things from universities as they do from commercial establishments, such as convenience, customer-centred service and product guarantees (Singleton-Jackson, Jackson and Reinhardt 2010; Molesworth, Nixon and Scullion 2009). The University of Regina recently set the bar for "product guarantees" when it became the first university in Canada to guarantee career success.[1] As universities continue to broaden their customer service mandate, university professors — recast as "service providers" — are expected to provide a learning environment that is conducive to customer satisfaction. Accordingly, student consumerism has been linked to grade inflation. If student satisfaction is the responsibility of the service provider, there is considerable incentive for the provider to inflate grades in order to please the customer. A survey of faculty at the University of Western Ontario found widespread agreement that today's students expected higher grades for putting out the same or less effort than in the past (Côté and Allahar 2011). Moreover, 90 percent of faculty said they felt pressure to give higher grades than students deserved, and a majority admitted that they had recently changed their courses to make them easier for students. Although these results cannot be generalized, it would appear that many professors are aware of, and are catering to, student-consumer expectations.

Some student-consumers go further, claiming they are entitled to educational rewards regardless of their performance in the classroom. From this perspective, receiving high grades (and ultimately a degree) is an entitlement paid for by tuition fees. It follows that universities are obligated to provide students not simply with opportunities for academic success, but with *realized* academic success. In fact, some students are even appealing to judicial systems. Students and parents in many U.S. states, for example, are drawing on consumerist arguments to launch "educational malpractice" lawsuits (Steele 2010). Similar cases have arisen in Canada. In 2012, a political science student at Concordia launched a lawsuit against the university after receiving an unexpected grade. Seeking reimbursement for the $342 course fee, he stated that the credential was a "product they sold me for $342 and ... they haven't adhered to the terms of the service, so I just asked for a refund" (cited in Johnson 2012).

ACADEMIC DISHONESTY AS MARKET RESPONSE

Academic dishonesty has become a hot public issue of late. It has been discussed at length on Canadian talk and radio shows and has been the subject of numerous editorials. Research suggests that "cheating" has become far more prevalent among higher education students in the past couple of decades. Julia Christianson Hughes, dean of the College of Management and Economics at the University of Guelph, says surveys of Canadian students show that more than 50 percent admit to some form of academic dishonesty (Moore 2014). In fact, these practices have become so prevalent that a Montreal-based company, known as unemployedprofessors.com, is openly hiring academics and graduate students to write custom essays for students. Similarly, a U.K. survey of over eighty universities found that academic misconduct has increased dramatically in recent years (Barrett 2011). This readiness to engage in plagiarism is fuelling the U.K.'s online essay industry, estimated to be worth over £200 million (Henry 2010). Up to 100,000 U.K. students now use the services of these companies each year. Alarmingly, an undercover investigation by the *Sunday Mirror* found that some firms are even providing medical school essays for purchase, while others are offering full masters level dissertations (Wright and Cortbus 2014). One company representative stated that seventy students in the past year alone had obtained their degrees by purchasing the company's ready-made dissertations.

The documented rise in academic dishonesty can be viewed as a rational response on the part of the student-consumer in that it conforms to the logic of the marketplace and a commodified educational environment. Coleen Vojak (2006: 178) argues that students' "academic moral compasses" have undergone a profound shift as they "increasingly connect their educational experiences to 'career, money, and success.'" Students who engage in academic misconduct, Vojak says, mirror market principles as both use "a value system in which economic goods are prioritized, success is quantified, self-interest is narrowly defined, personal benefits are accrued by shifting costs onto others and appearances of virtue are more profitable than real virtue" (190). Instrumentalizing higher learning as a means to an end also alienates students from the process and product of their labour, which results in increased incentives to take shortcuts to obtain the end goal. As academic dishonesty is reframed as a viable alternative to effort and engagement, it is understandable why a growing number of university students do not understand why plagiarism is wrong (Levine and Dean 2012). The use of market ideologies by universities makes them complicit in the production of an educational climate where purchasing coursework is seen as a rational and enterprising strategy. In John McMurtry's (2010: 23) words, "if the academy follows market values, why shouldn't students buy their papers from sellers of their choice? ... The rising epidemic of Internet plagiarism is not anomalous, but symptomatic of the increasing dominance of market values in the academy."

THE STUDENT-CONSUMER PARADOX

For many proponents of corporatization, the transformation of students into educational consumers is a positive development that addresses the demands of neoliberal restructuring (to be accountable, efficient and relevant). This is largely because students, as consumers, are less tolerant of inferior educational environments and "useless" learning, so they will demand greater efficiencies and hold universities accountable for improvements in the educational product. Missing from this perspective is an understanding of the fundamental differences between a customer-supplier and a student-university relationship. For example, just as educational "services" are different from other services, the normative expectations, rights and obligations of students are different from those of traditional customers. Some of these differences can be explained using market terminology. Unlike traditional customers, educational "consumers" must commit considerable effort to co-producing the product with the service provider, and unlike a corporation, the university has an obligation to assess how a customer "uses" its product before allowing more of the product to be purchased and consumed. Moreover, unlike a corporation, which sells its products to anyone with the ability to pay, money alone cannot (or, at least, should not) buy a university degree. Finally, the ideal of customer assurance in a market context (that is, "the customer is always right") is antithetical to the contingent process of educational discovery. Thus, applying market principles to education shows that the overarching assumption that the educational experience is a product rather than a process is not only inaccurate, it is inappropriate.

It is important to note, however, that the rise of the student-consumer remains a contested process. Many students still desire (and receive) a rich and challenging university education that is not solely linked to monetary rewards or job preparation. Yet, as the corporatization process accelerates and the costs of higher education and student debt continue to rise, more and more students will identify as customers.

CUSTOMERS PAY: TUITION, DEBT AND THE HIGH COST OF LEARNING

In Canada, successive federal administrations and most provincial governments have adopted a "customers pay" orientation to university financing that has resulted in Canada having some of the highest tuition fees in the world. Average tuition fees in Canada fell in constant dollars through the 1970s. Although fees began to rise in the 1980s, by 1986–87 they had still only reached 88 percent of their 1974–75 level (Cameron 1991). It was in the 1990s and 2000s that tuition fees climbed dramatically. The cost of undergraduate tuition has grown from an average of $1,706 in 1991–92 to $5,772 in 2013–14, an increase of 238 percent (CAUT 2012). These trends are mirrored by changes in university operating revenues. Between 1979 and 2009, the proportion of operating revenues provided by governments declined from 84 to 58 percent. At same time, the proportion funded by tuition fees increased from 12 to 35 percent. In 2009, government funding as a share of university operating revenues ranged from 75 percent in Newfoundland and 70 percent in Quebec, to just 50 percent in Ontario and 48 percent in Nova Scotia.

Tuition increases in Canada are most evident in professional programs, primarily because of tuition deregulation. Between 1990 and 2003, medical fees, adjusted for inflation, rose by 320 percent. At the same time, law school tuition rose by 217 percent and dental school tuition increased by 400 percent (CAUT 2003). By 2012–13, undergraduate students in dentistry were paying the highest average annual fees in the country ($16,910), followed by medicine ($11,891) and pharmacy ($10,297) (Statistics Canada 2012). At the graduate level, the most expensive program continues to be the Executive Master of Business Administration (MBA) — with average fees of $38,508 — followed by regular MBA programs at $23,757. McGill University is one institution where fees for MBA students have sharply increased in recent years. In a move supported by forty-five of Quebec's leading CEOs, in 2011 McGill began charging $29,500 a year for its two-year MBA program, an increase of nearly 900 percent.

Of course, escalating costs have not had an equal impact on all Canadians. Between 1980 and 2007, for example, undergraduate tuition as a proportion of average net income grew from eight to 18 percent for those in the lowest income quintile. For those in the highest income group, it grew from just two to three percent (Motte, Berger and Parkin 2009). In 1990 in Ontario, a middle-income family could earn the equivalent of four years of tuition in eighty-seven days; by 2012, the average time required had increased to 195 days (CCPA 2013a). According to BMO Financial Group, two thirds of Canadian parents say that they cannot afford the costs of sending their children to university (Singleton 2010). TD Canada Trust's 2011 education and finances survey goes further, showing that 93 percent of Canadians report that saving for their children's education was a top financial priority, but only 33 percent said they had any chance of saving enough money to pay for more than 10 percent of these costs (CBC News 2011).

Table 4.1 Average Undergraduate Tuition

Year	Province										
	NL	PE	NS	NB	QC	ON	MB	SK	AB	BC	CA
1991–92	$1,544	$2,141	$2,232	$2,046	$1,311	$1,818	$1,848	$1,859	$1,544	$1,970	$1,706
2013–14	$2,644	$5,696	$6,185	$6,133	$2,653	$7,259	$3,779	$6,394	$5,670	$5,029	$5,772
% Increase	71.2	166.0	177.1	199.8	102.4	299.3	104.5	243.9	267.2	155.3	238.3

Source: Canadian Association of University Teachers Almanac of Post-Secondary Education in Canada, 2014-2015.

Table 4.2 Tuition and Compulsory Fees, 1993–94 to 2017–18 (Current $)

Year	Province										
	NL	PE	NS	NB	QC	ON	MB	SK	AB	BC	CA
1993–94	$2,120	$2,801	$2,910	$2,520	$1,755	$2,497	$2,502	$2,436	$2,524	$2,441	$2,320
2013–14	$2,866	$6,380	$6,851	$6,592	$3,456	$8,162	$4,334	$6,882	$6,695	$5,657	$6,589
2017–18	$2,888	$7,060	$7,760	$7,572	$4,714	$9,483	$5,446	$8,365	$7,471	$6,111	$7,755

Source: Erica Shaker and David Mac. 2014. "Tier for Two: Managing the Optics of Provincial Tuition Fee Policies."

PROVINCIAL VARIATION IN TUITION FEES

The decentralized nature of Canadian post-secondary education is particularly evident in variations in tuition trends across the provinces. Tuition rose by 155 percent in British Columbia between 1991–92 and 2013–14, yet this overall increase was highly uneven over the two decades. For instance, between 1996–97 and 2001–02 tuition declined as the New Democratic Party (NDP) implemented a tuition freeze. As a result, B.C. students paid the second lowest tuition in Canada at the beginning of the 2000s. When the freeze was lifted by the incoming Liberal government, tuition increased over the next several years, bringing tuition levels closer to the national average. In Manitoba, tuition rose sharply in the 1990s under successive Conservative governments. In the early 2000s, however, the NDP government froze tuition, implemented a 10 percent tuition rollback, and then resumed the freeze at the third lowest level in the country after Newfoundland and Quebec. In Saskatchewan, tuition was lowered in 2006–07 and then frozen until 2010–11, but these policies followed three decades of successive tuition growth. Between 1990–91 and 2004–05, tuition climbed by an average of 8.5 percent a year under NDP leadership, almost four times the average annual rate of inflation (Gingrich 2011). Since the end of the tuition freeze in 2010–11, tuition in Saskatchewan has increased; today, students in the province pay the second highest tuition fees in the country. In 2013, an average undergraduate had to work over triple the number of hours required in 1975 to cover tuition, the largest increase in Canada (CCPA 2014).

It is especially instructive to contrast Ontario with Quebec. In 2003, the election of Liberal governments in both provinces brought different outcomes in the area of student financing and accessibility. In Quebec, the government implemented policies to deregulate tuition and reduce financial assistance, whereas in Ontario the Liberals increased tuition regulation. Of course, the different policies of the two governments need to be understood in the context of the nature and impact of previous policy environments. Despite Quebec moving to increase the amount of tuition paid by students in 2003, the province still had the lowest fees in Canada, and the Parti Québecios' partial commitment to the principle of universal access helps to explain the province's distinctive status in this area. In contrast, the actions of the Liberal government in Ontario followed the "common sense revolution" of Premier Mike Harris' Conservative government. In the area of higher education, the Conservatives' policy agenda included sharp reductions in public funding and the deregulation of tuition fees that saw tuition levels in Ontario rise to among the highest in the country (see Fisher et al. 2009).

Today, there are dramatic differences between Ontario and Quebec. Tuition grew faster in Ontario over the past two decades (nearly 300 percent) than in any other Canadian province. At $7,259 in 2013–14, Ontario now has the highest tuition fees in Canada.[2] Over the same period, fees in Quebec increased by just

102 percent and its undergraduate tuition of $2,653 sits alongside Newfoundland as the lowest in the country. Although the province's Liberal government had promised significant tuition hikes beginning in 2012–13, massive student protests and the victory of the Parti Québecios in the 2012 provincial election ensured that the proposed increases were repealed. The unique history of student militancy in Quebec — which has included a total of nine student strikes since 1968 — is one reason why students have consistently paid lower tuition than students in other provinces. Indeed, the 2012 student strikes were all the more impressive given the slanted media coverage of the tuition issue. In addition to the negative response that student activists have elicited in the national media (see, for example, Wente 2012), a content analysis of 143 Quebec editorials and columns about tuition fees revealed that 125 firmly supported a large fee increase, while only four unequivocally opposed it (Tremblay-Pepin 2013). It should be noted, however, that Quebec universities charge much higher fees for out-of-province students, a practice that does not exist elsewhere in the country.

With Quebec, Newfoundland has the lowest tuition rate in the country. In the late 1990s, per capita student debt in Newfoundland was the highest in the country. In 1999, the province's Liberal government implemented a tuition freeze in response to student unrest. Two years later, the government rolled back tuition by 25 percent. When the Conservatives took power in 2003, they maintained the tuition freeze and added additional measures to increase affordability, such as reducing interest rates on student loans and implementing a non-repayable needs-based grant system for all post-secondary students. In 2013, the government continued these policies by providing $25.8 million to help reduce student debt, which included $3.8 million to Memorial University to maintain its tuition freeze for 2013–14. These policies are in stark contrast to those of the other Atlantic provinces, which have allowed tuition to steadily increase.

Another way that Canadian universities are transferring the costs to their "customers" is by charging higher user fees (such as fees for health, dental and athletic services). Additional compulsory fees, which are largely unregulated by the provinces, rose by 134 percent across Canada between 1993–94 and 2008–09, with documented increases in every province (Gingrich 2009; Shaker 2006). According to Statistics Canada (2012), additional compulsory fees for undergraduate students in 2012–13 were lowest in Newfoundland and highest in Alberta. Erika Shaker and David Macdonald (2014) combine compulsory fees with tuition fees to offer a more complete picture of higher education costs. Their data shows that when these additional fees are included, Newfoundland is actually the least expensive province, followed by Quebec. At the other end of spectrum, Ontario is the most expensive province. Shaker and Macdonald also consider current policy trends to estimate the overall cost of university education for the 2017–18 academic year. They show that fees are expected to increase the most in Saskatchewan, Ontario and Quebec, and the least in Newfoundland, British Columbia and Prince Edward Island.. The continued affordability of education in Newfoundland is especially noteworthy.

CANADA IN CONTEXT

Despite variation across provinces, for Canada as a whole the trend is clear: most students are paying more and will continue to pay more as the costs of higher education are privatized. Of course, Canada is not unique in this regard. Consider the case of England. In 2010, the coalition government in the U.K. announced that university tuition fees would be allowed to rise by nearly 300 percent to a maximum of £9000, ostensibly as a way to compensate for public funding cuts. By 2014–15, three quarters of all institutions were imposing the maximum possible fee for all courses, up from one half the previous year (Paton 2014). According to one estimate, when interest charges on student loans and other fees are considered, the true cost of a university degree for students starting university in 2012 will increase up to £100,000 (Gallagher 2012). Not surprisingly, over the past several years demand for disciplines such as English, history, languages and philosophy has fallen significantly, while demand for business-related programs has increased (Paton 2013). Universities have also cut thousands of "soft degree courses" in programs associated with weaker employment prospects (Loveys 2011).

While England offers an extreme example of how the costs of higher education are being transferred to students, many public higher education systems are moving in the same direction. In nations where tuition fees have been in place for a long time — such as the U.S., Australia and the Netherlands — costs have increased considerably. According to one estimate, the cost of obtaining a degree in the U.S. has increased by 1,120 percent over the past 35 years (Jamrisko and Kolet 2012). In other countries where higher education has traditionally been free or inexpensive, "non-tuition" fees have been introduced or increased. In Ireland, for example, no tuition fees are charged but the "student contribution" or registration fees — which increased by €500 in 2011 to a total of €2,000 in 2012 — are comparable to tuition costs in many countries. In France, universities have added supplementary fees that range from €10 to over €2,000 depending on the institution (Marcucci and Usher 2012).

Yet, these trends are not universal. There remains considerable cross-national variation in university fee structures. In Europe, public university students in Greece, the Czech Republic, Hungary, Germany, Denmark, Finland, Sweden, Iceland and Norway study virtually free of charge. There are also distinct differences within the U.K. While tuition has skyrocketed in England and Wales, fees remain more affordable in Ireland and free in Scotland. In fact, Scottish higher education has moved in the opposite direction by abolishing student fees and setting ambitious targets to widen access for disadvantaged groups (see Denholm 2012a, 2012b). Research by the Scottish Parliament Information Centre found that while the staggering fee hikes in England have cost students around $14 billion over the past three years alone, Scottish students have saved $1 billion as a result of fee-free access (STV News 2014). It is interesting to note that although Quebec is often singled out as having exceptionally (and unrealistically) low fees in the North American context, attending university in Quebec is still far more expensive than in many OECD countries.

Many countries in Latin America, such as Brazil and Venezuela, have also maintained free public higher education. Several years ago in Mexico there was an attempt by the government to modestly raise tuition at the national university, the Universidad Nacional Autónoma de México (UNAM). This led to a national student strike that forced the government to reverse its position. It is interesting to compare the UNAM in Mexico with the University of California, which was hit with enormous budget cuts, tuition increases and student unrest in 2009. In 1960, tuition was free for California residents; today it costs nearly $13,000 per year. Noam Chomsky (2009) recently visited both university systems and his comments are worth quoting at length:

> I had a startling experience a few weeks ago. I travelled to Mexico City for talks at the National University, an enormous and very impressive institution with high standards of achievement and scholarship. Entrance is selective, but the university is virtually free. I then visited an even more remarkable institution, the college in Mexico City ... It is not only free, but has open admissions ... Shortly after I went to San Francisco for talks, and learned more about the California institutions of higher education. They have been at the very peak of the international higher education system. By now tuitions are quite high, even for in-state students, and cutbacks are affecting teaching, research, and staff. Needless to say, Mexico is a poor country with a struggling economy, and California should be one of the richest places in the world, with incomparable advantages. I mention these recent experiences only to emphasize that the recent cutbacks in higher education seen in much of the world cannot simply be traced to economic problems. Rather, they reflect fundamental choices about the nature of the society in which we will live. If it is to be designed for the wealthy and privileged ... then these are good choices. If we have different aspirations for the world of our children and grandchildren, the choices are shameful and ruinous.

Escalating education fees, whether in California, the U.K., Canada or elsewhere, do not merely reflect an economic strategy or the inevitable impact of public funding cuts. Rather, downloading the costs of higher education to students and their families is a political choice that reflects particular assumptions about education and what constitutes a just society.

INTERNATIONAL STUDENT RECRUITMENT AND FEES

The number of international students studying at Canadian universities has increased every year since the mid-1990s. By 2010, approximately 8 percent of undergraduates and 20 percent of the graduate student population were international students (AUCC 2010b). In 2011, the number of international university students reached 100,000, which is a fourfold increase since 1995. To be sure, international student mobility has positive elements. It can be a source of cultural enrichment and foster cross-national research collaboration. According to the AUCC's 2006 internationalization survey, "academic" rationales for international student recruitment are common within the university community. In fact, 92 percent of respondents stated that their institutions recruited international students to promote a more globally diverse campus (AUCC 2007b).

I would argue, however, that it is critical to understand the economic function of international students within the context of corporatization and recurrent public funding cuts. For university administrators in Canada and around the world, international student mobility is viewed less in terms of enriching campuses and expanding cultural knowledge and more in terms of using specific recruitment strategies to attract private income and maximize revenue. These students are seen as a lucrative investment because they often pay extraordinarily high fees. In Canada, international students were not charged differential tuition prior to the late 1970s. Yet, in recent years, tuition fees for international students have increased sharply (up 86 percent over the 2000s). By 2012–13, average tuition for international undergraduate students in Canada was $18,641 — more than three times the average rate paid by Canadian citizens (Statistics Canada 2012). This figure rises to over $25,000 for many graduate programs and $57,000 for some professional programs. Not surprisingly, a recent survey by the Canadian Bureau for International Education found that cost was one of the biggest obstacles for students wishing to study in Canada (Senate of Canada 2011).

Under corporatization, international student recruitment has also become saturated by the language of the market and virtually synonymous with marketing and branding. The first phase of Canada's international education plan began in 2007, when the federal department responsible for foreign and international affairs selected Bang Marketing, a Montreal-based company, to develop a distinct education-Canada brand. A year later, a multi-million dollar "Imagine Education au/in Canada" brand was officially launched to sell Canadian education around the world. More recently, the federal government has produced a new fifteen-point marketing strategy to draw international students away from more prestigious universities in the U.S. and U.K. (Ipsos Reid 2012). Selling Canadian education abroad is also featured prominently in the government's 2014 international education strategy, which seeks to "brand Canada to maximum effect" using "customized marketing strategies" (Government of Canada 2014: 4). University presidents have also launched a series of their own international recruitment ventures, including when a delegation of fifteen presidents visited India in 2010, with the goals of improving the Canada brand and convincing the hosts that they were "not in their country simply to try and boost Canada's international student enrolment numbers" (Fine 2010).

As part of the drive to recruit international students, there has been an increase in private for-profit "educational" providers, such as Australian-based Navitas and its competitor Study Group International. Navitas is a transnational corporation that has operated in Canada since 2006. Under partnership agreements with universities (for example, Simon Fraser University and the University of Manitoba), Navitas has established a presence on university campuses in the form of international study centres that recruit and educate international students for the university. Navitas provides the university with a share of the tuition revenue it receives in exchange for being allowed to use university facilities, and university names and logos in its marketing campaigns. The recruited students — many of whom would not have qualified for admission to the university — are provided with English-language training and other preparatory courses in various disciplines, and are guaranteed a transfer to a regular university stream. For both the company and the university, the benefits of this partnership are largely economic.

Many have criticized these companies, but fail to locate their critiques in the fact that their existence depends on the corporatization of the larger university system. In fact, Navitas' corporate strategy acknowledges that public funding reductions and the increasing reliance on full-fee-paying international students are essential to its success. And like many partnership arrangements under corporatization, these deals are often implemented with little discussion or debate. Given the threat that these "partnerships" pose to public universities, it is encouraging that faculty and student resistance has forced many administrations — at McMaster, Dalhousie, Carleton, Windsor and elsewhere — to back away from these deals in recent years.

PROPONENTS AND CRITICS OF TUITION INCREASES

Regardless of whether one is a domestic or international student, there have been significant increases in tuition costs across Canada. But, proponents and critics of corporatization hold radically different views about this trend. Overall, proponents of rising tuition costs argue that increasing the proportion of university funding paid for by individuals is in the best interests of students, higher education and the public — that is, it is for the public good. Because they see the benefits of higher education as accruing primarily to individuals, they contend that education should be viewed as a private rather than a public good, and that students (redefined as consumers) should pay most of the costs. Proponents often point to earning statistics, such as those put out by the Canadian Council on Learning (2010a), which claim that people who hold a Bachelor's degree earn nearly $750,000 more than a high school graduate over a forty-year period. This figure fits with the common assertion that a university degree holder earns, on average, $1 million more over his or her lifetime because of educational credentials. From this perspective, shifting the costs from taxpayers to students results in greater equity between those who pay and those who benefit.

These kinds of arguments are often bound up with purported concerns for social justice. For many advocates of tuition deregulation, low or regulated tuition means that middle and upper class individuals, who account for a disproportionate share of university attendees, are accessing higher education at a fraction of the cost of what they can actually afford to pay. Not only that, but low-income taxpayers, who presumably receive fewer benefits from higher education, are required to finance the education of more financially privileged groups (see, for example, Usher 2014) Following this line of argument, low tuition policies and, by extension, increased public investments in higher education discriminate against the poor because they represent a net transfer of wealth from lower to higher income families. Some proponents go one step further to argue that consistently high enrolment rates mean that increased tuition does not render university education inaccessible for low-income families. For this group, to the extent that tuition does lead to financial hardship, expanded access to student loans and grants is sufficient to mitigate the problem (see, for example, Pakravan 2006).

Opponents of tuition increases argue that, on the contrary, university students are actually not subsidized by taxpayers. Rather, publicly funded university education is a profitable *investment* by the public treasury for the public good. This is because the social rate of return to public education spending significantly exceeds its cost. The direct public benefit of investing in higher education has been estimated at $100,000 per individual, or a 160 percent return on each dollar invested (CFS 2012). Looking just at university graduates in British Columbia, Iglika Ivanova (2012) found that they pay much more than the full cost of their education through their increased tax contributions and reduced reliance on government transfers. Compared to individuals with a high school education, Ivanova found that men with an undergraduate degree contribute, on average, $159,000 more to the public treasury over their working lives, while women contribute $106,000 more. In contrast, a four-year undergraduate degree costs approximately $50,000 (of which tuition fees make up 40 percent). In short, public investment in higher education generates significant fiscal benefits in the long term. Furthermore, because the affluent pay more taxes in absolute terms, financing higher education through general government revenues amounts to a transfer of income from higher to lower income families, not the other way around. As university funding shifts from income taxes to higher tuition, poor families, who pay very little income taxes, end up paying considerably more as the progressive elements of the post-secondary finance structure are reduced (Mackenzie 2013).

While corporatization's supporters emphasize the individual benefits of higher education —both market-related benefits (such as improved labour marketability and higher wages) and non-market-related benefits (such as greater personal health, happiness, longevity and quality of life) — it is equally important to consider the social benefits of higher education. The creation of new knowledge often benefits current and future generations, especially if this knowledge is widely disseminated and not subject to exclusionary mechanisms. Other social benefits include reductions in poverty and inequality, lower health care costs, environmental sustainability, higher levels of civic participation and increased community cohesion. Indeed, government involvement in the financing and provision of higher education is based on the premise that it accrues social benefits. While the study of non-market social benefits from education is still in its infancy, evidence suggests that these benefits have been underestimated (Klein 2006; McMahon 2009). There is also evidence to suggest that the individual benefits of higher education — such as the $750,000 to $1 million earning premium discussed above — have been overestimated. According to the Canadian Federation of Students (2007a), when inflation is factored into the equation, the additional potential earnings of a university education is closer to $150,000. Relying on more recent data, the Federation (2012) asserts that this earnings differential may be even lower than it previously claimed, sitting at just $80,000 for men and $46,000 for women.

The social benefits of public funding were also evident during the recent global economic crisis. While many private U.S. universities experienced severe financial hardship resulting from investment losses, Canada's public system was largely protected because of the relatively small proportion of university revenues drawn from investments. Seen in this light, not only has there been considerable *underinvestment* in higher education, but government funding cuts coupled with increased tuition are also highly inefficient from both an economic and social perspective.

Finally, it is important to note that relatively small changes in the tax system could dramatically reduce tuition levels. For example, the total cost of rolling back undergraduate tuition rates in Ontario to their 1990 level — from $6,500 to $2,500 a year — would cost approximately $1.5 billion (adjusted for inflation and the growing student population). In contrast, the corporate tax cuts the province introduced in 2009 were estimated at $1.6 billion (Macdonald and Shaker 2011). Tuition in Ontario could be eliminated if Ontario families paid an average of $170 more per year in taxes. Since 2000, Canadian federal governments have also chosen to forgo $48 billion in revenues through tax cuts, with much of it going into the pockets of corporations. Just 10 percent of that money could have been used to eliminate tuition fees for all students currently enrolled in Canadian universities (Falvo 2012).

WHAT DOES THE PUBLIC THINK?

Compared with most governments and university administrators, the Canadian public tends to be remarkably agreeable to tuition reductions and public funding increases. Survey results indicate that the public strongly disagrees with a "customers pay" model of university financing. One 2009 poll found that 86 percent of Canadians believe tuition fees should be frozen or reduced, 9 percent said they should be raised and over half think that university and college tuition should be eliminated altogether (CAUT 2009b). Moreover, a majority of Canadians rank reductions in tuition and student debt as the top priority for government investments in education. These results are not surprising, given that 93 percent of Canadians agree that cost should not prevent qualified students from attending university. National surveys have also found that a majority of Canadians, in all regions of the country, believe that governments should invest more in universities and colleges, even if it means they would personally have to pay more in taxes (CAUT 2011a; CCL 2009a; CFS 2011, 2012; Ipsos Reid 2004).

These national results mirror provincial surveys. In Nova Scotia, for instance, 83 percent of respondents stated that tuition should be reduced (CFS 2011). In Ontario, a large majority of the population — close to 80 percent — opposes increasing tuition as a measure to reduce university costs. Furthermore, one third of Ontarians identify lowering or capping tuition as the "single most important thing" the provincial government should do for university education in the province (OCUFA 2013). Just as the public opposes rising tuition fees, it also supports generous public funding for higher education. For instance, approximately 80 percent of Ontario residents believe that governments rather than students should pay a larger share of the costs of post-secondary education (Ekos 2005, 2003). And a survey by the Ontario Confederation of University Faculty Associations (2013) found that cutting public funding for universities received the lowest support rating amongst a list of twelve stimulus and cost-cutting strategies designed to help manage Ontario's financial situation.

STUDENT DEBT AND STUDENT AID

Not surprisingly, increases in tuition fees and changes to national and provincial policies have had a significant impact on student debt. In 2012, student debt in the U.S. surpassed $1 trillion and it continues its upward climb. While faring somewhat better than their American counterparts, student debt is a significant and growing problem for Canadian students. During the 1990s, debt among Canadian undergraduates doubled (CCL 2010a). Between 1982 and 1995, the average student loan amount for Bachelor's degree graduates rose by 121 percent for men and 145 percent for women. From 1995 to 2005, the proportion of student loan borrowers that owed $25,000 or more at graduation increased from 17 to 27 percent, while the proportion owing more than $50,000 tripled (Luong 2010). Today, federal government student loan debt in Canada is approximately $15 billion; when provincial and commercial bank loans are included, the total is closer to $20 billion. Sixty percent of Canadian students currently graduate with average debts of over $27,000 for an undergraduate degree. Based on an average salary of approximately $40,000, it takes students about fourteen years to pay off this level of debt (Mangaroo 2012). This $27,000 figure does not include private debt accumulated by students, nor does it include parental support. As costs escalate, students have also been forced to diversify their sources of funding. According to the Canadian University Survey Consortium, between 2002 and 2011 the proportion of undergraduates who relied on four or more funding sources nearly doubled, from 21 to 39 percent (Prairie Research Associates 2002, 2011). Moreover, the average amount from each funding source increased from $9,000 to nearly $12,000.

Of course, tuition increases are not the only source of rising student debt. A series of changes in student aid policies have also played a role. Beginning in the 1990s, federal financing policies shifted from universal to targeted programs and from funding institutions to funding individuals. Consistent with this ethos, the federal government has initiated specific initiatives in response to increases in student debt load, including altering the definition of "student loan" to exclude $1.5 billion in student debt, and raising the legislated ceiling of student loans owed to the government, set by the Canada Student Financial Assistance Act, from $15 to $19 billion. As a part of corporatization, there has also been a shift in student aid from grants to loans. In some countries, student loans have been introduced where they did not exist before (for example, France in 1991, Hungary in 2001). In others, like Canada, funding systems have tilted towards loans and away from grants and scholarship programs. According to the OECD's *Education at a Glance 2014*, grants now cover a much smaller proportion of the direct costs of post-secondary in Canada (less than 5 percent) than they do in most other OECD countries.

There has also been an increasing reliance on tax expenditures as the preferred form of direct student assistance, through the Education Tax Credit, Student Loan Interest Tax Credit, Tuition Fee Tax Credit, Textbook Tax Credit and the Scholarship, Fellowship and Bursary Tax Credit. Tax credits are designed to offset tuition costs and help families save money for post-secondary education. While some argue that these measures are highly beneficial (Usher and Duncan 2008), most of the evidence suggests that tax credits are a regressive and inefficient policy measure. For example, all students qualify for education tax credits regardless of socio-economic status and financial need, which disproportionally benefits those from higher income backgrounds. Indeed, tax credits have little impact on accessibility because most students are unable to claim these credits while in school, so the money is not available to meet tuition and living expenses. Not surprisingly, those students who delay claiming tax credits until after graduation tend to have lower incomes and are more likely to come from poor families. According to Christine Neill (2013), while only 10 percent of tax filers have incomes above $80,000, they account for 42 percent of the total tax credits that are transferred to parents (and other eligible family members). Meanwhile, approximately one half of tax filers have incomes below $30,000, but they use only 7 percent of transferred credits. Because tax credits are ultimately dependent on sufficient taxable income, even the ability to make full use of them after graduation is uncertain given the employment realities facing many university graduates.

Registered Education Savings Plans (RESP) and the associated Canada Education Savings Grant (CESG) suffer from similar inadequacies in that they primarily help students whose parents have money to invest in their education. These programs were introduced to incentivize savings for post-secondary education at a time when tuition fees were rising sharply in the 1990s. The RESP allows educational savings to grow tax-free until the beneficiary is attending college or university full-time, so the program is only accessible to those who can afford to save. The CESG is a direct matching grant offered by the government to anyone who is investing in an RESP (to a maximum of $7,200). Again, those parents who cannot afford to save receive little benefit. Despite moderate changes in 2004 that made these programs more accessible to low-income Canadians, they still represent a disproportionate system of student aid that primarily benefits families who need it the least. A 2007 survey of RESP subscribers found that children from households with incomes under $20,000 comprised only 4.7 percent of families that were saving for post-secondary education through the RESP. In contrast, households with incomes over $80,000 accounted for 34.6 percent of RESP subscribers (Government of Canada 2009).

Tax credits are also associated with enormous costs. In 2009, the much-maligned Canada Millennium Scholarship Foundation[3] was replaced with the Canada Student Grants Program (CSGP). According to the CCPA's (2013b) *Alternative Federal Budget 2013*, the CSGP distributed roughly $614 million in 2013, while the Canada Student Loan Program lent $2.3 billion. While significant funds were being distributed through the CSGP, it was very little compared to the $2.81 billion the government allocated to education-related tax credits and savings schemes. So, if the money provided through tax credits was shifted to direct, upfront grants distributed by the Canada Student Loan Program (CSLP), it would turn every dollar loaned by the CSLP into a non-repayable grant, which would dramatically reduce the need for students to borrow. As it stands, however, the aggregate of student loans disbursed by the CSLP (minus the aggregate of loan repayments received) has been increasing at approximately $1 million per day (CFS 2012).

Of course, student aid policies and student debt also vary by province (MacLaren 2014; Shaker and Macdonald 2014). While the average debt load for Canadian students enrolled in their final year of a bachelor's program is $27,000, it is only $15,000 in Quebec, the lowest in the country (Martin and Tremblay-Pepin 2011). This lower debt load is a product of lower tuition fees as well as the province's relatively generous financial aid programs. Likewise, in Manitoba, tuition freezes and increases in non-repayable student aid have resulted in the second lowest levels of student borrowing and per capita student debt. In the late 1990s, student debt in Newfoundland was the highest in the country, with over 20,000 students owing more than an average of $30,000. Years of subsequent tuition relief and generous student aid have since led to a steep drop in the number of students relying on financial assistance and significant reductions in overall debt load. From 2002–03 to 2008–09, the proportion of full-time university students receiving a Canada student loan in Newfoundland declined from 57 to 31 percent (CAUT 2011b). In 2014–15, Newfoundland became the first province in Canada to entirely replace its student loans system with needs-based grants. In contrast, since 2000, student debt in the other three Atlantic Provinces has increased faster than the national average, with student debt load in Nova Scotia being among the highest in the country.

In Ontario, despite the increasing number of borrowers, student debt has been mitigated to some extent by recent increases in grants and other non-repayable aid. In 2011–12, for example, the province implemented the "30% Off Tuition Grant," which refunds a portion of education costs for undergraduates who qualify for the program. In Saskatchewan, three decades of successive tuition growth meant that, by 2006, 36 percent of university graduates reported debt loads of more than $20,000 (Gingrich 2009). While the tuition freeze and several non-repayable assistance programs for low and middle income students have provided some debt relief, the number of university graduates in the province reporting debts of more than $20,000 has continued to increase (Gingrich 2011). In British Columbia, student debt in the 2000s also mirrored national trends. Rising fees and the elimination of the province's needs-based grant program in 2004 meant that undergraduate debt grew faster in B.C. than in any other province over the course of the decade (Berger 2009).

Not only do provinces differ in the amount of upfront aid they offer students, they also have different repayment and after-the-fact debt relief policies. In 2009, Newfoundland became the first province to eliminate interest on the provincial portion of student loans. Prince Edward Island and Nova Scotia now also have a zero interest policy on provincial loans. In sharp contrast, interest rates on student loans in B.C. are the highest in the country and interest begins accumulating immediately after studies are complete, whereas many other provinces have a six-month grace period. Ontario, Nova Scotia and New Brunswick all have a "debt cap" that limits the degree to which students can go into debt; Quebec has a debt cap as well as a deferred payment plan for students who have difficulty making loan payments; Prince Edward Island offers a debt reduction grant for students with large amounts of debt; Manitoba has a bursary program designed to limit student debt; and Saskatchewan provides financial incentives for graduates who choose to remain and work in the province. Although Alberta cancelled its Student Loan Relief program in 2012, it was replaced with small grants for students who complete their programs or find work in particular occupations.

Considerable sums of public money are devoted to offsetting tuition increases and helping to mitigate student debt. However, most debt relief policies in Canada are applied after the fact. Student-consumers must still provide most of the money upfront, and tuition cannot be paid with tax credits. Summarizing Canada's approach to student financial assistance, Shaker and Macdonald (2014: 11) write that the use of targeted, retroactive approaches instead of universal public support has resulted in a "highly complex, non-transparent system of student assistance programs that are in many cases unpredictable and extremely difficult for students to navigate."

THE NEGATIVE CONSEQUENCES OF RISING TUITION AND STUDENT DEBT

High tuition and debt have a major impact on the decisions and choices that students make. According to a 2006 national survey, nearly 40 percent of Canadian post-secondary students stated that debt concerns were a major factor underlying their personal life decisions, including their living and working arrangements (Ekos 2006). Of those students whose academic decisions were also impacted by debt, a significant proportion said it led them to choose schools with lower tuition, attend school part-time and take reduced course loads. Moreover, nearly one in five stated that it led them to attend college instead of university. These results varied by province. Students in Quebec, for example, were far less concerned about debt and it was less likely to impact their educational choices. In my view, however, decisions that are motivated by financial hardship should not be viewed as simple matters of "choice." For example, 30 percent of the students surveyed indicated that personal decisions made on the basis of cost/debt were entirely or mostly involuntary (roughly the same proportion said they were "somewhat" voluntary). In reality, debt performs a kind of "disciplinary" function on students. The impact of cost and debt on student decision making — and the resulting outcomes — can be broken down into three sets of "choices": those made by students before or upon entering (or not entering) university (access choices); those made by students during the course of their studies (completion choices); and those made by university graduates (post-graduation choices).

Access to Higher Education

Financial considerations often influence where students choose to study. In Canada, tuition levels have impacted provincial enrolment trends, especially in Atlantic Canada. Between 1997 and 2009, the number of students from Nova Scotia attending Memorial University in Newfoundland increased by over 1000 percent, while the number of students from New Brunswick attending Memorial increased by 800 percent. By 2010, approximately one sixth of Memorial's 14,000 undergraduate students (or approximately 2,300 students) were from out of province, compared with just 137 out of province students in 1997. The primary reason given by these students for choosing Memorial is the university's low tuition fees (Macdonald and Shaker 2012). Taking a step back from decisions about which university to attend, what about the more fundamental decision of whether or not to attend university in the first place? University "access" can be viewed in two ways. From a supply-side perspective — where a primary consideration is the supply of trained graduates — the key question is "how many." That is, the greater the level of participation or attendance, the greater the level of access. From a social welfare perspective, the more important question is "who attends" because it takes into account the characteristics of university attendees. From this perspective, an accessible education system is one in which everybody has an equal opportunity to participate.

Unfortunately, much of the public discussion about post-secondary attendance narrowly equates participation with access. If university access is measured solely in terms of "how many" students attend, then access has increased steadily over the years, even in provinces with higher tuition fees (in economic terms, demand for higher education is sometimes said to be "inelastic" — that is, independent of the cost). These high enrolment rates are often used by proponents of increased tuition to refute the claim that escalating costs have made university education unaffordable (Milway 2005). The relationship between access and the socio-economic characteristics of university attendees, however, is more complex. To begin with, post-secondary students in Canada have always been disproportionately drawn from higher income families. In 2006, youth between the ages of 18 and 24 with parents earning more than $100,000 in pre-tax income were nearly twice as likely to attend university compared to those whose parents earned less than $25,000 (CAUT 2012; see also de Broucker 2005 and Finnie, Childs and Wismer 2011). The fact that university attendance is stratified by social class is not in dispute. The question is whether or not poor and other disadvantaged groups have an equal opportunity to participate.

To answer this question, it is useful to begin by surveying public opinion polls. As noted above, an overwhelming majority of Canadians believe that cost should not prevent qualified individuals from attending institutions of higher learning. At the same time, polls also show that most Canadians believe cost does reduce access for low-income groups and these concerns have become more acute as fees continue to rise (CCL 2009a; CFS 2009). Public opinion on this issue aligns with the behaviour of secondary school graduates. Cost and finances are the most commonly cited barrier to post-secondary participation (Barr-Telford et al. 2003; CCL 2009b; Market Quest Research Group 2005). As the CFS (2009: 11) notes, "two thirds of students who decide against enrolling in university say that student debt affected their decision."

Moreover, studies suggest that access to university has become more difficult for underprivileged families (Coelli 2005, 2009; Neill 2009), especially in the case of professional programs, and that high tuition/high debt has had an especially detrimental impact on racialized groups in Canada (CFS 2010). Evidence also points to a shifting social class composition among students in particular universities and provinces. For instance, John Conway's (2004) influential report on university accessibility in Saskatchewan demonstrates that increasing tuition and other financial barriers have been severe impediments for rural, low-income and Aboriginal students.

Proponents of tuition deregulation argue that needs-based programs of financial aid allow the vast majority of (if not all) students to attend university if they choose. What they often fail to consider are the financial and other hardships resulting from excessive debt loads, as well as the deterrent effect of "debt aversion." Debt aversion is the personal calculation that debt accumulation and repayment are not worth the returns from higher education. It is one of the most common reasons given by students who never pursue post-secondary studies, especially those from disadvantaged backgrounds who are more averse to borrowing and the possibility of default (CCL 2010a; R.A. Malatest and Associates 2007). Students from racialized groups, those from lower income backgrounds and single parents are more likely to hold negative views about taking on student debt (CFS 2009).

Unequal access to post-secondary education and the divergence of participation rates among socio-economic groups is not solely, or even primarily, tied to tuition costs (or the university's "sticker price"). Differences in the socialization of working- and middle-class youth, parental education levels, early educational advantages and countless other privileges and barriers associated with social class are all important variables. Nevertheless, rising costs and the impact of debt aversion are creating access barriers for disadvantaged families. The fact that enrolment levels have continued to rise and that higher fees can be partially offset by targeted grant and loan assistance does not negate this reality.

Completion Time, Persistence and Employment
Financial concerns also impact students during the course of their studies, including their completion times and completion rates. According to one Canadian survey, nearly half of those students who said they were completing their studies at a slower pace than others reported that finances were a major reason (Ekos 2006). An additional one in four said that finances were somewhat related to slower completion. Others studies indicate that as student debt rises, persistence declines; the more money students borrow on an annual basis, the lower their level of persistence (McElroy 2005). Debt aversion may underlie this negative association. According to the CAUT (2007), students who borrow more than $10,000 are less than half as likely to complete a degree program (34 percent) as those who borrow less than $1,000 (71 percent). Students who discontinue their studies often cite financial obstacles as an explanation (Diallo, Trottier and Doray 2009). As a result, financing higher education though increased loans may actually be widening (not narrowing) the gap in educational opportunity and degree attainment by social class. That debt has an adverse effect on persistence is also affirmed by Joshua Mitchell, President of the Canadian Association of Student Financial Aid Administrators, who told the Standing Senate Committee on Social Affairs, Science and Technology that "those who are most at risk with post-secondary participation, in particular students from low-income families, first generation students and Aboriginal students, will abandon post-secondary education if their loan debt is too high" (Senate of Canada 2011).

Obtaining paid employment is another decision that can impact if and when students complete their studies. The proportion of students who were employed while attending university has increased from roughly one quarter in 1976 to nearly one half in 2008 (CFS 2012). According to Statistics Canada (2009a), the proportion of 20- to 24-year-olds who were employed while in school increased in every province between 1997–98 and 2007–08. Not only are more students taking on paid employment, they are also working longer hours (Motte and Schwartz 2009). While working at the same time as attending university may have a positive impact in some instances, research suggests that students — especially those from poorer backgrounds and/or with higher levels of debt — are far more likely to report adverse rather than positive impacts (CFS 2012; OCUFA 2010c; Prairie Research

Associates 2010). And not surprisingly, the more students work, the more likely they are to report negative impacts. One study found that 40 percent of first year students who worked 10 hours a week or less reported that it negatively impacted their studies, compared with 70 percent of those working over 30 hours a week (Prairie Research Associates 2007a). Adverse effects of paid employment include negative correlations with class preparation and attendance, study time, grades, as well as course and degree completion (Callender 2008; Côté and Allahar 2007; Motte and Schwartz 2009). As more and more young people are forced to complete their studies between periods of employment, they are arguably losing their identity as students. In other words, "student life" — a time of growing independence, "voluntary" poverty, leisure, exploration and free intellectual inquiry — is being redefined as a mode of contingent labour. Under corporatization, the categories of "student" and "worker" increasingly overlap, with students becoming workers who happen to study.

A very different but no less serious problem is that many students are unable to find work in order to finance their education and lessen their debt loads. Student employment prospects were significantly affected by the global economic crisis. In 2013, the youth unemployment rate in Canada was 13.7 percent. Although this is slightly below the unemployment peak of 15.2 percent in 2009, these numbers do not reflect that many young people have since given up looking for work and are therefore not counted in official unemployment statistics. For higher education students especially, one serious impact of the crisis was the significant jump in the number of students who were unable to obtain summer employment beginning in 2009. And the federal government is making things worse. Summer hiring of students in the federal public service declined by 36 percent between 2009 and 2013 (Hatt 2014).

Post-Graduation: Less Education, Less Desired Careers
Students who borrow to finance their first post-secondary degree are significantly less likely than those who do not to pursue further study. Likewise, university graduates with high levels of debt are less likely to pursue a second degree than those with less debt (Maritime Provinces Higher Education Commission 2007; Prairie Research Associates 2007b; Williams 2012). The influence of financial considerations on pursuing additional education is especially dramatic in the case of professional programs. Over the last fifteen years, entry into these professions has become far more difficult for families at lower income levels. In Ontario, for example, there has been a precipitous decline in participation rates among poorer students in law, dentistry and medicine (Conlon 2006; Frenette 2008).

Student debt also impacts career decisions. Upon graduation, many indebted students discover that their career choices are restricted to jobs that allow them to pay off their loans. For this reason, many find it difficult to consider public service or other less lucrative occupations. Once again, this tendency has been noted in the case of professional programs, such as law:

> A recent survey found that two-thirds of law graduates say that debt is a primary factor in keeping them from considering a career in public interest law … Other surveys have found that about half of the students who begin law school with stated public interest law commitments go into private practice law upon graduation, in large part because of their debt burden. For those students who do take a public-interest law job after law school, many find that they are unable to keep on working in this sector for more than two or three years, at which point they transfer into more lucrative positions. (Tannock 2006: 48–49; see also Field 2009)

It was these kinds of concerns (as well as concerns about access) that prompted a highly critical response on the part of the Canadian Bar Association (2003) to law school fee increases.

Of course, the effects of debt are not limited to the legal profession. Robert Chernomas and Errol Black (2004) have considered the impact of debt on medical school graduates. For them, physician shortages can be explained, in part, by the fact that graduates are taking longer to begin their careers because they are specializing rather than pursuing general practice. They also note that financial considerations are having an impact on speciality choice and practice location, which could exacerbate the divide in medical services between urban and rural communities.

Although the personal life choices of those with high debt are not addressed in detail here, it is worth noting that Canadians who hold student debt are less likely to have savings and investments and are less likely to own a home. Those that do own a home are more likely to have a mortgage (Luong 2010). High student debt also leads many graduates to "postpone marriage, to postpone having children, or, in general, to be unable to participate fully in adult life" (Schwartz 1999: 316). Jeffrey Williams (2012) likens growing student debt to a form of bondage, similar in principle and practice to "indentured servitude." Indeed, student debt is an exceptionally punishing form of debt and it has been designed that way. Most people can get out of debt by declaring bankruptcy, but with student debt there is no expiration date.

Student debt also permeates everyday life in ways that impact political culture. Students in earlier generations were relatively free to devote themselves to social and political causes prior to entering the workforce. However, as more and more students are forced to confront the debt "time bombs" that await them after graduation, participating in social activism becomes less tenable. In other words, debt dependence serves a disciplining and individualizing function. It contributes to the creation of a fragmented society where individuals are focused on individual concerns and less likely to be engaged in collective struggles. Not coincidently, the possibilities for a social movement against growing tuition and debt have been pre-empted, at least in part, by the political discipline imposed by customer-pay models in higher education. This context may help explain why students outside of Quebec — who in general pay greater fees, work longer hours and take on more debt — have been less willing or less able to oppose corporatization and defend their rights. There is little doubt that this broader disciplinary function of debt is well understood by those who control the policy-making process in this country.

The transformation of higher education has significant impacts on teachers and students, both in terms of what they teach and learn, and how they are financially compensated or expected to pay. Another segment of the university population — administrators — is also implicated. Recast in the role of corporate managers, administrators have increased their political influence within the university by appropriating power from faculty and academic bodies. They have also adopted a more corporate management style, in which faculty are increasingly treated as subordinate workers rather than autonomous professionals.

NOTES

1 The "UR Guarantee Program" stipulates that all students who complete the program (which includes mandatory job-training seminars) are assured a job within six months of graduation. If students are unable to secure employment within that time, the university provides them with an additional year of undergraduate education free of charge.
2 In 1989, tuition fees cost Ontario families in the lowest income quintile 17 percent of their net income. By 2004, the cost for this same group was 46 percent of their income. It has been projected that by 2027, the overall cost of an undergraduate degree in Ontario could rise to more than $137,000, a considerable increase over the $77,000 cost in 2010 (OCUFA 2010c).
3 The Canada Millennium Scholarship Foundation (CMSF) was created in 1998 by the Liberal government to administer an endowment of $2.5 billion. The CMSF was charged with providing bursaries and scholarships to hundreds of thousands of Canadian students. The foundation also carried out a well-funded (though transparently partisan) higher education research program. An independent review of the Fund in 2003 found that incompetent administration and a lack of federal oversight allowed some provinces to divert CMSF money into provincial coffers, or use it to replace existing provincial aid programs. For a more detailed critique of the CMSF, see CFS (2007b).

CHAPTER FIVE

MANAGING UNIVERSITIES LIKE A BUSINESS

In the 1950s, Canada's universities were ruled by a strict academic hierarchy where professors rarely contested managerial decisions. By the end of the decade, however, critical challenges to the prevailing mode of governance had begun to take shape. During the 1960s, these challenges increased along with the rise of university-based social activism. Students and professors claimed that the management of universities was overly secretive and targeted the "corporate university," or the "knowledge factory," where campus relations and governance practices were said to resemble those of a business establishment. Writing at the time, Vernon Fowke (1959) argued that university boards of governors were inappropriately modeled on the structure of the business corporation. Similarly, Donald Rowat (1964) claimed that the top-down systems of managerial control found in corporations had no place in universities, and called on academics to free themselves from hierarchical structures and their "master-servant" relationship with administrators. These movements for governance reform were also supported by the Canadian Association of University Teachers (CAUT) and a prominent national commission headed by James Duff and Robert Berdahl (1966) that called for more open and democratic systems of university management.

These combined pressures led most Canadian universities to review and revise their governance arrangements over the 1960s and 1970s. In concrete terms, this meant that academics expanded their representation in governance bodies and new systems of review were created to allow faculty greater input into hiring, tenure and promotion decisions. Likewise, students won places on faculty councils, departmental committees and senates. University boards of governors also underwent significant change. The proportion of university boards with faculty representation increased from 9 percent in 1955, to 32 percent in 1965 and to 92 percent in 1975 (Cameron 1991). There was also a significant rise in student participation. In 1965, not one university board of governors in Canada had a student representative. By

1975, more than three quarters of boards had students as members. While the impact of these changes should not be exaggerated, they did mean that collegial governance was becoming institutionalized.

The growing corporatization of higher education has challenged these modest but significant gains. Over the past forty years, the management of Canadian universities has shifted back to a more corporate model of organization and control. Not only have university administrations expanded in size, but there has also been a change in the social characteristics and commitments of administrators. Concomitantly, "managerialism" has moved into the university, through the centralization of administrative power, the incorporation of performance indicators, ranking systems and marketing techniques into university management, as well as the suppression of academic freedom. These administrative aspects of corporatization have had negative impacts on university governance and have tied curriculums, infrastructure and program development much more closely to corporate interests, to such a degree that the future of liberal education is in jeopardy.

CHANGING OF THE GUARD: UNIVERSITY ADMINISTRATORS IN THE ERA OF CORPORATIZATION

During the "golden age" of Canadian higher education, upper level university administrators — those primarily responsible for major departmental, faculty and university decisions — were largely drawn from the academic community and assumed a collegial leadership role. The primary responsibilities of the administration were to support teaching and research and protect the university's autonomy from outside interests. The corporatization of the university has meant changes in the role of university administrations and in the makeup of individuals who occupy their leading positions.

THE IMPACT OF FISCAL RETRENCHMENT

A major impetus behind the transformation of university governance was fiscal retrenchment. In response to government cuts to universities in the 1970s, faculty members in many provinces responded with calls for unionization and collective bargaining. The unionization process first took hold in Quebec, where over 60 percent of professors were unionized by 1975 (Newson and Buchbinder 1988). By the early 1980s, over half of the Canadian professoriate belonged to certified bargaining units. The movement for unionization and collective bargaining was an important development for university employees, and essentially helped to democratize the university. Benefits included providing faculty with some protection against budgetary cutbacks, improved salaries and working conditions, as well as preserving their active role in university governance. At the same time, unionization inadvertently facilitated a more corporate administration apparatus, where the interests of administrators (management) were pitted against those of faculty (workers). It also served to legitimate the existence of the administration as a separate entity within the university or, as some have argued, to equate the administration with the university itself. According to James Cameron (1978: 79), for faculty to negotiate with "the university" was to accept the administration as "denoting an employing authority, like Bell Canada or Imperial Oil."

Also part of the corporate agenda, universities increasingly turned to private sources of financial support, which meant that administrators devoted a greater share of institutional resources to external relations, such as fundraising and the expansion of public-private partnerships. The assumption was that these new priorities required "better management" in the form of centralized executive leadership, in part because the business community favoured secretive deals between senior university administrators and corporate executives. In other words, administrators needed to be freed from faculty influence and cumbersome democratic procedures to deal with growing financial concerns. As Stanley Aronowitz (2000: 165) explains, university administrators assumed the "standpoint of the institution against those who would resist the 'necessary' and 'rational' decisions that any administrator must make in the face of relative scarcity — a perspective emblematic of even the most profitable corporations." As a consequence, there was a further differentiation of the administrative/managerial apparatus from the academic community. Stepping outside of their collegial leadership role, administrators began to be viewed — and to view themselves — as resource and personnel directors rather than representatives of the broader academic community. Increasingly, "career administrators" were hired from outside of the academy and those within the university no longer returned to their academic posts. As the austerity agenda deepened, administrative and academic functions became "specialized and structurally distinct" and administrations acquired a "place of their own" within the university (Newson and Buchbinder 1988: 16).

EXPANDING RANKS AND SALARIES

University administrations have expanded considerably under corporatization. In part, the rise in the number of administrative positions reflects an increased demand for administrative services due to program expansions and growing enrolments. However, evidence suggests that this growth has been disproportional to other dimensions of educational expansion (for example, student enrolment and faculty hiring). While there is no reliable information on administrative growth at the national level, several provincial examples illustrate this shift. At the Université de Montreal, the relative weight of administrative personnel increased from 10 to 15 percent of total university staff between 2000 and 2008 (or from 817 to 1,712 employees). Over the same period, the proportion of professors fell from 26 to 22 percent (Martin and Tremblay-Pepin 2011). At the University of Saskatchewan, the number of full-time equivalent academic staff increased from 984 in 2003–04 to 1,119 in 2009–10 (13.7 percent increase), whereas the number of full-time equivalent positions increased by 33.2 percent for administrative, technical, clerical and other support staff, or from 2,993 to 3,986 employees (Gingrich 2011). At the University of Calgary, one of the university's six vice-presidents — the one in charge of fundraising — has an administrative team consisting of one senior director, four executive directors, thirteen directors, four associate directors and thirteen officers and co-ordinators.[1]

Another indicator of administrative expansion is that administrations are consuming a greater and greater share of institutional resources. Using information from Statistics Canada and the Canadian Association of University Business Officers (CAUBO), W.D. Smith (2010) calculated that twenty cents is now spent on central administration for every dollar spent on instruction and non-sponsored research, up from twelve cents in 1987–88. Also using CAUBO data, Polster (2011) found that between 1973 and 2008, the growth in administration and general costs outpaced the growth in faculty salaries by a wide margin.

Similarly, the salaries of senior administrators in Canada appear to have risen disproportionally. For example, even though faculty at the University of Manitoba remain among the lowest paid in the country, senior administrators have enjoyed huge pay raises. Between 2003 and 2006 alone, the salaries of nine top administrators increased by 27 percent, or more than $400,000 (Guard et al. 2007). Administrative salaries at the University of Saskatchewan increased from 8 to 14 percent of total university expenditures between 1990–91 and 2001–02, while academic salaries declined from 41 to 36 percent. At the University of Regina, total administrative pay constituted 75 percent of total faculty pay in 2000; by 2008, administrative salaries exceeded those of faculty (Gingrich 2009). In their research, Azim Essaji and Sue Horton (2010) found that executive compensation across Ontario universities increased by 40 percent in real terms between 1996 and 2006, this at a time when these institutions were ostensibly under severe financial stress. According to the Association of Professors at the University of Ottawa, administration expenditures rose by an average of 40 percent between 2003 and 2009. In contrast, overall university expenditures increased by an average of just 4 percent over the same time period (CAUT 2010b). In Quebec, the percentage of payroll expenditures for university managers and administrators grew by 83 percent between 1997 and 2004 (Martin and Tremblay-Pepin 2011). Looking specifically at the Université du Québec à Montreal (UQAM), between 2000 and 2006 payroll expenditures for professors increased by 19 percent, which was significantly less than the 30 percent increase for management staff and 40 percent increase for senior executives.

Under corporatization, compensation trends for administrators are very similar to those for executives in the business world. Just as escalating corporate salaries are justified by the "pressures" associated with downsizing, cost cutting and labour market restructuring, university administrators are getting paid more to pursue a similar mandate. The similarities between business managers and the new type of university executives are especially evident in the case of university presidents. As Randall Nelsen (2002: 133) notes, the "leaders of universities and their partners representing other corporate businesses have evolved to a point where they are thought of, and think of themselves, as one and the same."

THE NEW UNIVERSITY CEOs

The roles and expectations of a university president have traditionally been more complex than those of a corporate CEO. Before the onset of corporatization, university presidents were expected to act as a representative of the faculty *and* the administration, in addition to their responsibilities as a colleague, an advocate for students, a negotiator with governments, a public servant and a scholar. It was also common for university presidents to play an esteemed role in social and political life through their capacity as public intellectuals. In Canada, there are many cases of past presidents functioning as public intellectuals, most noticeably in their writings on higher education. Examples include Claude Bissell (*The Strength of the University* 1968), James Corry (*Farewell the Ivory Tower* 1970) and Murray Ross (*New Universities in the Modern World* 1966). While a president's role remains varied and complex, corporatization has simplified it considerably by aligning its roles and responsibilities more closely with those of top business executives.

Unlike years past, few university presidents today assume positions of intellectual leadership or rise to the status of public intellectuals. The reluctance of today's presidents to speak out on matters of social and political concern reflects changes in university recruitment strategies as well as presidential job requirements. In *Leadership Under Fire*, Ross Paul (2011: 54), former president of the University of Windsor, states that university boards of governors in Canada are increasingly seeking presidents with "corporate leadership styles more akin to those of a chief executive officer than to those of the more traditional academic leader of previous generations." Private fundraising, in particular, has become a "critical component of presidential success, sometimes misconstrued by search committees as a singular talent unrelated to the more traditional skills of academic leadership and good management" (182). Paul gives the example of Robert Prichard, former president of the University of Toronto (U of T), whose legendary fundraising abilities helped to build an endowment of more than a billion dollars. According to Doug Owram (2010), few presidents today spend less than a quarter of their time (and most spend more) on the fundraising trail. This division of labour is in sharp contrast to just a few decades ago, when presidential fundraising in Canada was a marginal activity. These requirements also make it more difficult for presidents to speak out on public issues, as taking a moral or political stand on controversial topics risks alienating private donors and sponsors.

Given their changing roles and characteristics, it is not surprising that university presidents tend to support corporatization. Buchbinder and Newson (1990: 370) note that in the 1980s there was a "surprising degree of unanimity" among presidents with respect to corporate-university linkages (and in their willingness to use their institutional positions to discredit alternative agendas). More recently, increased corporate involvement with universities — particularly university research — is being viewed as positive by most university presidents. In fact, presidents tend to argue that corporatization does not have a detrimental impact on arts-related disciplines, university research agendas or intellectual and institutional autonomy (Mount and Bélanger 2001). There is also a high degree of support among presidents (and other administrators) for increased tuition fees (Woodhouse 2009). For example, Robert Campbell, President of Mount Allison University, argues that tuition in Canada should be fully deregulated and that Canadians need to overcome their "tuition phobia" (cited in Anderson 2012). Although Canadian university presidents have not said much publicly about hiring and tenure, in the U.S. most university leaders favour a contract system of employment.[2]

Of course, university presidents differ in the extent to which they support corporatization. While some may offer only tacit support, others are more proactive. The above-mentioned Prichard was a zealous supporter of what he called a "market-driven, deregulated, competitive and differentiated" university system (cited in Woodhouse 2009: 230). For Prichard, key features of this system included the "production of better services to customers" and bringing a greater variety of products to market. Market discipline was a source of freedom in Prichard's view because it allowed administrators to raise tuition and aggressively court private donors. The former president's pro-corporatization stance is also reflected in his lobbying efforts. Prichard aggressively petitioned the federal government in support of the drug company Apotex — one of the U of T's most prominent donors — earning him the undistinguished title of "drug lobbyist" (Washburn 2005: 124). A more recent example of a pro-corporatization president is Mamdouh Shoukri, now in his second term as president of York University. Shoukri's mandate has been heavily focused on research commercialization in science, engineering and medicine. Before his tenure at York, Shoukri pursued corporate-university partnerships at McMaster, where he served as Research Vice President. His previous experience in the private sector (Hydro Ottawa) may help to explain his institutional stance. Canadian university presidents who are actively involved in inter-corporate networks, such as service on corporate boards of directors, are more likely to support a corporatization agenda (Budros 2002).

As mentioned, the salaries of university administrators have increased in recent years. This trend is especially evident for university CEOs. In many cases, presidential salaries are now more than double the level that would have been considered generous in the 1990s. In part, this is because board compensation committees increasingly view the salaries of top executives as a reflection of institutional status and a logical corollary of new job requirements. This vision is exemplified by Colum Bastable, Chair of McMaster's board of governors in 2008, who defended executive pay increases by noting that university presidents "should be compared with chief executive officers because of the growing demands to run universities like businesses" (*Calgary Herald* 2008). The fifteen highest paid university presidents in Canada all earn in the neighbourhood of $500,000 per year in 2010.

Table 5.1: University Presidents' Compensation, 2010

University	President	2010 Salary	2010 Benefits	2010 Total
University of British Columbia	Stephen Toope	$378,000	$201,332	$579,332
University of Alberta	Indira Samarasekera	$502,000	-	$502,000
York University	Mamdouh Shoukri	$480,030	$18,066	$498,096
Simon Fraser University	Andrew Petter	$303,956	$175,877	$479,833
University of Calgary	Elizabeth Cannon	$449,000	$24,000	$473,000
Athabasca University	Frits Pannekoek	$362,000	$110,000	$472,000
University of Western Ontario	Amit Chakma	$440,000	$29,742	$469,743
University of Guelph	Alastair Summerlee	$440,590	$23,651	$464,241
Memorial University	Gary Kachanoski	$430,000	$30,000	$460,000
University of Victoria	David Turpin	$303,246	$156,507	$459,753
Dalhousie University	Thomas Traves	$385,635	$62,733	$448,368
University of Lethbridge	Michael Mahon	$337,000	$100,000	$437,000
University of Toronto	David Naylor	$380,100	$51,409	$431,509
University of Manitoba	David Barnard	-	-	$426,212
University of Saskatchewan	Peter MacKinnon	-	-	$425,000

Source: *Canadian Association of University Teachers Almanac of Post-Secondary Education in Canada, 2012–2013.*

Stephen Toope of the University of British Columbia and Indira Samarasekera of the University of Alberta topped the list, with compensation packages of $579,332 and $502,000 respectively.

BOARDS OF GOVERNORS AND UNIVERSITY-CORPORATE BOARD INTERLOCKS

Like university presidents, the profile and characteristics of university governing boards have shifted under corporatization. The vast majority of Canadian universities operate under a bicameral structure of governance that includes a division of labour and responsibility between a senate and a board of governors. In the corporate era, the role of senates has declined, while the role of boards has expanded. Senates are generally controlled by elected faculty members (with significant student representation) and are formally responsible for all key academic decisions in the university. These decisions include setting educational policy goals, awarding scholarships, overseeing student evaluations and exams, as well as approving new courses, programs and admission standards. The senate is also a venue where the academic concerns of the entire university community can be discussed in a public forum. University boards of governors manage institutional resources and attend to the university's relationship with governments and other external stakeholders. Their principle statutory obligation is to ensure a university's financial well being, and this control over budgetary processes often means that they have a considerable degree of control over academic priorities. Boards of governors are composed of university representatives and representatives from the community. When provisions are made for community members to join these boards, business leaders often represent "the community."

Business executive membership on boards of governors is partly honourific, but appointments to these boards can benefit corporations in a number of ways. For one, these ties project corporate power into the educational sphere. Through corporate-university board interlocks, business leaders gain input into university research agendas and the training of skilled graduates. Not only can these ties serve the particular interests of corporations and corporate elites, they strengthen their broader, hegemonic power to influence the direction of educational reform. They also facilitate the creation of a community of mutual interests across the university-industry divide and within the business community itself. For Canada's economic elite, university boards provide an additional forum for communication and decision making and a venue to work out their common concerns. In this way, university boards provide a similar function to the boards of policy organizations, think-tanks and philanthropic foundations.

The presence of Canadian business leaders on university boards is not new. In *The Vertical Mosaic* (1965), John Porter observed that, in 1951, eighty individuals identified as members of the Canadian economic elite held positions on the governing boards of fifteen major Canadian universities. At the time, Porter remarked that the boards of certain prominent institutions, such as McGill and the U of T, "positively glitter with stars from the corporate world" (301). Michael Ornstein (1988) found that the average number of corporate-university interlocks via university boards doubled from 12.4 in 1946–50 to 24.9 in 1961–65. According to Ornstein, these interlocks declined in subsequent years in line with governance reforms of the 1960s. Nevertheless, corporate executives were still amply represented on boards during and after the "golden age." Wallace Clement (1975), for example, found that 240 members of Canada's economic elite in 1972 held a governing position in one of Canada's private schools, universities or other institutions of higher learning. Clement drew particular attention to the unique position of elite institutions such as the U of T, which had thirteen members of the economic elite on its twenty-one-member board in 1972, eight of which held directorship positions in multiple corporations.

As corporatization accelerated, the corporate "withdrawal" from university governing boards ended. Looking at changes since the mid-1970s, William Carroll (2004) found that the presence of economic elites on boards of governors remained relatively stable from 1976 to 1996. However, other changes in the corporate-university network were used to integrate universities into the world of corporate capital. Carroll pointed to evidence of increasing ties "*emanating from inside universities,* as major university presidents become members of the corporate elite." This suggested a "*deepening of corporate-university relations,* as chief executive officers of universities and corporations rub shoulders in corporate boardrooms and participate in a common managerial culture" (2004: 197, emphasis in original).

Carroll also found that the network of corporate-university ties became more "inclusive" during this period. Growing inclusivity or integration was achieved through several mechanisms. For one, the network expanded to include most major universities in Canada, and the integration of the two spheres was enhanced by the increasing number of "organic intellectuals" — individuals who link corporations and universities through their participation in the governance of both institutions. Second, several "third party" organizations, such as the National Council on Education, the Corporate-Higher Education Forum and the Canadian Foundation for Innovation, emerged as additional fora where corporate and university leaders could discuss business-education concerns and establish a neoliberal policy consensus in the area of higher education. Third, more and more university boards had representatives from capital investment and (Canadian-based) high technology firms. These executives may provide links to funding or be used to support the university's role in providing high-technology products and services for the global economy. Others have documented a more insidious trend where "expert consultants in privatization" are being recruited to university boards (Tudiver 1999:

194). This practice gained prominence in the 1990s as executives from companies such as Price Waterhouse, KPMG and Ernst & Young (all of which specialize in the privatization of public services) joined the governing boards of several Canadian universities, including Queen's, Toronto, Regina, McGill and Concordia. In sum, although business leaders may not necessarily be joining university boards in significantly greater numbers, the network of corporate-university interlocks became deeper and more inclusive in the 1980s and 1990s.

There have been no detailed analyses of Canadian university-corporate board interlocks in the 2000s, but some researchers have documented the backgrounds and corporate affiliations of board members at particular universities (Arsenault 2007; CCPA 2005) as well as the ties between universities and particular industries (Cohen 2008). Also, the CAUT has tracked corporate involvement on university boards through its *Directory of University and College / Corporate Board Linkages*. The most recent version of the Directory, 2007–08, identifies hundreds of public university board members that held corporate directorship positions. Of this group, thirty-five university board members held between three and four corporate positions simultaneously, while ten held five positions and another ten held six or more.

This latter group of heavily interlocked directors included Peter Harder at the University of Ottawa, who held corporate positions at ARISE Technologies, Canada Life Assurance, Canada Life Financial, Great-West Life Assurance, Great-West Lifeco, IGM Financial, Kria Resources, London Life Insurance, Pinetree Capital and Power Financial Corporation; David O'Brian, who as chancellor of Concordia also held directorships at EnCana, Enplus Resources Fund, Molson Coors Brewing, Royal Bank of Canada, TransCanada, TransCanada PipeLines and Vale Inco; and David Peterson, chancellor at the University of Toronto, who sat on the boards of BNP Paribas (Canada), Franco-Nevada, Industrial-Alliance Life Insurance, Ivanhoe Cambridge, Rogers Communications, VersaPay and Shoppers Drug Mart. As well, John Manley, current head of the Canadian Council of Chief Executives, sat on Waterloo's board while serving at CAE, Canadian Imperial Bank of Commerce, Canadian Pacific Railway, DG Acquisition Group, IPSA International and Optosecurity. It should also be noted that seven university presidents held corporate directorships in 2007–08. They included Indira Samarasekera at Alberta (Bank of Nova Scotia); Stephen Toope at UBC (ENMAX); Carleton's Roseann Runte (National Bank of Canada); Thomas Traves at Dalhousie (Clearwater, InNOVAcorp); Heather Munroe-Blum at McGill (Four Seasons Hotels); David Johnston at Waterloo (ARISE Technologies, Masco, CGI Group, Fairfax Financial); and the University of Winnipeg's Lloyd Axworthy (HudBay Minerals).

In addition to strengthening the influence of corporations in the educational sphere, these ties can generate conflicts of interest. In 1969, Paul Axelrod (1982b) found that York University had millions of dollars invested in companies such as the

Toronto Dominion Bank, Simpson's, General Motors and Ford. Not coincidently, the membership of the board at that time included the president of the TD Bank, the vice-president of Simpson's, the vice-president of General Motors, and a former director of Ford. Although there is not significant research on direct conflicts of interest in Canada, at the very least, corporate representation on university boards (and vice versa) generates conflicts of commitment. Corporate executives have a fiduciary duty to advance the interests of their shareholders, and these interests often conflict with what is best for universities. Similarly, university officials serving on corporate boards may find that their values, ideological dispositions and even their educational priorities are affected by their corporate obligations. Also of note is that some governments are actively trying to increase the ties between the corporate sphere and higher education. The government of Quebec, for example, is currently in the process of changing the composition of university boards to give majority power to "independent" board members, thereby opening the door to greater corporate involvement.

All of these changes in the makeup of university administrations have been complimented by the growth of university governance models that are more corporate and bureaucratic in nature, as administrators adopt "the values, management styles, cost-cutting procedures, and the language of 'excellence' that has been the hallmark of corporate culture" (Giroux and Giroux 2004: 225).

CORPORATE GOVERNANCE MODELS

Proponents of corporatization argue that corporate governance models make universities more efficient. This argument rests on the assumption that the public sphere is inherently inefficient — burdened by bureaucracy, waste, convoluted decision making and a culture of incompetence — whereas the private sector is well managed, cost-conscious and accountable. It follows that reorganizing institutional governance in the image of the corporation is seen as a sensible choice, as it shifts governance from being guided by public policy to being grounded in business principles. More specifically, corporate management styles are seen as necessary to introduce more efficient budgetary processes and accounting controls as well as improved incentives for optimizing faculty productivity. These perspectives are grounded in a new organizing philosophy in the governance of public institutions known as "managerialism."

According to Rosemary Deem (2008), the roots of the new managerialism can be traced to cuts in public expenditures and the introduction of quasi-markets in public services that were part of the more general shift to neoliberalism. The ideology of managerialism holds that public institutions, including universities, should emulate the efficient organizational models in the private sector. These models include close monitoring of employee and institutional performance, the pursuit of key financial targets, benchmarks and "best practices," and the widespread use of accountability measures. Another underlying assumption is that management is of greater importance than the activities of those being managed. In this vein, the success of the public university depends on the effectiveness of its managerial apparatus rather than the quality of its teaching and research. Within higher education, managerialism can be analyzed both as a discourse and as a set of administrative practices.

THE DISCOURSE OF MANAGERIALISM

Eric Gould (2003: 86) characterizes managerial discourse as "corporate-styled eduspeak." On the one hand, this language is often ill defined. Managerial discourse is associated with vague terms like excellence, accountability, efficiency and quality, which have become over-simplifications devoid of specific content. This language is used, in part, to substitute the clichés of managerialism for rational discourse on higher education. On the other hand, it would be a mistake to assume that the language of corporate eduspeak is devoid of meaning or impact because this language is often associated with managerial and market criteria. For example, the term "excellence" signifies how well a university is performing in its delivery of knowledge and skilled labour to the corporate economy. It is also used to denote high rankings on a number of quantifiable indicators, such as the dollar value of incoming grants and the level of research commercialization. In this way, managerialist discourse is highly political and provides an important cover of legitimacy for the corporatizing university.

In contrast, academic discourse about excellence and quality typically emphasize things like well-equipped libraries, low faculty-student ratios, open and democratic governance procedures and broad public accessibility to the products of university research, all of which are steadily losing ground. Of course, managerialism entails more than a change in language; it also embodies a new set of management practices that enforce and overlap with corporate governance models in the university.

CENTRALIZING POWER IN THE ACADEMY

Like the strong faculty and student cultures of the 1960s and 1970s, managerial cultures are dominant today. Campus administrations increasingly view themselves as a culture apart from — or against — the values and norms of collegial governance. This is part of a move toward what Benjamin Ginsberg (2011) calls the "all-administrative university," a university where the faculty has no significant governance role.

In recent years, university administrations have assumed greater command over institutional objectives and policies. On some campuses, a stronger administrative presence has manifested as enhanced "security" measures (such as more cameras, police and student monitoring) and centralized control over resource allocation and messaging (including room bookings, campus advertising). More importantly, there has been a significant shift in the power of administrations in relation to the professoriate. Administrators have appropriated power from faculty and academic bodies in many ways. At some institutions, administrators have replaced collegial processes — where decisions affecting faculty and students are made collectively by the professoriate, not the employer — with "consultation" exercises that limit faculty participation in governance (Polster 2011). At others, educational issues have been redefined as purely administrative, and therefore not subject to collegial input, especially those that involve finance. A corporate management style also means that faculty members are increasingly treated as subordinate workers, or as "managed professionals," through intensified workloads, closer monitoring, enhanced performance evaluations and less access to institutional decision making (Rhoades 1998). Typically, these models do not dismantle faculty governance structures; rather, they supersede them.

A national survey of senate members in Canadian universities found large discrepancies between what these members believed senates should do and what they accomplished in practice (Jones, Shanahan and Goyan 2004). For instance, while 89 percent indicated that senates should play a role in determining the future direction of the university, only 43 percent agreed that they did. Moreover, 93 percent stated that senates should ask "tough questions" of senior administrators, but less than half felt that senates held administrators accountable in this way. Overall, only 44 percent agreed that senates were effective as decision-making bodies, while 60 percent said they primarily approved decisions made elsewhere. One of the most common reasons given for declining senate influence was the challenge of making decisions within the context of fiscal austerity. In this context, decisions about enrolments, admission standards, curriculums, performance reviews, hiring policies and research priorities — all important academic matters — are increasingly defined in terms of financial or budgetary criteria. This change is critical because financial decisions are generally under the purview of senior administrators and boards of governors, not university senates.

A more centralized administrative apparatus has gone hand-in-hand with growing administrative secrecy. In Chapter Three, I discussed how universities in Ontario have refused to disclose information on contract faculty hiring. This kind of management secrecy also appears in other areas, including in negotiating and regulating partnerships with the private sector. In 2010, the CAUT began investigating twenty university-industry-government partnerships to assess the extent to which these agreements contained provisions to protect academic freedom and the integrity of academic research.[3] Their report was not released until late 2013 because, in nearly every case, these deals were negotiated in secret and university administrators refused to make them public (see CAUT 2013). In fact, the CAUT had to compel universities (as well as industry and governments) to provide them with access to the agreements through requests under access to information legislation (by 2013 they had managed to obtain twelve out of twenty).

The fact that these agreements were put in place without academic or public oversight is problematic on multiple grounds. In a public university, any and all academic partnerships should be open and transparent. In addition, the content of these agreements raises serious questions around academic integrity, academic freedom and accountability. Ten of the twelve partnership arrangements clearly violated standards for academic integrity. The collaboration between the University of Alberta and the Centre for Oil Sands Innovation, for example, contained ineffective policies for handling conflicts of interest, no requirement for a non-partisan external review of research, and provisions that placed the direction and control over research priorities in the hands of the private sector. The deal also violated the university's intellectual property policies as well as the collective agreement between faculty and the university.

PERFORMANCE INDICATORS

The shift toward greater market accountability in university management can be seen in the linking of budget allocations to performance indicators (PIs). While PIs have long been used by universities as a means of evaluating different aspects of academic quality, their purpose has changed in the context of corporatization. Under corporate governance models, PIs open up routine evaluations of academic activities to non-academic considerations. Judgments of teaching quality and pedagogical formats, previously made within collegial forums, are being replaced by standardized "facts" such as class size, completion times and "costs per student." PIs in Canadian universities are also being used to monitor and support corporate priorities such as research commercialization (for example, how many patents a department has registered), the training of graduates with relevant skills (for example, how many "employable" graduates a university produces), and the generation of public-private partnerships (for example, how many matching grants a department has obtained).

All provincial governments collect performance data for universities, with Alberta and Ontario being the two provinces where PIs most closely reflect the corporatization agenda. Alberta's experiment with PIs began in the 1990s. Many of the indicators devised by Ralph Klein's Conservative government were borrowed directly from the private sector and designed to serve private sector needs. Not only did the government track student employment outcomes, it also generated data on employers' "satisfaction" with the education and skill level of recent graduates. Alberta's research PIs were also heavily market based. These included: the level of external grants, contracts and other sponsored research income, with an emphasis on industry funding; research output as measured by the quantity of publications and their citation rates; and the level of technology transfer as measured by licensing revenues and invention disclosures (Conlon 2004; Gauthier 2004). William Bruneau and Donald Savage (2002: 198) note that by the early 2000s, the effects of the Albertan PI regime were "numerous and depressing," and included the disappearance of entire university departments and large staff reductions.

In Ontario, the introduction of PIs in the 1990s began as a mechanism to help student-consumers make "market-relevant" choices among programs and institutions. However, their purpose soon shifted to provide a basis for allocating a portion of annual operating funding and influencing institutional behaviour. It was the Harris Conservatives that introduced Key Performance Indicators (KPIs) for all colleges and universities. These KPIs included graduation rates by program as well as graduate employment and student loan default rates. Many analysts have pointed to the irrationally narrow and punitive nature of these indicators and the fact that they ignored issues of educational quality. Critics also note that these measures were not within the control of universities; rather, they were largely a function of prevailing economic conditions. According to Axelrod (2002: 98), the KPI system coerced universities into "making academic decisions (including curricular development) on the basis of expected market conditions — betting, as it were, on the programs most likely to meet immediate economic demand." Recent Liberal governments in Ontario have maintained the same accountability mandate by allocating millions of dollars to "quality improvement" schemes, which in practice has meant accountability to the corporate interests that fund the Liberal party.

Overall, PIs have little to do with quality or accountability. They have been put in place largely to subvert the mission of universities toward private ends. As a managerial tool, PIs make it possible to decide on and control the internal activities of universities from outside of the settings in which academic work takes place. In this way, PIs shift the control over academic work upward and outward, toward administrators, governments and the private sector, supporting the notion that academics must be held accountable by external pressures because they cannot be trusted to make informed judgements or perform quality work.

UNIVERSITY RANKINGS

Accompanying the use of PIs, ranking systems have become an increasingly popular method with which to assess universities around the world. In Canada, the most prominent ranking system is the annual *Maclean's Magazine* ranking of universities. The perceived benefits of university ranking systems are that they respond to consumer (student and parent) demands for easily interpretable information about higher education, help to differentiate among institutions, programs and disciplines, stimulate competition among institutions (which enhances institutional quality) and function as a mechanism of accountability and quality control.

Despite these purported benefits, many have questioned the use of university rankings. Critiques include methodological concerns that indicators are often selected on the basis of convenience or what can be measured, rather than what is most relevant and important. For example, several global ranking systems — including the *Times Higher Education Supplement World Rankings* and Shanghai Jiao Tong University's *Academic Ranking of World Universities* — rely on research indicators, which assumes that institutional quality derives from research and research alone. Other critics point to the arbitrary weighing of indicators, as well as their lack of reliability or consistency as a measurement tool (Harvey 2008). In Canada, critics have repeatedly exposed the indicators used by *Maclean's* for being internally inconsistent, statistically insignificant and unreliable (Page 2012; Page, Cramer and Page 2010). There is little difference, for example, between high- and low-ranking institutions for most comparison measures, which means the rankings exaggerate variation and mask similarities between institutions.

While rankings are notoriously problematic in and of themselves, they also have a detrimental impact on higher education, students and the public at large. Jennifer Washburn (2005: 181) claims that ranking systems fuel a "competitive frenzy" in higher education and lock universities into a positional "arms race," where they are constantly scrambling to improve their rankings and prestige. She notes that any small change to an institution's rankings can have enormous financial and academic repercussions. For this reason, these systems are "encouraging schools to use a variety of gimmicks and accounting tricks to manipulate their statistical data in ways that may be contrary to the public interest." For example, some U.S. universities make SAT scores "optional" for applicants (thereby omitting the scores of less qualified and economically vulnerable students) and falsify acceptance and yield rates (Slaughter and Rhoades 2004). Several years ago, administrators at the University of British Columbia were exposed for pressuring faculty to manipulate course enrolments and cap class sizes in order to boost their *Maclean's* rankings. Internal documents showed that the administration advocated "lying to students about room capacity even if it meant denying students the opportunity to major in a discipline or graduate on time" (Doherty-Delorme and Shaker 2004: 20). Moreover, ranking systems that include student-selectivity threaten access for disadvantaged students by creating incentives for schools to recruit only those students who will be "assets" in improving their ranked positions.

In the era of corporatization, the primary purpose (and effect) of higher education rankings is not to improve universities but to move them further into the embrace of the market. The approach of university rankings is very similar to that of publications like *Consumer Reports*. Rankings rely on and encourage the belief that consumers and markets should determine university curriculums, teaching and research. Although these systems are unlikely to disappear in the short term, it is important to note that many Canadian universities are now refusing to participate in the *Maclean's* survey. Some senior administrators have even spoken out publicly. David Naylor (2006), former president at the U of T, candidly stated that his university "found *Maclean's* useful for one thing only: marketing."

MARKETING THE CORPORATE UNIVERSITY

Aside from a modest amount of recruitment advertising, marketing activities were outside the purview of university administrators for much of the twentieth century. Some even considered these practices to be an anathema. During his tenure as president of the U of T, Claude Bissell (1968: 174) warned of the dangerous implications that advertising had for education and society, noting that relying upon "over-simplification and exaggeration leads to the substitution of mass instinct for thought; the aim of the advertiser is, after all, to fix attention and not to engage the mind." Nearly half a century later, advertising and marketing have become permanent fixtures in the activities of most university administrations (Kirp 2003). These practices are part of the transformation of higher education from a site of educational activity to one of material consumption. In Canada, there has been a considerable increase in the resources devoted to marketing by universities. Branding and other image-enhancing activities are designed to attract corporate sponsors and, just as importantly, to attract student-consumers.

This new marking focus has created expensive and escalating public relations wars between public universities in Canada and a significant growth in the share of institutional resources devoted to advertising and promotional campaigns. Like private fundraising, marketing and branding require an expansive administrative apparatus (such as public relations specialists). Furthermore, as rivalries among universities have become more intense, the scope, reach and consumer orientation of student recruitment activities have followed suit. For example, it is now common for universities in one city or province to market themselves — in newspapers, magazines and on the internet — to "target markets" in other jurisdictions. At the same time, universities have developed innovative program offerings, promotional strategies and student guarantees. According to Ken Steele (2010):

> [Universities] are conducting online contests for prizes ranging from iPads to SmartCars to tuition discounts. Many institutions guarantee residence accommodation for first-year undergraduates; some, such as Lakehead University, guarantee scholarships at particular grade averages, while the University of Calgary guarantees completion of a four-year degree within four years. The University of Regina now guarantees

employment within six months of graduation. Although these 'guarantees' actually require significant commitment and effort from the student, the overall impression is increasingly one of education as a product for sale, satisfaction guaranteed.

Although the corporate reorientation of student recruitment may appear to empower student-consumers, the risk of deception and exploitation inherent in promotional (as opposed to informational) advertising is cause for concern.

Academic scholarship is also being used to define and strengthen university marketing activities. The very existence of the *Journal of Marketing for Higher Education* demonstrates just how far a student-consumer discourse has been embraced in some segments of academia. For example, some submissions in this journal move beyond "rational" student motives for choosing a university, such as educational quality, to assess the impact of market imaging, "brand personalities" and impression management (Angulo, Pergelova and Rialp 2010; Opoku, Hultman and Saheli-Sangair 2008). Others are devoted to measuring and enhancing student "brand loyalty," including the impact of institutional size on "relevant and desired marketing outcomes" (McAlexander and Koenig 2010: 69); how student trust in educational providers is translated into consumer allegiance (Carvalho and Mota 2010); and the linkages between brand perceptions and students' "conative, affective, and cognitive responses" (Bennett and Ali-Choudhury 2009: 85). Clearly, there is little difference between this literature and marketing literature in the business world.

Preoccupation with brand image also means that criticism of universities by faculty and students, as well as public displays of dissent or resistance on campuses, are increasingly viewed as a threat to the university's brand name. As a result, academic freedom has become yet another casualty of administrative efforts to market the corporate university.

SUPPRESSING ACADEMIC FREEDOM

Concerns about market reputation and corporate funding have been associated with a growing intolerance of "controversial" research and institutional criticism. This intolerance is a logical outcome of corporatization. The private sector has no tradition or recognition of freedom of expression, and workers are generally not permitted to criticize their employers in public. In the U.S., courts have recently ruled that academics who speak publicly against their institutions are not protected under academic freedom. In Canada, the right to criticize a university administration is expressly incorporated into faculty collective agreements across the country, but there have been efforts to circumvent the application of this protection. For example, the AUCC's new "Statement on Academic Freedom" (2011b) makes no reference to the right to criticize one's institution. It also tends to conflate academic freedom with institutional autonomy, a position that ignores the increasing threats to academic freedom coming from inside the university.

Similarly, Kenneth Westhues (2004) argues that academics who raise questions about the policies, priorities or partnerships of their universities can become victims of "administrative mobbing." Penalties for speaking out can include threats to tenure and promotion, public vilification or even dismissal. The 2009 firing of University of Ottawa professor Denis Rancourt is one such example. Rancourt's dismissal was said to be related to his grading scheme and pedagogical methods (supposedly under the purview of his academic freedom). Yet there is little question that his social activism and public criticism of the University of Ottawa under President Allan Rock — including how the institution's corporate orientation led to administrative malfeasance — played a role in the decision (see Rancourt 2011; Westhues 2009). Another example is the case of Robert Buckingham, former Dean of the School of Public Health at the University of Saskatchewan (U of S). In 2014, Buckingham spoke out publicly about an administrative initiative called TransformUS — a cost-cutting plan involving layoffs and program reductions at the university. The response of President Illene Busch-Vishniac and the larger administration was to assert that Buckingham was guilty of "egregious conduct and insubordination." He was promptly fired, stripped of his tenure and escorted off campus (Urback 2014). Buckingham's is a clear case of administrators trying to run their university like a corporation, operating as a secretive corporate elite and insisting on the unquestioned loyalty of those "beneath" them. In this instance, however, the administration went too far. Following widespread public outcry, the university eventually "reconsidered" its decision to dismiss Buckingham, although he was never allowed to return to his position as Dean. Furthermore, less than two days after the university provost was forced to resign, the U of S board of governors announced that President Busch-Vishniac had been fired.

Student activists have also been targeted by corporate-minded administrators. One infamous case was the administrative crackdown that took place at York University several years ago. In response to student unrest in 2004, the York administration overhauled the university's Temporary Use of Space Policy by outlawing any unauthorized use of university buildings and restricting freedom of assembly. The administration also stipulated that students and faculty needed permission to bring guest speakers to York. As David Noble (2005: 24), writing at the time as a professor at York, explains "in the manner of all private-sector owners and managers, [the administration] deemed the ... university campus ... to be 'private property' and formulated official policy on its use." The following year, police were invited onto campus by the administration and subsequently violently dispersed students who were protesting, among other things, the corporate representation on

York's Board of Governors. According to Howard Woodhouse (2009: 237–238), these student actions were deemed to be "a threat to York's relations with powerful business interests" and administrative intervention was meant to "stem their opposition to the corporate agenda." Like a more corporatized version of *in loco parentis*, coercive student conduct and use-of-space policies are denying students the opportunity to assemble and speak freely on many campuses.

In addition to policing teachers and students to protect their own brands, administrators also prioritize shielding corporate sponsors from criticism. It was this concern that motivated the University of Ottawa to prevent a prominent Burmese human rights activist from speaking on campus in 2007. The subject of the activist's talk was the unethical Burmese business activities of Total SA, a French oil company whose board members included the wealthy Desmarais family, one of the university's largest benefactors. According to documents obtained by the Canadian Friends of Burma through access to information requests, members of the senior administration used a number of strategies to block the event. In internal correspondence, university officials appeared to be aware that they were violating elementary codes of academic freedom in the service of their corporate sponsor; in an email to then university president Gilles Patry, one vice president noted that preventing the talk "flies in the face of many principles we hold dear in the University world, but I think we have other interests at stake" (Morgan 2010).

These changes to academic freedom align with broader political efforts to transform the university. Universities are being pressured to depoliticize their curriculums. Typical of this viewpoint is Tom Flanagan, former professor of political science at the University of Calgary. Flanagan (2007: 27) has mocked the "faux disciplines" of "women's studies, native studies, queer studies, and cultural studies," which he says have been invented to get around the objective standards of traditional scholarship. Practitioners in these fields, according to Flanagan, "practice advocacy scholarship in support of social movements," creating a "monolithic" climate of intellectual leftism. Limiting the boundaries of discussion on Middle East politics has been a cornerstone of efforts to delegitimize independent and dissident academics. Consistent with the Conservative government's record on academic freedom and freedom of speech,[4] in 2009 Minister Gary Goodyear's office threatened to withhold federal funding for the Social Sciences and Humanities Research Council over its decision to fund an academic conference at York entitled "Israel/Palestine: Mapping Models of Statehood and Paths to Peace" (Thompson 2011). Attempts to restrict the boundaries of debate have also included repeated efforts to ban Israeli Apartheid Week events, as well as attacks on the Sociology and Equity Studies program at the Ontario Institute for Studies in Education (OISE) regarding the thesis project of graduate student Jenny Peto on holocaust education (Moon 2014; Nadeau and Sears 2011). The treatment of Norman Finkelstein and his tenure denial at DePaul University in the U.S. is one of the most obvious examples of how the career of a leading scholar can be derailed by these kinds of campaigns.

Campaigns to restrict dissent and academic autonomy have a number of impacts. For one, they promote a narrow, vocational conception of university education, at the same time as reconstituting the campus as a corporatized space with an apolitical veneer. Further, the idea that there is an ingrained ideological bias among the professoriate has reinforced the assumption that academics regularly violate reasonable standards of professionalism under the guise of free expression and, therefore, must be held more "accountable" for their teaching and scholarship. The university's growing reliance on private funding only makes them more vulnerable to these kinds of political pressures.

CURRICULUM REFORM, CAMPUS INFRASTRUCTURE AND CORPORATE CONTROL

Within the rubric of corporatization, a centralized management structure is seen as being less burdened by collegial decision making and having benefits beyond increased efficiencies and economic returns. Proponents claim that popular and economically relevant fields of study would not have emerged if administrators lacked the power and flexibility to divert scarce resources and deploy faculty to areas of high demand. According to the Business-Higher Education Forum (2001), programs like computer science would have languished if professors controlled the curriculum. Similarly, in a paper produced in association with the World Bank, D. Bruce Johnstone (1998: 24) claims that academics routinely resist curricular reform by drawing upon "the idea of the university as a proper and necessary bastion of continuity and tradition" and an army of "politically volatile" students who are easily enlisted to support the status quo. Milton Greenberg (2004) goes further, arguing that professors cling to a "university is not a business" mantra whenever administrators push for market-led curriculum changes, which shields them from reasonable standards of service and accountability. Implicit in all of these arguments is the idea that faculty are too self-interested and/or backward thinking to make decisions in the interests of the university, its students and the economy. In line with these assumptions is the notion that job training should take precedence over the goals and values of a liberal education. As a result, academic departments more removed from labour and commercial markets have been deemed less important to the university's mission, which has led to greater differentiation by program and an inequitable distribution of funding. On campuses across the country, the neglect of liberal arts programs has been accompanied by the growth and construction of new management schools, medical research labs, engineering facilities and other "relevant" curricula and infrastructure.

KILLING LIBERAL ARTS

As student enrolment numbers have shifted from basic arts and sciences to more practical, applied and business-related fields, so too have the types of programs provided by universities. In part, this shift from liberal arts to career focused programs is premised on a "skills gap" in the Canadian economy. Since the early 1990s, business groups, think-tanks, politicians and the media have promoted the idea that our universities and training programs are not producing enough highly skilled graduates. Federal Human Resources Minister Diane Finley recently referred to the labour and skills shortage as "the most significant socio-economic challenge ahead of us in Canada" (Weston 2013). According to another Conservative party insider, "there are too many kids getting BAs and not enough welders."

Yet, there is reason to question the legitimacy of such claims. For one, Canada produces more post-secondary graduates than ever, and a large proportion of these are college and technical school graduates. In fact, the OECD's *Education at a Glance 2014* notes that Canada has the highest proportion of adults (25 to 64 years) that have completed post-secondary education among all OECD countries. In large measure, this position is explained by the country's high proportion of college students, which includes the unique CEGEP program in Quebec. Canada has approximately three times more post-secondary non-university graduates than the OECD average. Rather than there being a shortage of skills or skilled graduates, it is more accurate to say that there is a shortage of high quality jobs and that many Canadian workers are over-qualified for their jobs and underemployed (Livingstone 1999; Stanford 2014; Tal 2013). A 2014 study by Statistics Canada confirms that large numbers of young Canadians are indeed overqualified in their current positions, particularly university graduates. The study found that among university graduates aged 25 to 34 who were not in management occupations, 18 percent worked in occupations normally requiring a high school education or less, and 40 percent worked in jobs requiring a college-level education or less (Uppal and LaRochelle-Côté 2014b). Another review of the "best peer-reviewed research in Canada" on labour and skills supplies concludes that there is "no evidence of a national labour shortage at present or into the foreseeable future" (McDaniel, Watt-Malcolm and Wong 2013: 2–3). In the words of economist Jim Stanford (2013: 23), "Canadians are the best-trained workers in the industrial world, and 1.4 million of them are officially unemployed. Throw in discouraged workers, involuntary part-time workers, and those whose current jobs underutilize their training, and it's clear that the 'skills crisis' is a self-serving myth."

Further, and contrary to popular belief, liberal arts graduates have performed well in the Canadian labour market compared to university graduates from other disciplines (Council of Ontario Universities 2011b, 2012; Finnie et al. 2014; Liu, McCloy and DeClou 2012). A paper commissioned by the Social Sciences and

Humanities Research Council (SSHRC) found that "social sciences and humanities-based industries" account for more than three quarters of all employment in Canada and that these disciplines influence more than $388 billion in economic activity, which is roughly equivalent to the amount influenced by science, technology, engineering and medicine (Impact Group 2008). While the importance of the liberal arts cannot and should not be measured primarily by economic or employment criteria, these trends run counter to the widely-held assumption that a liberal arts education has little "value" in today's economy.

The rhetoric of a skills gap and the irrelevance of the liberal arts has, at least in part, been employed as a political tactic to restructure university education to areas in demand by dominant business sectors. Not only are universities devoting more resources to vocational and applied fields, but liberal arts programs are moving in a more marketable direction in order to sell themselves (for example, sociology departments that offer new specializations in applied criminology) and to increase the "applicability" of their degrees (such as the addition of new "business and society" courses). This utilitarian approach has also influenced how money is distributed to the arts through external research bodies. A good example was the announcement in the 2009 federal budget that scholarships granted by the SSHRC would be focused on "business-related degrees."

In the corporate university, where introspective questions about morality, society and the common good are deemed irrelevant (or worse, "political"), no area of study is more under threat than the humanities. Humanities programs have been downgraded; books and articles documenting their incompatibility with neoliberal restructuring saturate academic and popular presses (see, for example, Burgan 2008; Cohen 2009; Donoghue 2008; Mignolo 2003). In contrast, courses and programs that are seen as augmenting university revenues — often those curriculum streams most attractive to profit-generating foreign students — are being expanded. To this end, many universities have introduced new and exclusive "boutique" programs, such as executive MBA degrees. As Erika Shaker (1999) documented years ago, MBA and executive MBA programs in Canada have become important "status symbols" for corporatizing universities and are developed in close consultation with the private sector. Indeed, the expansion and proliferation of business schools has been at the forefront of many trends that have taken shape under corporatization, including the following:

> The push for more professional education, donor-driven expansion, responsiveness to student and employer demands, highly integrated business-campus relations, high tuition fees for market-based programs, greater autonomy for professional schools, unequal distribution of resources on campuses, the marginalization of traditional disciplines, the

rise of new commercially based research and teaching, and increased student emphasis on career opportunities. (Coates and Morrison 2011: 61)

University administrations share much of the responsibility for the recent proliferation of corporatized curriculums. Just as corporate managers tend to downsize unprofitable branches of their companies, university managers are doing the same with those faculties and programs with limited revenue or market potential. For example, the University of Alberta recently announced that it is suspending admission to twenty programs within the Faculty of Arts. This decision followed the elimination of 100 sections of arts courses over the previous year (Migdal 2013). These assumptions also underlie recent administrative initiatives such as "resource optimization" programs as well as new cost-cutting exercises known as "program prioritization" that place a heavy emphasis on program cost, student demand and student outcomes (Bradshaw 2012). Similarly, some university administrations have adopted a "profit-centre" model of governance, where individual academic units are treated as self-contained entities and are expected to pay their own way by chasing outside funding and increasing student headcounts. A variation of this model was recently adopted by the University of Toronto. Faculties at the U of T now retain most of the revenues they generate and are required to pay for the use of common university services out of their own operating budgets. Although the U of T has counterbalanced these changes with some measures to maintain equity, the new model provides an advantage to those faculties (such as business schools) that are able to generate outside funding and charge higher fees.

Governments have also played a role in redefining curricular relevance by assuming greater control over academic programs. In Manitoba, for example, legislation was passed requiring provincial approval to alter a university program. In the late 1990s, the government of Ontario initiated the Access to Opportunity Program, which aimed to "double the pipeline of computer science and engineering graduates" in the province (Jones and Young 2004: 199). The Alberta government has also introduced funding and other mechanisms to ensure that new programs correspond with its version of labour market needs. Most recently in 2013, the government announced it would be sending "mandate letters" to all colleges and universities to specify their roles and the government's expectations of them. Sometimes government intervention extends beyond program oversight. In 1999, the government of British Columbia granted university status to the Technical University of British Columbia (TUBC). During its time in operation, this "university" functioned like a high-technology online diploma mill supplying corporations with "just-in-time" employees.

Some would argue that putting the blame on university administrators and governments deflects attention away from the real source of the problem: increasing corporate control over higher education. It is true that corporate sponsors have become more actively involved in the development of university curricula. Industry scientists now regularly visit campuses and sponsor university conferences and workshops. Work placement programs, business internships and industry-sponsored courses are also on the rise. And, there is no shortage of business commentators calling for a university system driven by market forces and corporate demand. In these ways, the corporate sector pushes universities to respond to immediately perceived labour market needs, and to subsidize corporate job training by producing work-ready graduates. According to the Conference Board of Canada, between 1993 and 2013 there was a 40 percent drop in the amount of money Canadian businesses spent on employee training (Munro 2014).

Yet, the perspectives of business managers are not entirely uniform. Many of today's business leaders support liberal arts programs. In 2000, for example, the CEOs of thirty Canadian corporations issued a public statement endorsing the liberal arts. This kind of testimony from individual business leaders reinforces the conclusion that the creative skills and general talents of liberal arts graduates are still valued in the private sector. In the words of Thomas D'Aquino, former head of the Canadian Council of Chief Executives:

> Even as business leaders talk of the need for relevance of education to the job market, many have been expressing strong public support for the traditional liberal arts, which are at least as relevant today as they were a century ago. That is precisely because they teach young people how to think rather than attempting to instill in them a specific of soon-to-be-obsolete knowledge. (cited in D'Aquino and Stewart-Patterson 2001: 116)

Of course, sentiments by business leaders extoling the virtues of the liberal arts operate more in theory than in practice. As one former university vice-president puts it: "On Friday [a business executive] will speak in glowing terms of the value of the humanities. On Monday morning the money goes to engineering" (cited in Axelrod 1998: 9).

Whatever the ultimate source of curriculum reform under corporatization, private sector interests and values are increasingly shaping university disciplines, programs and course offerings. This influence can be further illustrated by looking at two other recent developments: the expansion of public-private partnerships in university infrastructure and the proliferation of donor agreements.

STRUCTURED INEQUALITIES: CAPITAL FUNDING AND PUBLIC-PRIVATE PARTNERSHIPS
Public-private partnerships (P3s) have become increasingly important in the delivery of public services in Canada (Loxley 2010). Although citizens and taxpayers

have the greatest stake in P3s and are largely responsible for funding them, the public is not a "partner" in any meaningful way. In reality, P3s are side deals between political parties and corporations in which corporations are afforded lucrative investment opportunities at low risk, and gain access to the physical and social infrastructure of public services at little cost. In the context of higher education, P3s shift research and infrastructure development towards those areas favoured by the private sector and allow corporations to appropriate the intellectual infrastructure of educational institutions.

Within Canadian universities, capital funding is used for the expansion of (or major renovations to) campus infrastructure. Universities rely on a number of sources to finance capital projects. Provincial governments often provide the majority of this funding, or it is paid through a combination of government funding and the universities themselves, often through fundraising. Capital funding for universities increased considerably over the 2000s. Its growth was largely a result of three initiatives: (i) a one-time jump in capital funding for Ontario universities under the SuperBuild program; (ii) funding for research infrastructure provided by the Canadian Foundation for Innovation (CFI); and (iii) the federal government's Knowledge Infrastructure Program (KIP). What makes SuperBuild, the CFI and the KIP so significant is that they are all "matching" programs. That is, each of these programs was designed to function like P3s and secure matching funds from the private sector.

SuperBuild, the CFI and the KIP
From 1999 to 2003, the Ontario SuperBuild program funded dozens of infrastructure projects on university campuses. Most of the required matching contributions were provided by corporations and wealthy individuals. As a result, funding for programs that provided the greatest strategic advantages to business were favoured over those areas deemed to be less profitable. For example, in 1999–2000, engineering, computer science and business received 51 percent of SuperBuild funds and 62 percent of money from the private sector. The natural and health sciences received 28 and 25 percent respectively (Robertson, McGrane and Shaker 2003). In contrast, the social sciences and humanities received just 3 percent of SuperBuild funds and 0.8 percent of private sector funds, even though more than 40 percent of students in Ontario universities were enrolled in these disciplines. Similarly, the fine arts received 2 percent of SuperBuild funds and 1.8 percent of private sector funds; libraries were given 0.14 and 0.18 percent; and education received nothing from either source. Although the private sector did not provide all the funding for these projects, the matching structure of the program gave it de facto control over much of the infrastructure development on Ontario campuses, including how public money was allocated. Corporate control was only strengthened by the fact

that many powerful Canadian companies — such as the Toronto Dominion Bank and Bell Canada — were represented on SuperBuild's advisory board.

The second example, the Canadian Foundation for Innovation (CFI), is an independent corporation that was established by the federal government in 1997. Its goal is to help universities and other research institutions modernize their physical research infrastructure and equipment. Generally speaking, the CFI pays 40 percent of university infrastructure costs for a program it funds, while universities and other partners cover the remaining 60 percent. Applications for CFI funding are assessed on the basis of need, as well as their potential to strengthen the capacity for "innovation" and potential benefits to Canada. Overall, these matching contributions have amounted to billions of dollars in new money, which has essentially guaranteed dependence on the private sector. Like SuperBuild, the CFI program has a "structural" preference for infrastructure projects in certain disciplines. Between 1998 and 2009, the CFI disbursed over $4.2 billion to various projects. Overall, approximately 90 percent of this funding went to the physical sciences and engineering and the health sciences. Moreover, these disciplines accounted for 5,590 out of 6,310 funded projects. In contrast, arts and literature and the humanities and social sciences received just five percent of funds, despite representing a majority of all research appointments (Guppy, Grabb and Mollica 2013). This disparity has reinforced the shift from basic to applied/commercial research in Canada, and has allowed the CFI and its "partners" to gain considerable leverage over curriculum priorities.

Third, the Knowledge Infrastructure Program (KIP) was announced as part of the 2009 federal budget. Administered by Industry Canada, the program allocated roughly $2 billion to support hundreds of post-secondary infrastructure projects as part of the government's economic stimulus plan. On the one hand, the KIP provided much needed material resources to Canadian campuses. On the other hand, it did little to address the gap in core funding across universities and its

Table 5.2: CFI Funding by Discipline, 1998–2009

Area	No. of Projects	Total Funds ($)	% of Funds
Arts and Literature	73	39,709,673	0.9
Health Sciences	1,177	1,394,523,033	32.5
Humanities and Social Sciences	561	176,315,717	4.1
Multidisciplinary	86	200,634,279	4.7
Natural Sciences and Engineering	4,413	2,473,718,765	57.7
Total	6,310	4,284,901,467	100

Source: Guppy, Grabb and Mollica 2013.

projects have primarily been oriented towards providing a "foundation for future economic prosperity" (Industry Canada 2012). KIP money was leveraged into an investment of more than $3 billion from municipalities, provinces and the private sector, resulting in a total investment of more than $5 billion. Like SuperBuild and the CFI, the KIP inherently favours projects that can amass matching funds. At the University of Western Ontario, for instance, KIP funding for the new $100 million Richard Ivey School of Business was chosen over a variety of other proposals. Other examples of KIP-funded projects in Ontario include: the Biosciences and Technology Convergence Centre at Algoma; the Energy Systems and Nuclear Science Research Centre and the Automotive Centre of Excellence at UOIT; and the Innovation Centre for Canadian Mining Industry at Toronto. Brock's KIP showpiece is the $111 million Cairns Family Health and Bioscience Complex. The ground floor of this complex houses Brock's "business incubator," where faculty and business leaders work together to market their discoveries. One more aspect of the KIP program is worth noting. The majority of KIP money has gone to infrastructure repairs and upgrades to existing campus facilities and not new infrastructure. According to the CAUT (2009c), less than half of what the government stated it was investing in higher education infrastructure actually went to new projects.

Deferred Maintenance and "Hidden" Costs

One reason why a large portion of KIP money — and other public funds — has been diverted to infrastructure upgrades is because university infrastructure in Canada has suffered from prolonged neglect. In 2009, the Canadian Association of University Business Officers estimated that the total value of deferred maintenance on Canadian campuses was over $5 billion, half of which is considered "urgent." In fact, university budgets are so strained that deferred maintenance is said to pose "serious health and safety risks" at many institutions (CFS 2012: 9). Likewise in Ontario, a 2007 report showed that nearly half of the total space in the province's universities is classified as operating in poor condition (Council of Ontario Universities 2010). P3s and matching programs have contributed to this problem. While some programs and disciplines are being equipped with new state of the art facilities, libraries and other publicly funded infrastructure that house most of the teaching and research space for arts, education and the social sciences have been excluded from this support.

Infrastructure projects also come with "hidden costs." In part, this is because funding for the operation, staffing and maintenance of new buildings is often entirely absent. New KIP projects, for example, do not generally account for operating expenses. Likewise, the CFI provides funding for construction, with only a small amount for operations.[5] As a result, the ongoing costs of maintenance must be absorbed by universities. Staffing and maintenance costs for campus infrastructure in Canada amount to more than $1 billion annually, and capital projects based on a P3 model have only increased this burden. In order to finance these costs, universities are dipping into their general-purpose and operating budgets. This means that some of the money that once supported arts-related disciplines is being diverted to servicing infrastructure in applied fields. Some universities are also incurring considerable debts because they are unable to meet fundraising targets. According to the AUCC (2008a: 40), the "increase in debt servicing of academic buildings is the result of government practices to leverage as much private sector funding as possible in support of university construction." The annual cost of debt servicing, which has grown substantially in recent years, also reduces the amount of money available to cover teaching and other expenses.

There is no question that applied and high-technology programs require more expensive facilities and infrastructure than other disciplines. Under corporatization, however, the inequality in infrastructure spending and development on Canadian campuses has become much more pronounced. Programs in the arts, social sciences and humanities cannot compete when funding arrangements are based upon public-private partnerships and matching contributions from the private sector. The reliance on P3 capital funding clearly illustrates expanding control by corporations and neoliberal governments over university governance.

DONOR AGREEMENTS

Another way that the private sector is asserting its influence over university governance is through donor agreements. As we have seen, Canadian universities are increasingly turning to private donors to compensate for public funding shortfalls. In exchange for monetary contributions, private donors are offered seats on university governing boards and their names are emblazoned on academic chairs, institutes, faculties, buildings and lecture halls. In *The Trouble with Billionaires*, Linda McQuaig and Neil Brooks (2010: 192) note that in contrast to past years, when buildings were often named in honour of distinguished academics, today "campus buildings and auditoriums have been named almost exclusively after people whose distinctive characteristic is the possession of lots of money." Examples include the K.C. Irving Chemistry Centre at the University of Prince Edward Island, the Schulich School of Business at York, the Michael G. DeGroote School of Medicine at McMaster and the Wayne & William White Engineering Design Centre at the University of British Columbia. McQuaig and Brooks also highlight that, in 2007, a group of professors at the U of T approached the administration with the idea of naming the university's Health Studies Program after Tommy Douglas, a Canadian health care pioneer who was selected as the "Greatest Canadian" of all time in a nationwide contest organized by the CBC. In its response, the university turned down the proposal because it offered little potential for fundraising.

Some argue that naming university buildings after rich donors is of little consequence. Yet, corporate and other wealthy patrons — who Jacques Barzun (1993: 157–58) once described as "danglers of gifts" and "false friends" — are not simply being granted naming rights. They are now claiming, and in some cases being allowed, control over academic decision making in the university. Under corporatization, there are many examples of universities entering into contracts with private donors that grant them considerable control over academic priorities.

In Canada, four 1990s donor agreements at the U of T are indicative of the changing relationship between universities and the private sector. In 1995, Canadian business icon Peter Munk donated $6.4 million over ten years to finance the Munk Centre for International Studies. Under the agreement, Munk was also free to withdraw his donation at any time if he was dissatisfied with the Centre's "progress." In 1996, the Joseph L. Rotman Charitable Foundation pledged $15 million to the university's Faculty of Management in return for matching funds to create six new endowed chairs. The deal also came with a number of other privileges, including control over faculty hiring, committing future university resources to donor prerogatives and allowing the foundation to redirect its funds (and the university's matching funds) to other purposes. This agreement was only terminated after protests by students and the U of T Faculty Association. Another 1997 agreement set up the Nortel Institute for Telecommunications. In exchange for $8 million, Nortel was given influence over hiring for the new institute, which also gave it de facto control over curriculum and instruction. It was later revealed that faculty and students were required, by virtue of a secret clause in the agreement, to sign over to Nortel exclusive rights to research and inventions produced with Nortel money. Similarly, a $13.5 million agreement with Bell Emergis (a division of Bell Canada) in 1999 created four matching-fund chairs and four tenure track positions in the Bell Emergis University Labs. Bell had significant control over hiring and research. The university also assured the company that faculty researchers would be required to sign over their intellectual property rights to the university — which in turn would be transferred to Bell — in order to be considered for funding under the agreement. More recent donor agreements are even more threatening to university autonomy and integrity.

The Munk School of Global Affairs
The Munk School of Global Affairs came into force fifteen years after the deal that established the Munk Centre for International Studies. Munk agreed to donate $35 million to the U of T over a period of seven years to establish the new school. Of course, Munk will not pay the full amount, as he will receive a $16 million tax reduction for his $35 million contribution, reducing his actual contribution to $19 million. As well, the Federal and Ontario governments each promised $25

million in matching funds, so the taxpayers have contributed at least $66 million. The agreement shows that Munk was effectively buying influence over academic decisions. Although the contract affirms the commitment of both parties to "vigilant protection for the rights of freedom of speech, academic freedom and freedom of research," this conflicts with the provision requiring the school's director to provide detailed annual reports to the Munk Board of Directors (see University of Toronto 2010: 3, 10). Moreover, a major portion of Munk's money is released only after the Board is satisfied that the school has achieved certain donor-defined objectives, and he has the authority to withdraw funds over any aspect of the school with which he disapproves. Munk already requires that the school include space and offices for members of the Canadian International Council, a right-leaning think-tank specializing in foreign affairs. Munk is also connected to mining giant Barrick Gold, meaning it is unlikely that the school will conduct any research that is critical of the crimes of Canadian mining companies, let alone Barrick's own dismal human rights and environmental record. Given the money at stake, university administrators will be unlikely to resist any demand made by Munk or risk alienating the corporations he controls.

The Balsillie School of International Affairs
In 2007, co-founder of Research in Motion, Jim Balsillie, donated $33 million to Wilfrid Laurier and Waterloo universities to establish the Balsillie School of International Affairs. The money was donated through Balsillie's private think-tank, the Waterloo-based Centre for International Governance Innovation (CIGI). This agreement specifies that the committees established to make hiring, budgeting, research and curriculum decisions include both university and CIGI representatives and requires unanimity. Hence, CIGI effectively had veto power over academic matters normally reserved for universities. The CAUT began investigating the agreement after Ramesh Thakur was fired from his position as the school's inaugural director (see Findlay 2010). Thakur claims he was fired because he resisted CIGI's intention to assert greater control over academic affairs, and stated, "had it been clear to me that the school was a wholly owned subsidiary of CIGI, I would never have taken the job" (cited in Valpy 2010). In 2012, another $60 million agreement was signed between CIGI and York University to establish a joint program in international law. This partnership arrangement, which included a $30 million contribution from both the Ontario government and CIGI, also ostensibly gave the think-tank veto power over budgetary matters, academic staffing, curriculum and research (Tedesco 2012). And, like many of the agreements previously discussed, Balsillie was given the freedom to pull his money if CIGI was not satisfied with the direction of the program. In this case, however, the deal was cancelled after widespread opposition from Osgoode Law School faculty.

The Clayton H. Riddell School of Political Management
In 2012, Carleton University signed a $15 million donor agreement with Calgary oil magnate and former chair of the Canadian Association of Petroleum Producers, Clayton Riddell, to create the Clayton H. Riddell School of Political Management. The $15 million provided by Riddell was the largest single donation ever provided to the University. From the outset, the Carleton administration was highly secretive about the deal, which was brokered by former Reform Party leader Preston Manning. When the agreement was requested under Ontario's Freedom of Information and Protection of Privacy Act, the administration refused to provide it. Following mediation, the University released a heavily redacted version of the agreement and, after stalling for nearly a year, was eventually ordered to release the full contract by Ontario's information and privacy commissioner. The contract revealed that Riddell's foundation effectively appointed three of the five members of the program's steering committee. Manning chairs the committee, while his former chief of staff, Cliff Fryers, and Chris Froggatt (former chief of staff to Conservative cabinet minister John Baird) are also represented. This committee was initially given "sweeping power" over the program's budget, hiring and curriculum (Henderson 2012). And, like the agreements noted above, a provision in the contract allowed Riddell's foundation to assess the school's performance after a period of time and to withhold the remaining $10 million if he was not satisfied with any aspect of its performance. The CAUT described the Carleton agreement as "unprecedented" (Cheadle 2012). After an outpouring of public opposition, Carleton announced that the deal did not reflect the university's academic policies with regard to budget management and staff selection and would be renegotiated. Under the revised agreement, the steering committee no longer has the power to "approve" hiring and curriculum decisions and assumes a more advisory role.

These kinds of private donor deals are a result of the ascendency of corporate management in higher education. Above all, they mean that universities are not only being run more like businesses, they are increasingly being run *by* members of the private sector. How universities are governed has been transformed. There is a new marketing ethos where corporate governance models tied to discourses and practices of managerialism proliferate, programs and curriculum offerings have changed and new public-private partnerships have been forged that threaten academic freedom. Corporate influence is not, of course, confined to governance relations. One of the key public service elements of universities — foundational and other research — is being appropriated and controlled by corporations and a corporate ethos. Rather than being of service to society, academic research is more and more (and more overtly) being used for corporate profit.

NOTES

1 These trends are not confined to Canada. In the U.K., the number of university managers increased more than three times as fast as the number of academics between 2003 and 2010 (Turner 2010). In the U.S., between 1975 and 2005, the number of administrators and administrative staffers grew by an "astonishing" 85 and 240 percent respectively, while the number of full-time professors grew by just 51 percent (Ginsberg 2011: 25).

2 In the U.S., less than one quarter of higher education leaders surveyed said they would prefer that full-time, tenured professors make up a majority of faculty at their institutions, and seventy percent expressed support for limited contracts (Stripling 2011). Also of note is that those presidents who had previously held faculty positions were much more likely those who had not to support tenure, which highlights the implications of the growing recruitment of administrators from outside of the academy.

3 The CAUT's investigation was inspired by a study by the Centre for American Progress, which looked at ten major collaborations between U.S. universities and leading energy corporations. The report exposed how these kinds of agreements have compromised academic integrity in the U.S. (see Washburn 2010).

4 Minister Goodyear's intervention fits within the Conservative government's record of silencing critics of its policy positions. The government's position on freedom of speech was revealed in 2009 when British MP George Galloway, a critic of the Israeli occupation and of Western military intervention in Afghanistan, was banned from entering Canada on grounds of national security (a claim that made Canada the object of international ridicule). Academic scholarship and scientific research have also been subjected to unprecedented political scrutiny. Professors critical of Conservative government policies have been targeted in the media and by party spokespersons. This kind of inspection extends to the government's own academics. Scientists working for Natural Resources Canada were informed in 2010 that they would be required to obtain "pre-approval" from the Minister's office before speaking to the media (Gergin 2011). A survey of federal government scientists commissioned by the Professional Institute of the Public Service of Canada (2013) found that 90 percent of them feel they are not allowed to speak freely to the media about their work, and 86 percent said they would face censure or retaliation for doing so. In the summer of 2012, 1,500 scientists, students and supporters rallied on Parliament Hill to protest the government's attack on scientific research and the preferential cutting of programs that do not align with the Conservative agenda.

5 In 2010, the CFI began to address the issue of operating expenses when it launched its first major competition for operating funds. The Major Science Initiatives program provided $185 million over five years to cover 40 percent of the operating costs (for up to five years) of science facilities that the organization had already funded.

CHAPTER SIX
THE CORPORATE CORRUPTION OF ACADEMIC RESEARCH

Universities have long had both teaching and research as core functions. Just as who teaches and what gets taught have been altered under corporatization, so too has who is directing research and what gets released. Historically, university research has been tied to external needs and interests, with the strength of these ties and their implications for research depending on the broader social and economic context. In the 1960s and 1970s, there was relatively little collaboration between Canadian academics and members of the business community. This lack of engagement can be traced, in part, to corporate reservations about the nature of university research, including the processes for performance and evaluation, procedures for sharing results, and the reward structure. It also resulted from the university's relative independence as an institution. Most university research during this period was organized along disciplinary lines and independently regulated by academics. Likewise, the process of research funding was, for the most part, academically controlled.

In the 1980s and 1990s, however, research alliances between universities and the private sector began to expand and have continued to increase ever since. Federal policy has played an important role in this expansion facilitating, almost forcing, universities to do research for corporations, or at least in ways that benefit industry. The appropriation of university research is especially evident in recent changes in practices around intellectual property and the commercialization of academic research. Corporate influence has, in effect, corrupted academic research in ways that are not always publicly transparent, including in the selection of research topics, keeping research secret, and through bias in the collection and release of information.

A HISTORY OF FEDERAL RESEARCH POLICY IN CANADA

From the 1970s onward, federal programs and policy changes have contributed to the corporatization of university research in Canada. While many provincial initiatives have also contributed to this trend, the federal government is the largest source of support for university research in Canada and, as a result, has had considerable influence over this aspect of post-secondary education.

Before the 1970s, there was relatively little research collaboration between universities and industry. Nevertheless, there were some new organizations created during this timeframe — many of them sponsored by the federal department of industry — to facilitate corporate-university alliances, including centres of advanced technology, industrial research institutes, industrial innovation centres, management advancement institutes and industrial research associations (MacAulay 1984). As well, between 1976 and 1981, the Natural Sciences and Engineering Research Council (NSERC) provided $1.2 billion in grants to encourage closer ties between universities and the private sector (Tudiver 1999). To support an ongoing mandate in this area, the NSERC Industrial Research Fellowship program was also created in 1980–81. Twenty-six awards were handed out in its first year; just two years later, the number of grants increased to 132 (MacAulay 1984).

In the 1980s, the federal Conservatives under Brian Mulroney oversaw a decisive shift in national research policy, resulting in a considerable growth in research alliances between university and private sector partners. The basic objective of the new policy regime was to redirect university research towards industrial ends. As part of this so-called "innovation" agenda, Canadian federal and provincial governments launched more than 100 intersectoral research partnerships to promote collaboration in science and technology (S&T) (Atkinson-Grosjean 2006). The mandate of the Science Council of Canada — the country's national advisory agency on S&T policy — also changed. In one of the Council's most influential reports, Philip Enros and Michael Farley (1986) coined the term "service university" to describe the desired relationship between universities and the private sector. Put simply, service in this context referred to a narrow, unidirectional focus on satisfying corporate interests. Other federal initiatives helped to shape and define the university's service role. For example, private sector representatives were incorporated into government policy-making bodies, including through the establishment of federally appointed advisory committees concerned with university research, such as the Intellectual Property Advisory Committee and the National Advisory Board on Science and Technology (now the Advisory Council on Science and Technology).

At the same time, the private sector became more involved in the activities of the federal granting councils (the NSERC, the SSHRC and the Medical Research Council). Their influence was evident in the introduction of the SSHRC's "strategic research grants" program, which was designed to entice researchers to pursue more applied and economically driven projects. The NSERC in particular became a major player in the government's drive to transform university research. Between 1981–82 and 1990–91, expenditures on NSERC's basic research program declined from 72.7 percent to 61.9 percent of the council's budget, while expenditures on targeted research rose from 11.6 to 18.5 percent. Over the same period, support for partnership research increased by 1,900 percent, from $1.9 to $37 million (Polster 1998). The corporate orientation of all three councils was strengthened in 1987 when the government launched its "matching funds" program. Strongly endorsed by the Corporate-Higher Education Forum, the program tied any additional funding through the councils to matching contributions from the private sector.

Another important development in the 1980s was the creation of the federal Networks of Centres of Excellence (NCE) program. Modeled on the Ontario network, federal NCEs were established as national research networks targeting commercial applications in partnership with industry. Janet Atkinson-Grosjean (2006: xiii–xv, emphasis in original), who conducted the seminal study on NCEs, describes the program:

> Scientific excellence, commercial relevance, and public-private collaborations are recurrent themes in all new programs. Funding is targeted to areas of strategic importance to Canada's prosperity and international competitiveness ... The radical goal (later modified) was to turn university researchers *away* from basic science and *towards* commercial application. Further, the tradition of serendipitous discovery was far too anarchic for the policy establishment; research should not only be 'managed' — a novel concept — but managed on private sector rather than academic principles.

From its inception, NCE research has been assessed on its ability to facilitate corporate-university partnerships and commercialization. In the first competition in 1988 (Phase I), evaluations of applications included a 20 percent weight for showing that results would lead to commercial products or processes, and 20 percent for demonstrating linkages between universities, industry and government. In order to be renewed in Phase II, NCEs had to demonstrate that they would strengthen their commercialization potential and relevance to industry. As a result, Phase II networks conducted more applied and less basic research and NCE participants expanded to include over five hundred corporations (up from less than two hundred in Phase I). It is important to note that although NCEs have always been based in universities (and universities have assumed much of their costs), their structure has made them largely unaccountable to the policies that normally guide academic work.

With the election of the federal Liberals in 1993, the emphasis on "innovation" in university research became more entrenched. The Liberals made their innovation agenda explicit in several major reports. In 1999, for example, the Expert Panel on the Commercialization of University Research produced a report arguing that universities should add a fourth mission — "commercialization" — to their customary missions of teaching, research and service. The Panel also asserted that commercialization potential should be a condition for federal research funding and that professors' commercialization track records should be incorporated into tenure and promotion policies. The resulting recommendations of the Panel were strongly opposed by many academics; in 2000, 1,400 researchers signed a letter rejecting the conclusions of the report.

Three years later, the Liberals released two companion documents: *Achieving Excellence* (Industry Canada 2002) and *Knowledge Matters* (Human Resources Development Canada 2002). *Achieving Excellence* specifically addressed university research capacity at the national level. What is most striking about the report is that it assumes (like the Science Council in the 1980s) that the primary purpose of the university is to serve business. To this end, the government promised to "support academic institutions in identifying intellectual property with commercial potential and forging partnerships with the private sector to commercialize research results" (Industry Canada 2002: 50). These commitments were reflected in a $50 million pilot project launched as part of the 2004 federal budget to strengthen the commercialization capacity of universities and research hospitals, as well as the growing corporate orientation of federal NCEs. Between 2002–03 and 2006–07, the number of private sector organizations involved in NCEs increased by 40 percent (AUCC 2008b). Somewhat surprisingly, the AUCC (2002) not only supported this agenda, but it secretly negotiated an agreement with the federal government where, in exchange for increased funding, universities promised to *triple* their level of research commercialization.

Federal investments in university research rose from $733 million in 1997–98 to $2.93 billion in 2007–08 (AUCC 2008b), and these investments were directed to support a particular policy agenda. A large proportion of the new money was provided through matching programs and other partnership arrangements. As a result, the number of corporate-academic research contracts sharply increased. According to the AUCC (2008b), Canadian universities undertook 6,000 research contracts with Canadian and foreign firms in 2006, more than double the number in 1999.[1] Large corporate investments in research infrastructure were also provided through the Canadian Foundation for Innovation (CFI), which channelled hundreds of millions of dollars in private sector funds to applied research fields (the natural sciences and engineering and health sciences received roughly 95 percent of CFI funding between 1998 and 2009). The CFI's applied research focus is evident in its matching fund structure and the fact that the number of corporate representatives on its board accounted for nearly 40 percent of all director and member positions between 1998 and 2009 (Guppy, Grabb and Mollica 2013). As of 2011, the CFI had provided 7,372 awards with a total value of more than $4.4 billion (CAUT 2012). Targeted research investments under the Liberals also included the establishment of the Canada Research Chairs (CRC) program in 2002. This program provided $900 million to establish and sustain 2,000 research chairs in Canadian universities. To date, the distribution of CRC chairs has heavily tilted in favour of some disciplines over others; natural sciences, health sciences and engineering have received 80 percent of all chairs, while the social sciences and humanities have been afforded just 20 percent. Moreover, because CRCs are awarded on the basis of each university's share of granting council funding, just twelve large institutions have received two thirds of all positions.

The Liberal's innovation strategy also put significant pressure on the granting councils to forge closer ties with industry. Many NSERC programs were initiated or expanded to encourage such collaboration, including the Industrial Research Chairs program, Industrial R&D Fellowships program and Strategic Grants program. In 2004, NSERC launched an award to encourage students to identify market products or services that could be enhanced through the application of their research projects. Shortly thereafter, it introduced the "Ideas to Innovate" program to create spin-off companies from council funded projects. Around the same time, another major granting council, the Canadian Institutes of Health Research (CIHR), launched its own commercialization and innovation strategy to strengthen the value of research related intellectual property. As part of this initiative, programs were set up to educate health researchers in technology transfer and entrepreneurialism. It should be noted that the intellectual property capabilities of all three councils were strengthened in 2001 when they collectively launched the Intellectual Property Mobilization Program. This tri-council initiative was designed to accelerate commercialization and assist Canadian universities engaged in academic capitalism.

Shortly after coming to power in 2006 the Harper Conservatives released their new S&T strategy in a document called *Mobilising Science and Technology to Canada's Advantage* (Government of Canada 2007a). The strategy further advanced the corporatization of higher education by including a strong emphasis on commercialization and private sector involvement, which was put into practice in the 2007 budget when the government launched a new NCE program to be "proposed and led by the private sector" (Government of Canada 2007b: 205). Some of the new NCEs were packaged as Centres of Excellence for Commercialization and Research (CECR), which are designed to facilitate commercialization in the "priority" areas of management, business and finance, natural resources and energy, health and life sciences, information and communications technologies and the environment.

An interesting example of a CECR with an "environmental" focus is the Canada School of Energy and Environment, which is a tri-party collaboration between the universities of Calgary, Alberta and Lethbridge. The School supports tar sands development and advises industry and governments on creating "sound regulations and appropriate legislation" to deal with energy expansion and environmental enhancement (Stewart 2011). Although it purports to be an academic research centre, one of the school's former directors, Bruce Carson, was a political appointee and long-time strategist for the Harper government. Before assuming his position, Carson served as vice chair of the Energy Policy Institute of Canada, whose membership includes numerous representatives from the oil and gas industries. Keith Stewart of Greenpeace Canada has describes Carson as "the political quarterback for the joint government/industry pro-tar sands campaign" (cited in Stewart 2011).[2] Of course, the Harper government's support for research that caters to the interests of Big Oil is well recognized. A survey of "senior people considered to be well informed on S&T in Canada" found widespread agreement that Canada's two strongest areas (out of fifty) of research and technology application are "Oilsands and Related" and "Conventional Oil & Gas Exploration/Extraction" (Council of Canadian Academies 2006: 3, 6). Notably, survey respondents also identified "Clean Energy Technologies" as the area where Canada should be developing its future S&T capacity.

In keeping with its S&T strategy, the Harper government also pledged $200 million over seven years — though the Canada Excellence Research Chairs program — to encourage nineteen internationally recognized researchers to pursue their work in Canada (along with $275.6 million to create 310 new/renewed "regular" CRCs). Similar to the Centres of Excellence for Commercialization and Research, these chairs are targeted in the areas of information and communication technologies, natural resources and energy, health sciences and the environment. This narrow focus not only excludes most researchers in the natural sciences, but it effectively excludes more than half of Canada's researchers in the social sciences and humanities. It has also excluded women; all nineteen current chair holders are men and not a single woman has been nominated for an award.

To implement their innovation agenda, the federal granting councils have been one of the Harper government's most consistent tools. At NSERC, new programs have linked hundreds of major corporations with university researchers. The University of Alberta alone currently holds twenty-two industrial research chairs, which is double the number of any other university. As part of NSERC's focus on innovation, the government has also redirected public funds to programs to help solve company-specific problems, which is tantamount to providing free labour for the corporate sector. According to Karen Seidman (2013), since 2009 "company specific research funding" has grown by more than 1,000 percent. Remarkably, in

2012, NSERC was even offering to organize "speed dating" events to bring interested researchers and companies together. At the same time, NSERC's Discovery Grants program — the main funding source for basic research in the natural sciences and engineering — has declined significantly, from two thirds of the council's budget in 1978 to one third in 2010. Between 2002 and 2010, the success rate for Discovery Grant applicants fell from 83 to 58 percent (CAUT 2010c).

Predictably, the CIHR's commercial mandate has also expanded in recent years. In 2009, controversy arose when Dr. Bernard Prigent, Vice-President of Medical Affairs at Pfizer Canada, was appointed to the CIHR's governing council. Given that Pfizer has every interest in diverting CIHR funds toward commercial drug studies and away from research that might challenge the pharmaceutical therapeutic paradigm, this appointment was an obvious conflict of interest. Steven Lewis, Saskatchewan health researcher and former member of the CIHR council, states: "It is hardly irrelevant that the company to which Dr. Prigent owes his livelihood and his allegiance has owned up to sleaze that stands out even among its shady peers" (cited in Munro 2009). Of course, many non-academic appointees sit on the governing boards of the granting agencies. Half of the NSERC's council members in 2010 (many of whom are not scientists) were from the private sector. One of these appointments was climate change skeptic and former head of the Fraser Institute, Mark Mullins. The governing council at the SSHRC has also expanded its industry representation. In 2013, for example, Jack Mintz was appointed vice-president of the Council. Since 2008, Mintz held the position of Director of the School of Public Policy at the University of Calgary. Donald Gutstein (2014) has exposed the extensive ties between the School of Public Policy, Big Oil and Alberta Energy. He argues that the School operates more like a right-wing think-tank than a graduate school in an accredited public university. Mintz himself is a director of Imperial Oil and the Imperial Oil Foundation. This enhanced corporate presence aligns with the government's announcement in 2007 of an additional $11 million earmarked for SSHRC research in management, business and finance, as well as its 2009 announcement that scholarships granted by the SSHRC would focus on business-related degrees.

Recent federal budgets have continued to neglect basic research in favour of commercial application. In budget 2012, $37 million was allocated to enhance council support for "industry-academic research partnership initiatives" in areas with promising commercial output. In budget 2013, all new money announced for the granting councils was targeted to support research partnerships with industry. In budget 2014, the government launched the Canada First Research Excellence Fund, which accelerated its support for targeted research in the interests of corporate Canada. According to James Turk, the new Fund "gives the private sector veto power over who gets grants" (cited in Seidman 2014). The Harper government has also overseen a transformation of its in-house research branch, the National Research Council (NRC). The current president of the Council, John McDougall, is a former Imperial Oil petroleum engineer with ties to Big Oil in Alberta. In 2013, the government formally announced that the NRC was "open for business" and would receive $121 million over two years to shift into its industry-oriented mandate (Allen 2013).

This growing entanglement of corporations in university research, facilitated by federal policy agendas, is especially problematic in Canada for a number of reasons. Canadian private sector research and development is weak, which means that a relatively high level of R&D is performed by universities, and there is a high level of corporate R&D investment in universities.

It is well known that Canada's private sector performs and funds a smaller share of R&D activities compared with other industrialized nations. In 2006, for example, Canada's private sector performed just 54 percent of Canadian R&D (valued at $15.8 billion), compared with 70 percent in the U.S. and 69 percent across all OECD countries. In contrast, Canadian universities performed an estimated 36 percent of Canada's R&D activities in 2007, which was much larger than the U.S. (14 percent) and the OECD average (17 percent). Also in 2007, Canada's private sector invested a higher proportion of its R&D expenditures in universities than was the case in all other G7 nations and all but three OECD countries. Furthermore, this level of investment appears to be accelerating. Between 2001 and 2007, private sector investments in university research increased by 28 percent. In contrast, business investments in its own research activities grew by just 3.5 percent (AUCC 2008b). In other words, the large corporations that dominate Canada cannot or will not do the research that is essential to their businesses, so they have succeeded in convincing, or forcing, universities to do it for them. Universities have become the publicly funded research arms of large, private corporations, many of whom may not actually be Canadian.

Not surprisingly, government efforts to corporatize university research have been opposed by many within the academic community. In 2005, forty prominent Canadian scientists spoke out publicly against the kinds of co-funding or matching programs favoured by governments, and the negative implications of corporate funding for university research. The comments of these scientists are worth quoting at length:

> Inevitably, co-funding steers resource allocation, as dictated by the partner entity, which may be to the detriment of some of the best science. In particular, co-funding is often biased against fundamental research that is far from commercialization and so at odds with the short-term goals of industrial partners ... In general, grants are best awarded solely on

the basis of scientific peer review, and funded in full without matches, strings, or contingencies that depend on outside agents. By eschewing scientific excellence as the primary consideration, co-funded programs imperil scientific credibility and fail to engage the breadth and depth of national scientific expertise. (Tyers et al. 2005: 1867)

In line with these policy changes, universities in Canada have become accustomed to operating in a more competitive funding environment and more adept at casting their activities in terms of the requirements set forth by funding agencies. As a result, many university administrations have adopted the same kind of "innovation" agenda as neoliberal governments, with the same restrictive focus on commercialization and intellectual property.

PRIVATIZING PUBLIC KNOWLEDGE: INTELLECTUAL PROPERTY AND COMMERCIALIZATION

For much of the twentieth century, academics (and universities) did not consider research-related intellectual property (IP) as an opportunity for economic enrichment. Many university inventors who were formally entitled to patent royalties did their best to avoid personal remuneration, preferring instead to channel the obligatory profits back into their laboratories. Others resisted patenting altogether. For instance, when Jonas Salk discovered the polio vaccine in 1954 (an invention clearly worth millions), he did not patent the vaccine because he believed that no individual should own or profit from discoveries made about the natural world. Similarly, Stanley Cohen and Herbert Boyer, who discovered the gene-splicing technique in 1973, resisted patenting because they recognized that their discovery depended upon the freely available work of other scientists. In short, the prevailing academic view was that knowledge should be placed in the public domain without proprietary restrictions, and that limiting access by commercializing research results was a suspect practice, or worse.

Under corporatization, these ideas about the role of IP in higher education have been largely abandoned. The result has been a plethora of new IP agreements designed to convert public knowledge into private profit. Proponents claim that IP rights serve a number of economic and social functions. Taking for granted the university-corporate research context, such IP agreements increase corporate profits, thus generating new revenue streams for universities. Moreover, essentially "privatizing" research provides incentives for academics to create useful products and services, rather than engaging in "useless" basic research (ignoring completely that it has been basic research that has formed the basis of almost every important industrial technology around). IP agreements will also encourage professors to move nascent discoveries out of the ivory tower and into the marketplace.

Contrary to these views, I believe the weight of evidence shows that the negative consequences of the commercialization agenda outweigh any perceived benefits. Under this agenda, basic research is typically viewed as mere curiosity or indulgence. Researchers in fields like the humanities and social sciences and speculative science, in particular — which lack the profit-making or power enhancing applications of other disciplines — have been deemed less relevant. According to Thomas D'Aquino, former head of the Canadian Council of Chief Executives, "research on its own, without the benefit of transformation into new products, processes, and services, is of little value" (D'Aquino and Stewart-Patterson 2001: 17).

Moreover, by attaching monetary incentives to discovery, a commercial orientation creates a preoccupation with particular kinds of outcomes, which can lead to research bias. It also enhances research secrecy and stifles scientific progress by restricting the free flow of information (discussed in greater detail later in the chapter). Related to this, IP does not provide incentives to engage in research (create/discover); rather, it merely generates incentives for academics to commercialize their discoveries (or "innovate").

Not only have the financial returns on IP for universities been marginal at best, but the costs to the public have been substantial. Although the Canadian taxpayer pays most of the costs of university research, they do not incur benefits at the same rate as research products become the property of corporations, universities or professors. Moreover, as Benjamin Ginsberg (2011: 189) describes it, IP incentives and reward structures have "institutionalized scientific avarice," thereby eroding the ability and willingness of academics to respond to a broad range of public needs and interests. This is not to suggest that all IP rights are counter-productive in the academy. Indeed, protecting certain ownership rights, such as course-related IP and other scholarly work covered by copyright, may be particularly important in the context of corporatization to protect academic freedom and the legitimate interests of the professoriate. At a more general level, however, the concept of intellectual property has been transformed from a mechanism of academic protection and freedom to a commercial obsession on the part of administrators, academic capitalists and members of the private sector.

CREATING THE COMMERCIAL INFRASTRUCTURE

The commercial orientation of university administrators is often stated clearly in academic planning documents. For example, the University of Guelph's (2008: 2) "strategic research plan" states that the university "is expected to figure prominently in the proposed national expansion of the commercialization of university research." While the University will try to remain "respectful" of fundamental, discipline-based research, the overriding priorities are commercial engagement and private sector collaboration. Similarly, a planning document from Brock (2009: 5) reads:

"Without losing sight of the importance of basic and inquiry-based research ... Brock University's faculty and student researchers will be particularly interested in the impact of their work upon the economic, social and cultural development of the Niagara Region." To fulfill this objective, the University will "support expanded commercialization opportunities through the development of appropriate intellectual property arrangements." Lakehead (2009) has a similar mandate and its administration explicitly recognizes that a key impediment to commercialization is the faculty research culture. To remedy these outdated ideas, it asserts that "faculty must be provided with additional education relating to the value of technology transfer to the University, particularly what technology transfer means, how it benefits research" and how the administration can assist professors in commercializing their discoveries (24).

To fulfill these commercial objectives and better align with the corporatization agenda, university administrators have been active in creating a commercial research infrastructure. Over the past few decades, most administrations in Canada have expanded their offices of research administration, diverted resources to disciplines with greater economic potential, and developed formal and informal IP policies that encourage academics to commercialize. Often in collaboration with governments and the private sector, administrators have also been key players in the establishment of two other instruments of commercialization to support corporatization: (i) technology transfer offices and (ii) university-industry research centres.

Technology transfer offices (TTOs), sometimes referred to as industrial liaison or business development offices, play a central role in IP management and the commercialization agenda. The function of TTOs is to translate the results of university research into concrete commercial applications. Professional staff in these offices assist faculty in commercializing their inventions and are sometimes involved in other forms of university-industry liaison, such as industry-sponsored contract research. In Canada, TTOs did not appear in their current form until the 1980s. Their rate of expansion has been rapid; by 1995, thirty-two universities had established such an office (Fisher and Atkinson-Grosjean 2002). Between 1999 and 2008, the proportion of Canadian universities actively managing IP through TTOs increased from 61 to 88 percent (AUCC 2008b; Statistics Canada 2010b). While their size, tasks and organization vary considerably,[3] all but the smallest Canadian institutions have active TTOs today.

A significant proportion of the work performed by TTOs is generated by university-industry research centres. These centres include a diverse collection of research associations, including research parks, research clusters and business incubators. For example, the University of Windsor/Chrysler Canada Automotive Research and Development Centre is a cooperative R&D facility where students, professors and corporate engineers work together on automotive research. One of Canada's most reputable business incubators is Digital Media Zone (DMZ), which opened at Ryerson University in 2010. Like other incubators, DMZ's facilities are designed to encourage entrepreneurship, largely in the form of public-private partnerships and spin-off companies, formed in order to commercially exploit academic inventions. According to Sheldon Levy (2011), president at Ryerson, DMZ helped spawn thirty-four spin-off companies in its first nineteen months of operation.[4]

Research parks located on or near university campuses have also become an important instigator of university-industry collaboration. Examples include Edmonton Research Park in Alberta, Innovation Place in Saskatchewan (one of the largest research parks in North America) and the University of Manitoba's "smartpark." Smartpark Development Corporation is a subsidiary corporation of the University of Manitoba with a mandate to develop land and lease space to companies who work in areas that coincide with research expertise at the university. Today, the university's smartpark is home to thirty corporations, most notably Monsanto, and employs 1,100 people. A recent survey conducted by the Canadian Association of University Research Parks claimed that the twenty-five research parks located in Canada in 2007 were home to more than 750 high technology corporations and research centres and employed over 39,000 people (AUCC 2008b).

In addition to TTOs, business incubators and research parks, a growing number of research "clusters" have emerged as part of the new commercial infrastructure. In these clusters, business, financial and academic institutions come together in a single geographic location. Located in Toronto's downtown "Discovery District," MaRS exemplifies the cluster concept and is a conversion innovation centre of biomedical research and expertise. It actively networks corporations with academic and medical researchers to enhance IP commercialization. Other prominent research clusters in Canada include Montreal's digital media and computer graphics cluster; Saskatoon's agriculture biotechnology cluster; and Waterloo's information technology cluster that is renowned for churning out profitable spin-off companies.

PUBLIC SUBSIDY, PRIVATE PROFIT: UNIVERSITIES AS PATENT HOLDING COMPANIES

Prior to 1980, universities in the U.S. were able to secure patents on publicly funded research only through special government approval, which typically followed a lengthy application process. As a result, only a small number of universities engaged in patenting activities. In 1980, the Patent and Trademark Law Amendments Act, more commonly known as the Bayh-Dole Act, was passed. This critical piece of legislation enabled universities to own and license patents on discoveries made through publicly funded research. In Canada, a similar change occurred in 1990 via Treasury Board fiat. In previous years, all IP produced under government contract was vested in the Crown. From this point forward, patents that had reverted to the Crown became property of the university. As a result, universities across

Canada had the capacity to grant patent licenses to industrial partners in return for corporate patronage.

Needless to say, these changes that allowed universities to claim IP rights on technologies developed in their laboratories greatly accelerated academic capitalism. As potential patent holders, administrators viewed more and more academic research as potential IP, while faculty were better able to conceptualize and advance their discoveries as commercial products. These changes also facilitated a massive giveaway of public assets to private industry. Speaking about the Bayh-Dole Act in the U.S., Leonard Minsky (2000: 98) describes how these changes impact the corporatization process:

> No longer acting as agents of the taxpayers who had paid for the invention, the universities were simply given ownership by the legislation. They, in turn, pass the invention on to the corporations for a price, a price that never reflects the true cost of the development of the invention, already paid for up-front by the public. This slight-of-hand dimension of "technology transfer," whereby public assets are basically handed over to transnational corporations for pennies on the dollar, remains invisible ... The act was a gift of public money to private investors using the universities to launder the money.

These IP arrangements essentially give corporations the rights (often exclusive monopoly rights) to inventions generated at public expense. This process typically requires the public to pay twice for the same invention; they pay once through taxes to support the research and again though restricted supply and higher prices when the invention reaches the market. Because universities do not work patents or manufacture anything, this means they have become, in effect, patent holding companies.

Because there is no national legislative framework, IP policies at Canadian universities vary considerably. Each university in Canada is free to develop its own policies, which are translated into practice by TTOs. At some universities, the IP belongs to the inventor; at others, the IP is owned by the university. Many other institutions have joint arrangements where IP ownership and the distribution of revenues are shared according to a prescribed formula. Most universities in Canada have tended to take the position that they should receive some IP revenue in exchange for providing researchers with facilities and resources.

COMMERCIALIZATION: THE IP PAYOFF

Most of the empirical work, by government agencies and by organizations like the Association of University Technology Managers (AUTM), use three key indicators to track the commercialization of university research: patents (and invention disclosures), licensing agreements (and royalties) and spin-off companies. While these indicators do not represent the full spectrum of technology transfer, they are useful for documenting the commercial output of universities and account for much of the work performed by TTOs. Together, they make clear that the commercialization of university research has increased sharply since the early 1990s. Between 1991 and 1997, for example, professional staffing for IP management doubled, the number of active patents and technologies tripled, and income from commercialization grew fourfold (Fisher and Atkinson-Grosjean 2002). In 1991, 10 Canadian universities participating in the AUTM survey reported an average of 4.9 licenses/options executed; by 2001, there were 22 participating institutions reporting an average of 14.2. Over the same period, the average number of invention disclosures rose from 25 to 43.5 (Kachur 2003). The rate of growth of university spin-off companies is equally noteworthy. According to Statistics Canada (2010b), of the nearly 700 spin-off firms created in universities and their affiliated research hospitals between 1980 and 1999, 78 percent were formed in the 1990s. This represented an average rate of 54 companies per year, versus less than 16 per year in the 1980s.

The commercialization of academic research continued to accelerate in the 2000s. In 2008, researchers in Canadian universities and research hospitals reported 1,613 invention disclosures, an increase of 81 percent over 1999. Also in 2008, these institutions filed 1,791 patent applications (173 percent more than the 1999 total) and the number of accumulated patents held by universities grew from 1,915 to 5,908, well above the OECD and EU averages (CCL 2009c). Universities and hospitals awarded 524 new licenses/options in 2008, a 126 percent increase over 1999. As

Table 6.1: University Spin-Off Companies

Years	Number*	Percent
Before 1980	45	3.7
1980 to 1984	64	5.2
1985 to 1989	92	7.5
1990 to 1994	181	14.8
1995 to 1999	359	29.4
2000 to 2004	312	25.5
2005 to 2007	123	10.1
Not Stated	47	3.8
Total	1223	100.0

*Note: These estimates represent an inventory of all spin-off companies reported by educational institutions since 1999, regardless of the status of those institutions (active, inactive, merged or amalgamated).

Source: Statistics Canada 2010b. Survey of Intellectual Property Commercialization in the Higher Education Sector, 2008.

well, the total number of active licenses/options grew from 1,165 to 3,343, or by 187 percent. The number of full-time equivalent employees engaged in IP management increased from 178 in 1999 to 321 in 2008 (an 80 percent increase). The rate of university spin-off formation also remained strong in the 2000s, with an average of 54 companies being created each year between 2001 and 2007. This information likely underestimates the number of university-based spin-offs because it only includes companies that are started in a formal arrangement with the university. The numbers would be significantly higher if spin-offs created independently by university faculty were taken into account. Some researchers claim that Canadian universities create twice as many spin-off companies as U.S. universities per dollar of research expenditure (see, for example, Robin 2004; Van Loon 2005).

All of this might lead one to conclude that Canadian universities have been highly successful in achieving their commercialization mandate. To be sure, some specific institutions have. While the University of Toronto leads the country in aggregate measures of commercialization, the University of Waterloo is Canada's most successful entrepreneurial university relative to its size. The depth and breadth of corporate-university research ties at Waterloo are illustrated by the relatively large amount of private funding it attracts and its cooperative education programs, where students complete work terms in industry as part of their curriculum. During a 2005 speaking tour, Bill Gates noted that in most years Microsoft hires "more students out of Waterloo than any other university in the world" (cited in Bramwell and Wolfe 2008: 1181–82). Waterloo has also shown a special aptitude for acquiring patents and generating spin-offs. This does not simply involve a few big companies (like Research in Motion); the entire Waterloo high technology cluster is effectively an off-shoot of the university. Many have credited Waterloo's commercial success to its entrepreneurial culture and its IP ownership model, which allows individual faculty (and students) to commercialize their ideas and retain full ownership rights.

Table 6.2: Intellectual Property in Canada's Higher Education Sector

	1999	2008	Increase
Invention Disclosures	893	1,613	+81%
New Patent Applications	656	1,791	+173%
Patents Held	1,915	5,908	+209%
New Licences and Options	232	524	+126%
Active Licenses and Options	1,165	3,343	+187%
Full-time equivalent employees engaged in IP management	178	321	+80%

Sources: Statistics Canada. 2010b. *Survey of Intellectual Property Commercialization in the Higher Education Sector 2008*; Statistics Canada. 2000. *Survey of Intellectual Property Commercialization in the Higher Education Sector 1999*.

Looking at the country as a whole, however, the financial benefits of commercialization have been limited at best. Even though Canadian universities have been adept at generating spin-off companies, these firms are much more likely to fail compared with U.S. firms, and their patents and licenses generate far less revenue. According to Karen Mazurkewich (2011), who co-directed a Canadian report on intellectual property, between 2002 and 2008 revenue from IP created at Canadian universities "was 1.14 percent of the total R&D expenditures, compared to five percent at U.S. schools ... While Canadian scientists are great at collaborating on publications, or sharing basic research data, our entrepreneurs are terrible at teaming up for the critical commercialization phase of business — helping carry an invention to market." Between 2004 and 2008 university revenues from IP were relatively small, at roughly $54 million per year. In 2004, the $51 million in income represented only 0.25 percent of total university revenues that year (Van Loon 2005). When the operational expenditures for IP management are factored in, this additional revenue is pared down to virtually nothing. And in 2008, the $53 million generated from IP paled in comparison with the nearly $2 billion in contract research undertaken by Canadian universities and hospitals (Statistics Canada 2010b). Increases in IP expenditures are also outpacing the income generated from these activities. Comments from technology transfer officers confirm that most universities in Canada generate little valuable IP and almost no revenue from commercialization. As one officer explained, "there are very few universities that actually make money off their patent portfolios" (Bubela and Caulfield 2010: 449). Just as the Expert Panel on the Commercialization of University Research recognized back in 1999, commercialization has yet to be proven as a viable way to augment Canadian university budgets.

Of course, Canadian universities are not alone in this regard. Very few universities around the world actually benefit from patenting and technology transfer. For the rest, these activities result in little additional revenue and, in many cases, financial losses (Bubela and Caulfield 2010; Slaughter and Rhoades 2008). Typical of market inefficiencies in the broader economy, market failure in higher education

Table 6.3: IP Expenditures and Revenues

	1999	2004	2005	2006	2007	2008
Total operational expenditures for IP management ($ thousands)	22,018	36,927	41,544	42,492	41,851	51,124
Total Income from IP ($ thousands)	24,770	51,210	55,173	59,689	52,477	53,183

Sources: Statistics Canada. 2010d. *Survey of Intellectual Property Commercialization in the Higher Education Sector 2008*; Statistics Canada. 2000. *Survey of Intellectual Property Commercialization in the Higher Education Sector 1999*.

is underwritten by the public in the form of higher tuition and other subsidies. Clearly, the financial problems of Canadian universities will not be solved (or even mitigated) by the commercialization of research. However, the lack of financial benefits is of small significance when compared with other outcomes associated with this aspect of corporatization. Corporate involvement in university research has corrupted academic scholarship, jeopardized the integrity of the public university and threatened the public interest.

CORRUPTING ACADEMIC RESEARCH

Supporters of corporatization present the benefits of university-industry research ties in clear, decisive terms. These purported benefits include financial support for universities, commercially valuable product development, faculty access to R&D opportunities, enhanced technological innovation and scientific progress. Some even claim that industry funding and public-private partnerships enhance customary measures of academic quality, such as publication productivity (Crespo and Dridi 2007). As the Corporate-Higher Education Forum put it thirty years ago, these partnerships generate "an economy of research effort and a synergy of results that generates genuine payoffs to the partners and to Canadian society as a whole" (Maxwell and Currie 1984: 83). Given the integrity of academic science and the safeguards of the peer review process, proponents also argue that concerns about academic freedom, research secrecy or conflicts of interest are largely unfounded. And, even if the process does result in reduced knowledge sharing or unethical research practices in some instances, the benefits are presented as overshadowing the costs. For its advocates, then, "the new ethos of academic commercialism, operating at all levels of research institutions, is largely viewed as a proper, favorable tradeoff of values, where conflicts of interest are manageable and impossible to eliminate and where the basic integrity of the university can be protected" (Krimsky 2003: 3).

The evidence, even just using the brief cost-benefit comparison above, suggests otherwise. The corporatization of academic research has not been beneficial for universities or for society, and the negative impact on academic research itself far outweighs any supposed benefits. Moreover, corporatization has corrupted the basic values that have historically defined scientific and other academic research, and compromised the ability of the university to act as a site of independent inquiry and thought. In large measure, the corrupting influence of corporate power stems from the fundamental antagonism between corporate and academic institutions and their opposing research cultures. This antagonism is evident in several aspects of the research process.

RESEARCH TOPICS

Corporate influence crosses all aspects of the academic research process, including at the outset with the selection of research topics and projects. Rather than setting their own research agendas in response to social needs, academics are increasingly joining with partners from the private sector to define their research priorities. As a result, the basis for deciding what knowledge is worth pursuing is defined more and more by the criteria of corporate demand. Many areas of university research have been affected by this shift. In agricultural research, for instance, the influence of agrochemical companies has moved research agendas in the direction of resource intensive production technologies, genetic engineering and chemical-based pest and weed control. In the latter case, hundreds of millions of dollars are being allocated to the development of new toxic pesticides and chemical herbicides in university labs, while the study of biological control and crop rotation — controlling agriculture pests through means other than pesticides — has all but disappeared. According to John McMurtry (2009: 17), independent agricultural research in areas such as "integrated pest management, organic farming for productive efficiency, management-intensive grazing, small-scale producer cooperatives, alternatives to factory-processed livestock and avoidance of ecological contamination by genetically-engineered commodities" have been "silently selected out" of universities because corporations are not interested in funding them.

The same is true in many areas of health research. In recent years, far more resources have been put into investigating the cellular/genetic basis for cancer than into environmental causes, which are now widely recognized to be key causal factors. Not only are corporations unwilling to fund research into the linkages between cancers and industrial toxins, but corporate and government funding programs have worked to redirect cancer research from causes to cures (Thompson 2008). It is often claimed that without the money and support of large corporations, universities would lack the capacity (and the incentive) to produce new life-saving drugs, medicines and therapies. The reality, however, is quite different. Corporate influence has diverted academic attention away from vaccine research and diseases that affect the world's poor (such as malaria, schistosomiasis, tuberculosis and dengue fever). In fact, a recent study of the top fifty-four Canadian and U.S. research universities found that less than 3 percent of research funding is devoted to diseases that affect the world's poorest people (Universities Allied for Essential Medicines 2013). The report also notes that more than a billion people currently suffer from "neglected diseases," or diseases that are "rarely researched by the private sector because most of those affected are too poor to provide a market for new drugs." For commercial reasons, the vast majority of research investments by the pharmaceutical industry (and increasingly universities) focus on what are called "lifestyle drugs" — high-profit treatments for obesity, baldness, wrinkles and sexual dysfunction. Of course, the impact of corporatization on academic research agendas is not limited to the natural and health sciences. Laureen Snider (2000, 2003) has documented a precipitous decline in social science research on corporate crime, for example. She attributes this decline to the unwillingness of private sponsors and governments to fund this type of research, and to political pressures both inside and outside of the academy.

In some ways, academics may be viewed as victims in this process. University researchers are under intense pressure to secure outside funding and many would be unable to continue their research programs without such support. A recent survey by researchers at OISE found that three quarters of Canadian academics said that pressures to raise external funds had increased since their first appointment (Tamburri 2012). Furthermore, the distinction between research choices made out of scholarly interest and those made because of funding availability is not an easy one to draw. Many academics believe they are engaging with particular topics out of their own free choice when in reality they are often "adjusting their curiosities" to match the interests of available sponsors (Schmidt 2000). Many funders are aware that they can arouse the necessary interest in academic circles without formally dictating research priorities. On the other hand, academics are also active participants in the selection of their areas of research. The fact that so many acquiesce to (or embrace) corporate lines of research suggests a high level of conscious complicity. According to Polster (2000: 30), many Canadian scholars freely admit to doing "whatever it takes" to strengthen their granting performance, including "switching their research topics to well-funded areas in which they often have lesser expertise." In sum, although corporate-university ties may reduce the ability of some academics to engage in alternative or critical research agendas, the selection of research topics are moral and political choices that cannot simply be blamed on financial necessity or the demands of funders.

RESEARCH SECRECY

Universities have often been an important source of the knowledge commons, the "cooperative human constructions that protect and/or enable universal access to the life good of knowledge ... This knowledge is shared, not privatized, packaged, priced, and profited from" (Sumner 2008: 193). The academy has similarly been described as a "gift economy" (Bollier 2002). The gift economy of academia presumes that research and scholarly resources are produced in accordance with publicly articulated purposes, and supported by the free production and circulation of knowledge, both within and outside of the university. Gift economies are also powerful systems for eliciting behaviors that the market cannot, such as honesty, information sharing and mutual collaboration. In their seminal work on the scientific enterprise, Robert Merton (1973) and Michael Polanyi (1969) reached similar conclusions about the nature of academic research. They argue that these are not simply proscriptions for the way academics ought to behave; rather, the open and disinterested nature of academic inquiry is precisely what makes it so innovative. As Jennifer Washburn (2005: 195) explains, the system "does a remarkably good job of speeding the creation of new discoveries, hastening public disclosure, and enabling peers to evaluate and replicate new research findings to ensure their accuracy — all of which helps to broaden the stock of reliable public knowledge that is available for future research and innovation." The knowledge commons and academic gift economies are idealized practices, of course. Research secrecy has always had a place in academia, as some professors have always been reluctant to share ideas out of fear that they will be appropriated by others. Nonetheless this practice runs counter to academic ideals and has increased under corporatization.

One of the ways that corporatization has fostered academic secrecy is through the creation of a more competitive, utilitarian and performance-based research culture. As publication productivity becomes more important for academic appointment and promotion, there are fewer incentives for collaboration and knowledge sharing among researchers (except in superficial instances of padding one's curriculum vitae through "honorary" publications). The same is true for graduate students, whose PhD experiences increasingly resemble competitive self-marketing marathons. And, as noted previously, greater pressures has been placed on faculty to obtain external grants, which has helped to transform the university from a knowledge sharing institution to a site of competitive fundraisers (Chan and Fisher 2008b). As Polster (2007a: 610) discovered in her research, the importance placed on grant acquisition "is reducing some colleagues' willingness to support one another in a variety of ways, such as reading or discussing research proposals and papers. It is also taking a toll on academic collegialism and morale." Polster (2000) also found that there is a growing tendency for Canadian academics to avoid scientific conferences for fear of disclosing valuable information, and, when they do attend, these "private academics" often refuse to provide details of their research or engage in discussions that might compromise funding or commercial interests. These trends are only amplified by the fact that researchers and departments that bring in more funding enjoy greater power and influence in the corporate university. The work of academic capitalists in particular, which is less likely to involve open knowledge sharing, is being prioritized over less lucrative forms of inquiry.

The culture of secrecy and competitiveness is produced in other ways too, including through non-disclosure and intellectual property agreements. Whereas academic secrecy is typically a short-term expedient to ensure publication, commercial secrecy can be a lengthy process that remains in place for as long as proprietors deem it to be in their interests. In some cases, contractual arrangements can force academics to transfer the results of their research to the firms who paid for it. In others, the publication of findings may be delayed until a corporate sponsor obtains a patent on its intellectual property. Selective disclosure and withholding of data may also occur if the research results are potentially damaging to the corporation and/or its bottom line.

Research secrecy can have important human consequences. Efforts to maintain research secrecy by certain industries, such as the pharmaceutical industry, have threatened the health and safety of individuals. Some drug companies go so far as to use "gag orders, appealing to trade secrets, concealing [drug risks] behind a veil of attorney-client privilege, settling legal actions out of court to hide data and documents, [and] stalking and harassing academic critics" (Healy, 2012: 119). Moreover, IP protections such as patents are highly protectionist and tend to restrict the diffusion of knowledge to and from universities (Murray and Stern 2007; Rosell and Agrawal 2009). As a result, they inhibit the amount of knowledge that is available in the public domain, including in areas such as food production and medicine. Roughly one quarter of patented inventions in agricultural biotechnology — which have been tied up in restrictive commercial agreements — originated in public institutions at the public's expense (Washburn 2005). The same is true of many medicines (such as drugs for AIDS) and even human genes, which have been patented and exclusively licensed to biopharmaceutical companies (such as the gene responsible for hereditary breast cancer).

Although the extent of research secrecy in Canada is not well documented, it has been explored extensively in the U.S. This evidence suggests that researchers with industry support are more likely to: (i) report that "trade secrets" resulted from their research (information kept secret to protect its proprietary value); (ii) be denied the information/data necessary to publish their results; (iii) delay publication of their research; and (iv) deny other academics access to their data and research findings (see, for example, Krimsky 2003; Washburn 2005). Graduate students may be especially vulnerable to secrecy agreements because they rely on the prompt publication of their findings in order to secure funding or employment, yet they are often prevented from publishing in a timely fashion or even from completing their projects. An investigation of graduate students and post-doc holders in computer science, chemical engineering and the life sciences found that one in four had been denied information relevant to their research, and this was especially prevalent in research groups with links to industry (Holden 2006).

Countless examples can be used to illustrate how corporate-university research partnerships stifle the free dissemination of knowledge. Professor Stéphane McLachlan and graduate student Ian Mauro, at the University of Manitoba (U of M), received a grant from the SSHRC in 2001 to undertake a project on the risks and benefits of genetically modified crops (GMCs). As part of the project, the researchers, along with local activists, produced a documentary film to "bring opinions, concerns and local knowledge of rural communities to the forefront of the GMC debate" (Sanders 2005: 34). Predictably, the opinions expressed by small farmers were highly critical of Monsanto's agricultural practices. Upon review, the U of M administration refused to allow the film to be screened and blocked its release for nearly three years, fearing litigation from Monsanto and not wanting to jeopardize negotiations that would see the company's Canadian headquarters moved to the U of M's smartpark. Public pressure and intervention by the CAUT eventually forced the administration to concede to screening the film, but with a disclaimer that it did not represent the views of the university. In the U.S., the oil giant British Petroleum (BP) has been involved in a similar conflict. In the first few months after the Gulf oil disaster in 2010, BP enlisted academic scientists into exclusive research and consulting contracts that were replete with secrecy clauses and barred them from making their findings public (Lea 2010). Not only was BP attempting to subvert the scientific process, but it was also putting measures in place to ensure it would control academic data and evidence about the disaster. Both of these incidents, and many others like them, clearly demonstrate how the deepening of corporate-university alliances under corporatization has the potential to stifle research in the public interest.

To conclude, research secrecy is incompatible with academic values and has negative implications for researchers, universities and the public at large. Within the academy, secrecy disrupts collegial relationships, reduces knowledge sharing, and promotes waste as researchers needlessly duplicate work that was not made freely available. Secrecy also restricts the course of knowledge production because scientific progress depends on researchers building on the findings of others. Most importantly, research secrecy inhibits the amount of knowledge that is available in the public domain.

RESEARCH BIAS

Corporatization has compromised university research by introducing a fundamental bias brought on by conflicts of interest. In general, a conflict of interest occurs when a person is inclined or obliged to pursue interests that compete with one another in a fundamental way. More specifically in this context, conflict of interest situations are those in which financial or other personal considerations may compromise (or have the appearance of compromising) a researcher's professional judgement in conducting research or reporting research results. For example, senior academic economists who occupy lucrative and high-ranking positions in governments and/or major financial institutions are clearly mired in conflicts of interest. As Charles Ferguson (2010) observes, "the economics profession — in economics departments, and in business, public policy, and law schools — has become so compromised by conflicts of interest that it now functions almost as a support group for financial services and other industries whose profits depend heavily on government policy."

What is particularly noteworthy about academic conflicts of interests is that they are rarely disclosed. One study examining 62,000 articles in 210 scientific journals found that only one half of one percent included relevant information about authors' research-related financial ties, even though all of the journals formally required such disclosure (see King 1999). In Canada, a CAUT investigation of twelve university-industry partnerships (seven research collaborations and five program collaborations) found that only one of the agreements required disclosure of individual or institutional conflicts of interest, and only one had a provision prohibiting financial conflicts of interest (CAUT 2013). Conflicts of interest may be especially damaging for universities; short of outright fraud, nothing is as threatening to the integrity of the university than the perception that it has been bought off.

One of the main consequences of these kinds of conflicts is research bias. In some cases, research bias results from direct corporate censorship or academic corruption. For example, an investigation of university-industry engineering research centres found that 35 percent allowed corporations to delete information from papers prior to publication (Washburn 2005). Likewise, a small minority of academics have deliberately falsified results to produce findings that accord with their interests or those of their sponsor. However, a much more prescient cause of research bias is the unconscious or internalized effect of financial benefit or career advancement. The logic is simple: researchers with a vested interest in reaching a particular conclusion will tend to weigh arguments and evidence in a biased fashion. The mechanisms through which this occurs are varied and subtle, including how questions are framed, how studies are designed, how contrary interpretations are emphasized and how conclusions are worded. Complicating matters is that the vast majority of academics perceive themselves to be objective and impartial, and corporate sponsors often recognize the importance of encouraging researchers to "feel" impartial (Freudenburg 2005). In any event, a substantial body of empirical evidence suggests there is a "funding effect," where even if corporate sponsors allow researchers free reign over the research process — which they often do not — projects financed by big business are far more likely to reach conclusions that support the interests of their sponsor (Krimsky 2013).

Many areas of academic research have been affected. One is food and nutrition. Researcher Marion Nestle (2007) has documented the extensive network through which food companies sponsor nutrition research, nutrition conferences, food and nutrition journals and the activities of professional societies. As a result, research findings in this area often favour the interests of their sponsors. In fact, Nestle reports that sponsorship almost invariably predicts the results of research into specific foods or nutrients. Similarly, Lenard Lesser and his colleagues (2007) looked at studies on the relationship between soft drinks and childhood obesity and found that while independent studies almost always find an association between habitual consumption of soft drinks and obesity, industry-sponsored studies almost never do.

Tobacco research offers another example of how industry funding distorts the research process. One study found that 94 percent of articles that had authors who were affiliated with the tobacco industry concluded that second hand smoke was not harmful. In contrast, only 13 percent of articles where the authors had no tobacco ties reached the same conclusion (Barnes and Bero 1998). Taking into account other variables (article quality, peer review status, article topic and year of publication), the study found that having an author with a tobacco-company affiliation was the only variable associated with the conclusion that second-hand smoke was not harmful. The basic strategy of the tobacco industry has been to use university scientists to make the dangers of cigarettes appear controversial. These companies depend on the fact that observers tend to associate academic research with independence and impartiality. Of course, this is not only true of tobacco companies. "Decency by association" is one of the reasons why most corporations that produce harmful products or engage in destructive practices actively seek academic partnerships. In the area of climate science, this is precisely why "academics, and not the president of Imperial Oil, are chosen to deliver the message that global warming is not occurring" (Gutstein 2009: 305). The ability of the tobacco industry to downplay the risks of tobacco consumption partly resided in the extensive network of ties it had created with medical researchers. Although these relationships have dissipated in recent years, the same cannot be said about the relationship between academic medicine and the pharmaceutical industry. More than any other area of academic research, conflicts of interest in biomedicine are threatening the health and well-being of people around the world.

BIG PHARMA, BIOTECHNOLOGY AND THE PERVERSION OF ACADEMIC MEDICINE

Historically, medical schools and researchers advanced medical science (and built their reputations) by maintaining clear boundaries between the academy and industry. In the area of pharmaceuticals, academic distrust of business ran especially high (Atkinson-Grosjean and Fairly 2009). In Canada, this changed in the late 1980s when government support for medical research declined and medical schools embraced the pharmaceutical industry as a way to maintain a stable influx of new funds. These efforts were facilitated in 1992 by the creation of the Council for Biomedical and Health Research to generate public support for drug-related research. At the same time, the field of biotechnology expanded in Canadian universities and set the stage for widespread commercial involvement in biomedicine.

Over the past few decades, the life sciences — mostly represented by biotechnology — has accounted for a disproportionate share of Canadian universities' commercial output (Niosi 2006). The integration of universities and biotechnology firms is now so commonplace that it has created the unusual situation where the field's leading academic scientists dominate technology transfer to industry, while many of the most influential publications are written by research teams from the private sector (Kleinman and Vallas 2001; Vallas and Kleinman 2008).

Today, the association between Big Pharma, medical science and university facilities and researchers is well established. Drug companies spend billions each year (more than they spend on consumer advertising or research) wooing physicians in order to generate support for their products, align medical research with corporate interests, and amass a network of well-respected consultants and lobbyists. According to one estimate, 94 percent of psychiatrists-in-training have accepted gifts from pharmaceutical firms by their third year (Ferrie 2013). Further, Canadian medical researcher Joel Lexchin (2010) notes that drug companies in Canada spend between $2.4 and $4.8 billion annually pushing their drugs to doctors. These figures are not surprising considering doctors have sole prescription power over thousands of pharmaceutical drugs that generate hundreds of millions of prescriptions every year. According to psychiatrist David Healy (2012), the industry monitors the prescribing habits of most doctors in the Western world, and data on who prescribes what is used by corporations to shape their marketing strategies. The fact that drugs are made available on a prescription-only basis has put a "relatively small group of people with no training in or awareness of marketing techniques — doctors — in the gun sights of the most sophisticated marketing machinery on the planet" (8–9). The pharmaceutical industry also provides hundreds of millions of dollars in financial subsidies to medical journals via the purchase of advertisements, special supplements and reprints, and it spends billions more on continuing medical education (CME) programs. The proportion of CME programs that are funded by industry has climbed steadily in recent years. Sales and marketing divisions dominate corporate decision-making around the distribution of CME money because the primary goal of these "public service" programs is to push new drugs.

Through these marketing and outreach efforts, corporations have infiltrated medical schools. In the U.S., one survey found that nearly two thirds of department heads at medical schools and teaching hospitals had financial or other ties to industry (Mangan 2007). According to the *New England Journal of Medicine*, a national sample of over 3,100 U.S. physicians revealed that 94 percent were involved with drug companies and 28 percent were paid consultants for the industry (Campbell et al. 2007). A further set of connections involves the millions of clinical trials for drugs and other medical treatments that are conducted in academic medical centres around the world. Industry funds approximately 70 percent of all clinical trials and 70 percent of these are run by contract research organizations that produce data that is wholly owned by their sponsors. Although clinical trials are ostensibly "research" activities, a large proportion amount to marketing exercises and commercial product testing. Remarkably, even members of institutional review boards and committees, whose job it is to "police the researchers" and protect human participants in medical trials, have extensive relationships with the drug industry (Brainard 2006; Campbell et al. 2003). A recent study of 288 panel members responsible for clinical practice guidelines in Canada and the U.S. found that over half of these individuals had financial conflicts of interest (Neuman et al. 2011).

As this cursory review makes clear, a myriad of potential conflicts and inherent tensions are involved in the relationship between corporations, the medical profession and biomedical researchers. In fact, medical journal editors now frequently complain that they can no longer find academic experts without conflicts of interest. Ellen Schrecker (2010) recounts an incident where the *New England Journal of Medicine* decided to ban authors with a financial interest in any company (or its competitor) that made a product discussed in the author's work. It eventually had to add the word "significant" because the editors could find only one submission over the previous two years that complied with the requirement. Likewise, the *Canadian Medical Association Journal* attempted to implement a similar conflict of interest policy but the editors could not find enough qualified researchers who did not have ties to drug companies.

The most common conflicts are financial in nature; these range from the provision of "hands-off" corporate sponsorships to situations where researchers hold a personal financial stake in their research outcomes. The latter cases are especially troublesome, yet surprisingly common. In his seminal study, Sheldon Krimsky and his colleagues (1996) studied the industry connections of the authors of 789 scientific papers published by 1,105 researchers in 14 major life science and biomedical journals. They found that 34 percent of the articles (267) had at least one lead author with a financial interest in the outcome of the research (not one article disclosed this interest). Moreover, the 34 percent figure likely underrepresented the actual level of conflict of interest because the researchers were unable to account for certain variables, such as authors who received consulting fees from companies involved in commercial applications of their work. Shortly after the release of Krimsky's findings, the leading life sciences journal *Nature* published a statement in which it acknowledged that financial conflicts of interests were common in biomedical research, but asserted that this was of little consequence. According to the journal, Krimsky's study provided no evidence that the "undeclared interests led to any fraud, deception or bias in presentation, and until there is evidence that there are serious risks of such malpractice, this journal will persist in its stubborn belief that research as we publish it is indeed research, not business" (Nature 1997: 469).

Since *Nature's* aggressive rejoinder, an abundance of evidence has been accumulated supporting the hypothesis that corporate funding and conflicts of interest are associated with research bias in the medical field. This pattern holds not only for research where investigators have a personal stake in the outcome, but for industry-sponsored studies more generally. For example, Mildred Cho and Lisa Bero (1996) found that 98 percent of drug studies funded by pharmaceutical companies reached favourable conclusions about drug safety and efficacy, compared with 79 percent of studies not funded by industry. Another investigation found that studies of cancer drugs funded by drug companies were nearly eight times less likely to reach unfavourable conclusions about the drug compared with similar studies funded by non-profit organizations (Friedberg et al. 1999). Similarly, medical researchers in Toronto reported a strong association between purported drug safety and financial conflicts of interest (Stelfox et al. 1998). More specifically, they found that 96 percent of authors whose findings supported the safety of a particular class of drug had a financial relationship with the drug manufacturers, compared with 60 percent of "neutral" authors and 37 percent of authors who were critical of the drug's safety.

More recently, several meta-analyses of the biomedical literature have provided extremely compelling evidence about the linkages between industry funding and research bias. The first by Justin Bekelman, Yan Li and Cary Gross (2003) looked at research published over a twenty-three-year period on the extent, impact and management of conflicts of interest in biomedical research. They found a strong and consistent correlation between industry sponsorship (mainly, but not all pharmaceutical) and pro-industry conclusions. In a similar review, Lexchin et al. (2003) found that studies funded by pharmaceutical companies were far more likely to have outcomes favouring their sponsors than studies sponsored by other organizations, and that "systematic bias" favours products that are made by companies funding university research. Some years later, Sergio Sismondo (2008) found that seventeen out of nineteen studies investigating the effects of drug company sponsorships showed an association (usually a strong one) between industry sponsorship and pro-industry conclusions.[5] Taken together, these studies illustrate the impact of corporate power in academic medicine and the important differences between publicly funded versus privately funded research.

It should be noted that in addition to research bias, outright research fraud is also on the rise. In a comprehensive review of retracted biomedical and life sciences articles listed in the PubMed database, 43.4 percent were found to be retracted due to fraud or suspected fraud (Fang, Steen and Casadevall 2012). The review also found that the percentage of scientific articles retracted due to fraud has increased tenfold since 1975. A second review of survey research on scientific misconduct found that falsifying data is far more common than previously estimated, and that this form of misconduct is reported most frequently in the case of medical and pharmacological research (Fanelli 2009). Further, approximately one third of respondents in the study admitted to some form of questionable research practice, such as altering the research design, methodology or results in response to pressures from funders. More evidence of biomedical fraud came to light in 2012, when a team of one hundred scientists tried to replicate the results of fifty-three of the most widely cited cancer research papers. This effort resulted in only six research studies being validated, while the rest could not be replicated. Many of the studies were apparently bogus (Sharav 2014). "Shockingly," writes medical journalist Helke Ferrie (2013: 284), "this was not Pharma-generated junk science, but came from university researchers who misled companies wanting to use their research for new cancer drugs. Indeed, there is no honour among thieves."

Corporate funding and conflicts of interest help to explain the preponderance of research bias in academic medicine, but it is not the whole story. Under corporatization, academics are ceding control over every stage of the clinical research process.

Ghost Writing and Ghost Management

As part of the biomedical research regime, corporate employees routinely write "academic" papers that emerge from corporate-sponsored research. This practice — often referred to as "ghost writing" — generally works as follows: when research results are ready to be reported, a corporation's marketing department will contract medical writers from a public relations or "medical communications" firm to produce a manuscript. After several drafts have been completed, the manuscript is then inspected by the company's marketing and legal departments for approval. It is usually around this time that an academic "author" will inspect and sign off on the article. When the article subsequently appears in a pre-selected journal, the ghost writer(s) either disappear(s) or is subtly acknowledged as providing some form of editorial assistance. Frequently, the academic who assumes authorship will not have had access to the data on which the study is based and, in some cases, is simply paid to have his or her name appear on the publication. The compensation rates for professors who participate in ghost writing generally range from $1,000 to $2,500 per article; however, payments can be as high as $10,000, especially if the writer presents the findings at conferences or in medical education lectures (Elliot 2010; Krimsky 2003). Meanwhile, professional ghost writers are often paid between $10,000 and $20,000 per article and have annual salaries that can exceed $100,000 (Mirowski and Van Horn 2005; Schafer 2004).

How prevalent is medical research ghost writing? Given the inherent secrecy of the process, not much information is available. What evidence there is suggests, however, that the practice is common, and even extends to medical textbook publishing (see, for example, Basken 2009; Lacasse and Leo 2010; Wilson 2010). In fact, one study estimates that the majority of articles on lucrative pharmaceutical drugs in leading medical journals may be wholly or partially ghost written (Healy and Cattell 2003). It is important to note that many ghost-writing campaigns are launched (or continue) after evidence of dangerous or deadly drug side effects are produced. Examples include Wyeth (now part of Pfizer) and the hormone replacement drugs Prempro and Premarin (breast cancer, heart disease, stroke); Eli Lilly and the antipsychotic drug Zyprexa (obesity and diabetes); and GlaxoSmithKlein and the antidepressant drug Paxil (suicidal ideation). Healy (2008, 2012) has even suggested that in some areas — such as on-patent drugs and the safety/effectiveness of antidepressants for children — virtually all of the published literature includes material that is authored by medical writers or pharmaceutical company personnel. It follows that studies of antidepressants in children "offer the greatest known divide in medicine between what published reports in the scientific literature say on the one side and what the raw data in fact show" (Healy 2012: 149). What published reports say is that these drugs are remarkably safe and effective. What the data show is that children are killing themselves at a much higher rate while they are on some of these drugs. For years, psychiatric drugs prescribed to children and adolescents have been associated with a long and adverse list of physical and emotional effects (Whitaker 2010). If medications that carry a high risk of disability and death in children are considered fair game for this kind of corporate-academic fakery, it would appear that there are few, if any, limits.

As disturbing as these practices are, ghost writing is only one part of an increasingly sophisticated system of "ghost management" in medical research (Sismondo 2007, 2009). Ghost management refers to the broader phenomenon whereby drug companies and their agents direct and shape the entire research process, from funding and design to publication and promotion. This process often begins before the onset of the research trials when company officials, in consultation with "publication planning" companies, shape the research design. The corporations participating in these networks sometimes manipulate trial design in ways that escape detection by peer review processes, including by conducting a trial drug against a treatment known to be inferior, excluding placebo responders, and testing a drug against too low a dose from a competitor's drug (Smith 2005). Many companies also conduct multicentre trials and artificially select for results that are favourable to their interests. In fact, 30 to 40 percent of clinical trials are never reported on because they fail to produce the "correct" results (Healy 2012; Kirsch 2010).

Before and during the trials, the corporate network will also select target journals and audiences, anticipate peer-review criticism and identify which academics (ideally key "opinion leaders") are going to be included as authors. Some of these opinion leaders — who are often considered the most distinguished in the field

— are creations of the pharmaceutical industry. In part, this is because they are repeatedly selected for ghost authorship, meaning their names may appear on eight hundred to one thousand articles. In addition to these recruitment efforts, industry can also fund their research and travel, make them investigators on clinical trials, put them on scientific programs, and arrange for them to present at continuing medical education events. It is especially important for publication planners to get involved early if "there is a need to create a market or to create an understanding of unmet need," otherwise known as "disease mongering" or "selling sickness" (Sismondo 2009: 177).

The size of the publication planning industry continues to grow. Over fifty different agencies now openly advertise publication-planning services, and many of them boast of having hundreds of employees who handle hundreds of manuscripts each year. Many of these companies are quite open about the kinds of services they offer. BioPharma Solutions, for one, explains that it specializes in "ghostwriting reviews and original papers" for peer-reviewed scientific journals. Phase Five Communications' website opens with the slogan, "Spin your science into gold." The industry is large enough that two international associations of publication planners exist to organize seminars and meetings. According to Sismondo (2009: 172), up to 40 percent of "important journal reports of clinical trials of new drugs (and, more anecdotally, perhaps a higher percentage of meeting presentations on clinical trials) are ghost-managed through to publication." As a result, not only are most published reports of clinical trials likely to be ghostwritten in some way, but roughly a quarter of published trials are altered so that a negative result for a drug will have been transformed into evidence that the drug is effective and safe (Healy 2012).

The large number of medical writing and medical education and communication firms, whose tasks are generally limited to ghost writing and preparing presentations, may be viewed as adjuncts to the more sophisticated work of publication planners. Medical journals should not be seen as dupes in this process, as many editors have extensive dealings with publication planners and are fully aware of the process. Ghost management and publication planning are primarily concerned with generating monetary value from scientific research. Needless to say, they amplify research bias because commercial interests are involved at virtually every stage of the research process. These practices should not be seen as a breakdown of ethical standards or editorial oversight; on the contrary, this is a well-organized industry that forms an integral part of the corporate production of knowledge.

Assessing the Impact
The corporatization of academic medicine has had a profound impact on universities, researchers and the public. For universities and the medical profession, it has

produced an unprecedented crisis of credibility in the published literature and severely tarnished the academy as a source of unbiased research. For researchers, it has reduced their ability to pursue independent lines of scholarship, increased restrictions on academic freedom and, in some instances, resulted in severe consequences for scholars who defy this corporate-university complex. The high profile cases of Nancy Olivieri and David Healy in Canada, the details of which have been documented elsewhere, are cases in point.[6]

The public impact, however, goes much deeper. For one, underwriting the costs of drug research is expensive. Canadian taxpayers pay most of the costs of discovering and developing new drugs, and they pay again as consumers for mass marketed treatments that offer little or no benefit. Evidence from Canada and France suggests that no more than 15 percent of new drugs represent any significant therapeutic advantage over those that already exist (Lexchin 2010). Likewise, some widely used drugs such as antidepressants have been shown to be only marginally more effective than placebos (Kirsch 2010).

There are also severe risks associated with corporatized medical research. Not only are violations of human research protection rules on the rise, but there is reason to believe that adverse trial events are increasingly treated as "confidential commercial information" and never made public (Washburn 2005). As well, the many drug scandals that have erupted in recent years illustrate the human toll that can result from corporate sponsorships, compromised clinical trials, research bias and data suppression. In the case of Merck's drug Vioxx, for example, millions of people took the drug before it was exposed as causing a serious risk of heart attack and stroke, a fact that was known to academic and corporate researchers but explained away and eventually suppressed (Nesi 2008; Schafer 2008). Of course, it was not only compromised research that allowed this deadly medication to remain on the market for so long. Merck executives also "discredited" and "neutralized" academics and medical researchers who were critical of Vioxx (Rout 2009). One estimate suggests that half a million premature deaths in the U.S. alone may have been caused by Vioxx use (Cockburn 2012).

Compromised research and publishing practices also explain, in part, why hundreds of thousands of Americans die each year from "correctly" prescribed drugs (Starfield 2000). Using data from the Canadian Medical Association, Ferrie (2009) contends that approximately 23,000 thousand people die in Canada each year from prescribed drugs, which is surely an underestimate since it only represents the incidence of reported deaths. Moreover, Canadians cannot rely on protections from Health Canada. Member of Parliament and drug activist Terence Young — who tragically lost his fifteen year old daughter to the drug Prepulsid in 2000 — reports that Health Canada has been "hopelessly compromised" because of its growing partnerships with the pharmaceutical industry and the resulting conflicts of interest (Young 2012). At the same time, the number of adults and children with a mental illness continues to rise, with some researchers concluding that pharmaceutical drugs are fueling, rather than alleviating, the epidemic of mental illness (Whitaker 2010). All of this calls into question whether it is safe for patients to trust any information about drugs that doctors and medical researchers provide. With approximately 20 percent of the North American population currently consuming pharmaceutical drugs for anxiety, depression and other ailments, and with pharmaceuticals and medicine accounting for the largest number of industry-sponsored research contracts in Canadian universities, these issues could not be more pressing (Council of Canadian Academies 2012b).

While there has been some effort to address these problems on the part of medical schools and journals in recent years, most research universities and medical centres remain heavily integrated with and influenced by the pharmaceutical industrial complex. There is also increasing corporate and government pressure to reduce regulations on drug research and eliminate independent watchdog groups. In 2011, for example, the Harper government put the interests of industry ahead of patient safety when the CIHR eliminated its internationally praised transparency requirement for full public disclosure of trial drug results. The policy, which was just three months old when it was scrapped, required scientists funded by the agency to reveal all their raw data to the public, regardless of what they chose to publish. More recently in 2013, the internationally acclaimed Therapeutics Initiative based out of the University of British Columbia, which had been conducting independent, evidence-based drug reviews for the B.C. government since the 1990s, had all of its funding suspended by the government due to pressure from Big Pharma. It has been reported, for example, that TI's work indirectly saved an estimated 500 lives in the province with its independent assessment of Vioxx (Canadian Health Coalition 2011). In the corporate university, marketing and profit continue to replace science as compromised research infiltrates the peer-reviewed literature and the "knowledge" base of physicians. "Medicine as we have known it," writes Healy (2012: 234), "is at death's door."

CORPORATIZATION AND SHIFTING RESEARCH AGENDAS

Corporatizing academic research — a process endorsed by the private sector, governments and universities alike — has gone hand in hand with the decline of basic research funding. It is useful, in closing, to briefly consider some of the long-term implications of this trend. For one, the importance of basic research to humanity is well documented. For hundreds of years, academic investigations that appeared to be irrelevant at the time have yielded many of the world's important scientific and technological advancements. In the area of medicine, these have included MRIs, x-rays and penicillin, just to name a few. Indeed, the majority of scientific breakthroughs in virtually every field have resulted from basic research conducted in academic settings built and supported largely by public funds. Although Canada currently ranks fourth in the world in terms of the quality of its basic peer reviewed scientific research, it continues to lag well behind other countries in the generation of intellectual property (Council of Canadian Academies 2012b). The response of the federal government has been to wind down basic research, hand over scientific resources to the private sector, and invest in research with immediate commercial application. It has also cut funding to dozens of world renowned research institutes, laid off thousands of federally employed scientists, closed down federal research libraries, and even resorted to old-fashioned "book burnings," presumably in an effort to undermine basic research on the environment and climate change (Nikiforuk 2013). Needless to say, such a strategy is highly damaging from the point of view of the public interest.

There is reason to believe that this strategy is also damaging to the economic interests it purports to serve. This is because most of the major scientific discoveries and breakthroughs of major commercial significance have also been produced through basic research. Simply put, basic inquiry yields economic benefits (see Salter and Martin 2001). In fact, many of the private sector's most dynamic industries owe their origins and livelihood (not to mention profits) to publicly funded curiosity-driven research. This includes biotechnology and pharmaceuticals, which are often seen as quintessential examples of successful corporatization.[7] According to Nobel Prize-winning scientist Paul Berg, the biotech revolution "would not have happened had the whole thing been left to industry. Venture-capital people steered clear of anything that didn't have obvious commercial value or short-term impact. They didn't fund the basic research that made biotechnology possible" (cited in Washburn 2005: 241). Of course, while the economic argument for opposing the commercial research agenda may be important from an overall policy perspective, I would place the profits of corporations at the bottom of the list of reasons why the commercial agenda in higher education should be opposed. In any case, it is important (and even ironic) to recognize that by reducing the university's relative freedom from market constraints, governments and the private sector are, in all likelihood, working against their own interests.

NOTES

1 University research investments by the private (and not-for-profit) sectors rose from $910 million to $1.7 billion during this period (AUCC 2008a). In the preceding years, corporate funding for academic research had already advanced more rapidly in Canada compared with other G7 nations (Fisher at al. 2006). Universities also funded a larger and larger share of their own research expenses in the 1980s and 1990s. According to one estimate, the reliance of Canadian universities on their own private funds outpaced

most other advanced industrialized nations between 1981 and 2003 (Vincent-Lancrin 2006). In part, this is explained by the growth in unfunded institutional costs associated with sponsored research. These costs grew by $600 million between 1996–97 and 2006–07 alone (AUCC 2008a).

2   Since leaving the Canada School of Energy and Environment, Carson has been charged with illegal lobbying and influence peddling, some of which was connected to his work with the School (Leblanc 2014).

3   The number of staff ranges from one to around thirty. At some universities, the TTO is located on campus and fully integrated into the university's structure (such as Simon Fraser). At others, the TTO operates outside the institution, either as a non-profit corporation (such as Queen's) or for-profit corporation (such as Victoria). In either case, the corporation is wholly owned by the university.

4   The number of business incubators on Canadian campuses has grown rapidly in just the past few years. In 2013, for example, the Co-operators Centre for Business and Social Entrepreneurship at Guelph opened its Hub incubator program; Brock started its BioLinc incubator operating under the Goodman School of Business; Carleton's Sprott School of Business launched a venture accelerator for students and recent graduates called Campus Entrepreneurs; and the University of Ottawa created an Entrepreneurial Hub to promote entrepreneurship across all faculties and schools.

5   Within this larger review, Sismondo (2008) reports that of 100 articles published in the pulmonary/allergy literature, 98 percent of articles sponsored by drug companies reported findings that were favourable to the drug being studied (compared with 32 percent of other articles). In a sample of 542 articles on clinical trials in psychiatry, 78 percent of sponsored studies favoured the sponsor's drug versus only 48 percent of those without industry sponsorship.

6   For firsthand accounts, see Olivieri (2000) and Healy (2008). For useful overviews, see Schafer (2004) and Woodhouse (2009: Chapter 3). What was most disturbing about the two cases was not the behaviour of the drug companies but the behaviour of the university. When Olivieri and Healy were removed from their positions at the University of Toronto, university and hospital officials failed to recognize — or, at least, failed to acknowledge — that their actions represented outrageous violations of academic freedom. The treatment of Olivieri was especially heinous. Professor Margaret Somerville, Founding Director of the Faculty of Law's Centre for Medicine, Ethics and Law at McGill University, has stated that the Olivieri case "reads like a horror story on the involvement of corporations in university-based research" (cited in Woodhouse 2009: 109). Both cases would eventually become flashpoints for larger political debates about whistle-blowers and the influence of corporate money in academic medicine.

7   One Massachusetts Institute of Technology study found that publicly funded research was a critical contributor to the discovery of nearly all of the twenty-five most important new drugs introduced between 1970 and 1995 (Washburn 2005).

CHAPTER SEVEN

RESISTING THE CORPORATIZATION OF THE UNIVERSITY

Higher education has undergone a series of dramatic changes under corporatization. More and more, teaching is focused on vocational training and carried out by casualized labour, governance models reflect business objectives and modes of operation and research is conducted to serve corporate interests. Based on this state of affairs, some hold a pessimistic view of the "runaway" changes that universities are confronting. Writing about the restructuring taking place in higher education back in 2002, Paul Axelrod (2002: 5) remarked:

> It is possible that a decade from now our universities will resemble little more than giant training warehouses, where short-term corporate needs dictate curricula to students who are increasingly taught not by professors but by advanced, impersonal technology. Research, funded primarily by private industry, will be designed to produce profitably-sold products, and will no longer engage the study of non-marketable ideas. 'Higher' education will be banal and completely regulated by external authorities. Those interested in exploring the world of ideas might have to set up new institutions (without public funding).

Yet, Axelrod's vision has not yet come to pass. Canadian universities have not been reduced to simple "knowledge factories" or "handmaidens of industry," and they have not been entirely corrupted by corporate values. Professors in many academic fields are able to define and regulate their own research agendas, and universities continue to produce independent research consistent with the public interest. The responsibilities and mandates of public universities still hold, albeit tenuously, to the ideals of critical research, teaching and scholarship.

Canadian universities are, however, approaching a critical juncture. If they do not reverse the current move toward corporatization, they risk being permanently transformed into institutions whose primary purposes are job training and enhancing corporate profits. The idea that universities are approaching a "crisis" is not new. For many, a major shortcoming of this claim has been a failure to provide convincing evidence for it. As Glen Jones' argues (1990: 3), it is not enough to identify a problem or elements of decline, "one must provide evidence that the problem is of such a magnitude that a failure to resolve the problem will lead to a decisive moment in which some characteristic of higher education will be threatened." The evidence presented in this book rises to Jones' challenge. Taken together, it demonstrates how many of the defining characteristics of the public university are deeply threatened, and the fundamental conflict between university and business priorities and practices. It also reveals how the corporate university's system of governance and its approach to teaching and research involve fundamentally negative consequences for instructors, for researchers, for students and for the public.

In the face of this crisis, there are several visions and strategies that have been or could be used to resist the corporatization of higher education. In my view, resistance efforts should be informed by evidence of the corporatization process itself. This evidence supports that there is a deep incompatibility or mismatch between university and corporate institutions, which means that strategies that simply aim to "regulate" corporatization — or accommodate the broader process through piecemeal reforms — will be ineffective in the long-term. To meaningfully challenge corporatization and its impacts, students and faculty need to locate resistance efforts within a wider critique of the capitalist system and form alliances with broader social movements operating outside of the university.

REGULATING CORPORATIZATION

"Centrist" critics, such as former Harvard President Derek Bok (2004), tend to support the use of regulatory strategies to address corporatization, thereby occupying the dominant, middle ground in debates over university restructuring. These critiques argue that corporatization is problematic, use a cost-benefit approach to evaluate it, and put forward a set of regulatory reforms to address it. In his work, Roger Geiger (2004: 265–66) presents some of the pros and cons typical of cost-benefit analyses of educational restructuring:

> The marketplace has, on balance, brought universities greater resources, better students, a far larger capacity for advancing knowledge, and a more productive role in the [economy]. At the same time, it has diminished the sovereignty of universities over their own activities, weakened their mission of serving the public, and created through growing commercial entanglements at least the potential for undermining their privileged role

as disinterested arbiters of knowledge. The gains have been for the most part material, quantified, and valuable; the losses intangible, unmeasured, and at some level invaluable. The consequences of the university's immersion in the marketplace are thus incommensurate.

Centrist critics also promote the principle of "institutional balance." This principle is based on the assumption that academic values and autonomy can be effectively preserved if corporate involvement in university affairs is kept within specific limits, and if university activities do not stray too far in the direction of corporate/government mandates.

Generally, centrist critics share the baseline assumption with supporters of corporatization that there is no alternative. Given that at least some degree of corporatization is inevitable, they see the goal as "making peace" with the market while trying to preserve academic values and some semblance of collegial governance. According to Bok (2003: 176), corporate involvement in university research may warrant radical action, but the only viable response at this point is to "tighten up the rules to limit the damage." By accepting the corporatization process as a given and focusing on the need to balance market forces and the public interest, the main issue for these critics is whether corporatization overshadows or unduly compromises the traditional functions of higher education. Their key questions of interest are: to what degree should higher education adapt to market forces and how can we reconcile commercial and academic values? In response to these kinds of considerations, centrist critics tend to favour a utilitarian model of higher education that is a blend of "traditional" and corporate features. It follows that these critics — who often include university administrators and faculty organizations — generally advocate targeted reforms or regulatory strategies to address the problems of corporatization. Some of the common proposed strategies include: institutional guidelines and model clauses for regulating corporate-university partnerships; conflict of interest regulations; stricter rules for governing the academic freedom of researchers; progressive accountability measures (such as "better" ranking systems); subjecting administrators to greater monitoring; and improving or "regularizing" positions for contract faculty. To be sure, these kinds of reforms have played an important role in "limiting the damage," as Bok suggests.

But the impact of these reformist strategies is limited to the short term and, in some cases, can even be harmful. For one, they provide the illusion that the problems associated with corporatization are being dealt with, which can reinforce the broader transformative process or render it invisible. Second, by focusing efforts on regulating corporatization, they do not allow for questions about whether the restructuring process itself is a legitimate one. Those who develop and implement these kinds of strategies tacitly concede that corporatization is acceptable so long as academic autonomy is protected and the harmful "excesses" of corporate involvement are kept in check. Reformist strategies tend to start from a defensive position where individuals and groups are reacting to symptoms of the process as they arise, rather than challenging the root causes. Finally, and most importantly, proponents of regulatory reform do not acknowledge the underlying problem of institutional compatibility. They assume that an appropriate "blend" of corporate and academic features in the university *can* be achieved. I would maintain, however, that it is neither desirable nor possible to reconcile corporate values, standards and structures with academic ones. As Thorstein Veblen (1918) argued nearly a century ago, there is a fundamental incompatibility between business enterprise and higher learning, such that they should properly be considered polar opposites or "two extremes." As a result, the risk is not that corporatization will overshadow or unduly compromise the university, it is that corporatization will irrevocably transform the university.

IRRECONCILABLE DIFFERENCES

Universities have always functioned to preserve class privilege and protect and legitimate the social order. At the same time, they are subversive institutions that are counted on to produce knowledge for the public good and to challenge systems of power and authority. The first of these functions aligns with corporatization. The second, which is rooted in academic freedom and collegial self-governance, does not, making it an ongoing source of tension for government officials, business managers and university administrators who are working to restructure higher education. The incompatibility between universities and corporate institutions is built into the two central mechanisms of corporatization: corporate-university alliances where universities collaborate with corporations (such as corporate sponsorships, research partnerships and donor agreements), and programs of internal restructuring where universities operate like corporations (such as academic capitalism, corporate governance models and the casualization of academic labour). This incompatibility also manifests itself in the outcomes or consequences of these practices and relationships (such as student consumerism).

Early critics of the role of business in higher education, like Veblen, were cognizant of the tensions between the university's missions and the demands of market capitalism. This stream of critique has expanded as corporatization has advanced. John McMurtry (1991, 2004, 2010) argues that the defining principles of education and the market — their goals, motivations, methods and standards of excellence — are not only distinct, they are also deeply contradictory. The market's preoccupation with proprietary rights, private-want satisfaction, the manipulation of intellect and ready-made product lines are necessarily opposed to education's emphasis on knowledge sharing, autonomous learning, critical thinking and intellectual depth.

According to McMurtry, to prevent the encroachment of corporatization into higher education, we must recognize that these two spheres are fundamentally, and irreconcilably, opposed. Similarly, Henry Rosolvky describes the growing entanglement of these institutions as "against nature" (cited in Duderstadt 2004: 72). Bart Giamatti — onetime commissioner of Major League Baseball and former president of Yale University — precisely describes this divergence:

> A college or university is an institution where financial incentives to excellence are absent, where the product line is not a unit or an object but rather a value-laden and life-long process; where the goal of the enterprise is not growth or market share but intellectual excellence; not profit or proprietary rights but the free good of knowledge; not efficiency of operation but equity of treatment; not increased productivity in economic terms but increased intensity of thinking about who we are and how we live and about the world around us. (cited in Tanguay 2003: 50–51)

Corporate-university conflict is exemplified by the differences between academic and industrial science. Whereas the ideals of academic research centre on disinterested inquiry and knowledge sharing, industrial science tends to be motivated by financial gain and encourages research secrecy. Likewise, academic research relies on peer review and the replicability of results, whereas industrial research does not involve the same verification process. Moreover, the goal of academic research is to advance public knowledge, whereas industrial research aims to produce proprietary knowledge or a product that succeeds in the marketplace. Finally, neither institution has yet to succeed when they step outside of their respective basic functions. Corporations are poor performers when it comes to knowledge sharing and research integrity, and universities are equally inept when it comes to venture capitalism and generating revenue from commercialized research. In my view, this institutional mismatch — which is evident in all the features of corporatization documented throughout this book — means that corporatization cannot be accommodated, reformed or managed. Radical programs of internal restructuring and institutional separation are required to effect change in the long term.

RADICAL REFORMATION

Regulatory strategies and reforms will not ever represent a real challenge to the corporatization of higher education. In the areas of the university that have been most affected by corporatization — including governance, research and the casualization of academic labour — more radical solutions are required in order to bring about substantive change

In the area of university governance, an effective response to corporatization needs to challenge the very legitimacy of managerialism. Strategies to reform or improve corporate management may be somewhat useful, but they are limited in what they can achieve and could even exacerbate the problems. Pushing for the construction of "better" accountability measures, like better performance indicators, legitimizes and entrenches the corporate notion of accountability (that is, accountability to management rather than to students, the academic community and the public). Similarly, initiatives aimed at improving the stock of university administrators (for example, by getting more academics into executive positions) does relatively little to influence how universities function under corporate models of managerialism (just as "progressive" business managers do little to influence how large corporations function). What is needed is to challenge the basic prerogatives of corporate management and construct concrete alternatives. In short, corporate management *itself* is the problem; its baseline assumptions and practices are fundamentally at odds with freedom of inquiry and effective governance in a university setting.

Calls for rules and guidelines for "managing" the innumerable conflicts of interest involved in corporate-university research alliances have also proven woefully ineffective. In his work, Arthur Schafer (2004, 2008) notes that corporate-university partnerships are almost "preordained" to produce research findings that favour the interests of business, meaning that the proprietary interests of corporations routinely win out and any attempt to regulate or manage conflicts of interest are destined to be ineffective. Building on Schafer's analysis, I would argue that an effective, long-term solution for addressing these problems would be an outright prohibition on corporate research funding, at least in those disciplines where the potential for harm is high. Critics of this strategy claim that denying corporate grants on moral grounds is a slippery slope that violates academic freedom, discourages valuable academic work and aggravates the funding crisis in higher education. However, so long as faculty are not prohibited from (or penalized for) speaking, writing, teaching or researching about a particular topic, restricting a funding source does not violate academic freedom. As Krimsky (2008: 94) explains, academic freedom "is not extinguished in the case that a university community takes responsible and transparent collective action, following accepted governance procedures, that prohibits certain funding from entering the university."

This is not to suggest that other kinds of sponsored research funding never result in problems, or that all corporate money is detrimental. The influx of private funding for applied research has, in some instances, accelerated scientific progress to an extent that would not have been possible without such support. Corporate money has also been directed to support the work of progressive academics. Henry Giroux, for instance, one of the most consistent critics of the corporate university, currently holds the Global Television Network Chair in Communication Studies at

McMaster University. Nevertheless, the harms that result from corporate funding and influence far outweigh these benefits, and the benefits that industry receives are wildly incommensurate with what it provides. At a broader level, universities are an inherited public resource that has been built up over decades by workers, students, scholars and taxpayers. Through funding and research partnerships, not only are corporations able to buy access to this inherited social investment, but they are under no obligation to share that access with others. There is also the question of whether corporations should be allowed to purchase the university's source credibility and accrue "decency by association" by aligning themselves with academic researchers. I would argue that private sources of economic power — especially those engaged in destructive social and environmental practices — have no right to appropriate the trust or integrity that public universities hold. It should also be noted that when the financial costs of partaking in corporate research alliances are taken into account (attracting partners, building infrastructure, hiring lawyers and other specialists to monitor complex agreements), the monetary implications of cutting these ties for universities would be far less than is commonly assumed.

There has been some movement in the direction of prohibiting corporate research funding and other institutional ties. Some medical schools have restricted ties between drug companies and physicians and eliminated industry support for continuing medical education. This trend is growing at some of the world's most prestigious universities. Several years ago, hundreds of Harvard medical students publicly demanded that the university cut its ties to Big Pharma, citing concerns about research bias, marketing disguised as education, and their own "indoctrination" into commercialized medicine (Wilson 2009). Moreover, academic associations like the AAUP (2014) are now calling for a prohibition on academics and/or administrators participating in certain industry-financed events, and for "barring" pharmaceutical and biotechnology companies from operating freely on campuses. Medical journals have also made some progress. The journal *Open Medicine*, for example, was formed in 2007 by former editors of the *Canadian Medical Association Journal* who resigned from their positions in part due to corporate threats to their editorial autonomy. The journal publishes its material freely online, has completely banned all pharmaceutical and medical device advertising, and has strict rules to prevent ghost writing (Willinsky et al. 2007). Similarly, in 2009, a collection of editors from the world's leading medical journals openly called for "a complete ban on pharmaceutical and medical device industry funding" to professional medical associations (Rothman et al. 2009: 1368). Drawing attention to the corrosive influence of corporate funding on medical science, these experts argued that "fundamental reforms" were required of medical organizations and academic medical centres in order to protect scientific integrity, patients and "the public's trust" (1372). These initiatives point to a growing recognition that academic medicine can and should "divest" entirely from the pharmaceutical industry.

Turning to academic labour, one of the greatest challenges is balancing the immediate interests of contract faculty with the long-term interests of the academic profession as a whole. On the one hand, some progress has been made in improving the lives and working conditions of contract faculty in Canada. The last two decades have seen a wave of union organizing by contingent academics; there are now relatively few faculty members in Canada who do not belong to a union. Some unions have succeeded in securing contract workers partial access to governance, such as committee participation and departmental voting rights. Other small inequities in the area of institutional support have been addressed, including greater access to conference travel and professional development allowances. A few faculty associations now also link per course pay to percentages of permanent salaries (a key element of a pro-rata model), while others have negotiated sabbaticals for long-term employees. Finally, a large number of departments have "regularized" one or more of their contract positions, providing full-time status, greater job security as well as access to pensions and other benefits. At York, for example, instructors with ten years of teaching experience can apply for a "Long Service Teaching Appointment," which guarantees them three full courses in each of the next three years as well as additional pay.

On the other hand, the efficacy of focusing on these kinds of piecemeal improvements for contract staff and/or "regularized" positions remains in question. Semi-permanent or full-time contract appointments are not the first choice of employment for most aspiring academics, and they do not offer an adequate long-term solution to the problems associated with contact work. Research has found that the work of full-time contract faculty in Canadian universities is still characterized by "heavier teaching loads, insecurity caused by contract status, little input into or control over teaching assignments, lack of time for research, relegation of their research role, and their consequent devaluation as 'teaching-only' faculty" (Rajagopal 2004: 62). Moreover, the majority of faculty are opposed to the separation of teaching and research (OCUFA 2012b), which necessarily takes place with contract and other teaching stream positions. At a broader level, it is important to emphasize that casualization in the academy is connected to a long-term strategy to transform the nature of academic work. As such, universities are systematically (and unnecessarily) under-producing quality jobs, and contract positions are being created where tenure stream positions can and should exist. Solutions should therefore be focused on demanding more tenure track appointments.

While we should not abandon the goal of improving the conditions of contract work, we need to devise strategies that improve working conditions at the same time as challenging the broader casualization process. If not, we risk institutionalizing casualization as a permanent feature of the academy and providing an official status to the academic underclass. There are a number of ways that this dual goal might be achieved. One would be to change the nature of academic labour organizing. As it currently stands, the labour movement has not succeeded in halting or reversing the move toward casualization. In fact, some claim that unionization has actually increased casualization because the majority of unions and faculty associations are focused on protecting the interests of existing tenure stream faculty, interests that are sometimes at odds with those of contract staff (Dobbie and Robinson 2008). A counter-measure might involve more consistently organizing non-tenure-track and permanent faculty into the same bargaining units in order to push for more radical solutions to problems that are sector-wide. Even where this is the case, many contract faculty still feel their needs are under-represented within bargaining units. What is required is solidarity across all segments of academic labour at the organizational level, including having permanent professors recognize the value in working with contract faculty to advance the rights of the entire academic labour market.

Developing a united front against casualization is critical and would reduce the ability of employers to play one side against the other. It might also be used to demand that sessional faculty receive proportionate compensation for their labour, which would make contract hiring more expensive for administrators. As a result, they may be more likely to create more permanent full-time positions. A national study of the wages of contract instructors would be a critical tool in evaluating the merits of such a strategy. These data would help organizers assess whether university administrators' desire for "flexibility" outweighs the potential costs of employing part-time faculty whose wages approach those of tenured professors. Until such alliances can be institutionalized, however, contract faculty need to continue to strengthen their own organizational capacity at the regional, national and international levels, through organizations like the Coalition of Contingent Academic Labour.[1]

To conclude, none of this is to suggest that universities should abandon applied research or "practical" education. The public continues to expect universities to find solutions to real world problems and teach people how to make a living within current institutional arrangements. In fact, a "pure" university divorced from "useful" education and research is not the desired end goal. Universities should be involved in contemporary issues and struggles, and they fail when they confine themselves to isolated "ivory tower" pursuits. However, these tasks do not require universities to integrate themselves with corporations or operate like corporations. There are many other ways for academics and universities to be relevant in the "real" world.

STUDENT AND FACULTY ENGAGEMENT: BUILDING INTERSECTORAL ALLIANCES

In Canada today, universities are simply one target, albeit an important one, of corporate/political forces that are attempting to weaken the public sphere and expand their impact on the general population. In this way, the problems confronting universities are akin to the problems facing other institutions and of Canadian society more broadly. As public intellectual and activist Ursula Franklin (2000: 21) explains, corporatization is "not so much a university problem, but the university manifestation of a general, technologically-facilitated shift of power and accountability. The impact of this new misdistribution of power is felt in many other public institutions in Canada." It follows that efforts to transform universities are inextricably linked to struggles to democratize social, political and economic life, and that there will be inherent challenges in trying to develop free and democratic universities in a society characterized by inequality. Educator Paulo Freire recognized these limitations, claiming that it is "naïve idealism" to believe that a "province on freedom" can be created within the university when "the material conditions of [the broader] society work against the affirmation of freedom" (Freire et al. 1994: 143). So did Canadian student "syndicalists" in the 1960s, who argued that the problems of education were rooted in socio-economic structures and that their solution entailed altering these structures in the direction of a more equitable society. One of the necessary conditions to successfully oppose corporatization is to connect efforts to broader social movements operating outside of the university.

RECENT DEVELOPMENTS IN THE STUDENT MOVEMENT

Historically, student movements have been at the forefront of large-scale social change. And in many countries around the world, there is now a renewed sense of commitment. This shift is evidenced by a substantial increase in the level of student participation in educational activism, the use of more militant tactics (such as occupations) and the creation of linkages with broader social movements. Student unrest has focused on a number of issues, including the impact of educational restructuring on their own lives. In the past few years alone, students in California engaged in a mass walk-out and a series of occupations across the entire University of California system; massive student demonstrations in England were followed by a wave of occupations that spread to dozens of universities; students and educators in Italy organized against public disinvestment by occupying campuses, train stations, highways and airports; students in Austria occupied classrooms and offices for an entire semester in defiance of financing reforms; in Greece hundreds of schools and university departments came under student occupation as the government faced mounting opposition to its higher education agenda; student groups in Puerto Rico engaged in a series of mass strikes and occupied university buildings for several months in opposition to tuition increases; and thousands of students, teachers and activists in Colombia organized actions against their government's plan to introduce for-profit universities. Students have also launched large and coordinated resistance campaigns in Germany, France, Denmark, Spain, the Netherlands, Finland, Croatia, Argentina, the Philippines, Taiwan and elsewhere.

Today, students have once again become a galvanizing force, and not just for their own personal concerns like tuition and debt. What is particularly striking about many contemporary student movements is that they are locating educational concerns within the larger context of government austerity agendas, attacks on worker's rights, declining social programs, ecological devastation, and the expansion of corporate power. These developments are indicative of some of the new intersectoral alliances that are beginning to form among university-based and other social movements. In Chile, for example, hundreds of thousands of students began a series of mass demonstrations in 2011 against tuition increases. Over the next few years, this initial upheaval progressed into a broad-based movement composed of students, teachers, academics, unions, civil servants and human rights organizations. As the diversity of its participants grew, the movement began to challenge class inequality, health care privatization, environmental destruction, the Chilean constitution, the activities of foreign mining companies and even the basic structure of the capitalist economy (Bernasconi 2012; Larrabure and Torchia 2011; Lavars 2012). By late 2013, inter-movement solidarity had reached unprecedented heights, united around what Dustin Ferretti (2013) calls an "anti-neoliberal master framework." This included roughly sixty universities and high schools where students and entire faculties were on strike. A similar series of events recently took place in Puerto Rico, where educational disinvestment led to protests, mass strikes and occupations in 2010–11. This student-based movement received broad public support from religious organizations, community and professional associations and labour unions, and quickly evolved into a nation-wide struggle against privatization, unemployment and cuts to public services (Rodriguez 2011).

Of course, there is also evidence of these kinds of alliances in the Canadian context. The 2012 Quebec student strikes, which began as a series of actions opposing planned tuition increases, evolved into action about issues much broader than tuition. One major branch of the movement — represented by the Coalition large de l'Association pour une solidarité syndicale étudiante (CLASSÉ) — consisted of students who located the tuition hikes as part of a broader neoliberal program and as a symptom of a failing and unjust social order. This vision was made explicit in CLASSÉ's "Share Our Future" Manifesto:

> This burden is one that we all shoulder, each and every one of us, whether we are students or not: this is one lesson our strike has taught us ... Our strike goes beyond the $1625 tuition-fee hike. If, by throwing our educational institutions into the marketplace, our most basic rights are

being taken from us, we can say the same for hospitals, Hydro-Québec, our forests, and the soil beneath our feet. We share so much more than public services: we share our living spaces, spaces that were here before we were born. We want them to survive us ... This is the meaning of our vision, and the essence of our strike: it is a shared, collective action whose scope lies well beyond student interests. (CLASSÉ 2012)

What started as a student protest was transformed into a broader social and economic agenda. Accordingly, the students held general assemblies, organized alternative education events and built alliances with outside organizations. According to Ingar Solty (2012), the success of the student strikes rested upon the solidarity and support the movement received from the "Red-Hand-Coalition" — an alliance of 125 organizations including anti-poverty groups, environmental groups and public sector unions that formed in 2009 to resist privatization and neoliberal restructuring. The students also received widespread support from teachers, parents, university professors and other civil society organizations in part because of the broad social and political mandate the movement had come to represent.

As impressive as its accomplishments were, there is understandably some disappointment among students and others that the movement was not able to impact public policy and the future direction of the province in a more profound way. In part, this may have been because the movement underestimated the amount of real power it had to influence decision-making. There were hundreds of thousands of participants in the student strikes, and they had a broad range of support from civil society organizations. If just ten percent of Quebec students had decided not to pay their tuition for a semester, this would have put enormous pressure on the government. The Quebec example can also be used to show how strikes are an effective tactical option for interested groups other than workers. In many respects, students are (unpaid) workers and their "education" is an essential component of economic activity. If a broad mass of students identified and organized as workers — through strikes, unionization and even salary demands – they would likely have an even greater impact.

Related to the growing organizing power of students, there are increasing alliances between students and organizations fighting climate change. Based on evidence that the world's oil, gas and coal reserves need to remain in the ground to avoid catastrophic climate change (see McKibben 2012), many Canadian student groups are joining the worldwide movement to pressure universities to divest from the fossil fuel industry. As Naomi Klein (2014: 354) points out, universities "are the institutions entrusted to prepare [students] for the future; so it is the height of hypocrisy for those same institutions to profit from an industry that has declared war on the future at the most elemental level." As students recognize, nearly every university has a large endowment, and every one of these endowments has extensive fossil fuel holdings. United under the Canada Youth Climate Coalition, the student-led divestment movement is active on over forty Canadian campuses, and ten campuses have held successful student votes in favour of divestment (faculty members at a smaller number of universities have also endorsed the idea) (see Prystupa 2015). Recently at UBC — an institution with some of the largest university holdings of fossil fuel investments in Canada — professors, librarians and program directors voted in favour of divestment.

University divestment is a political rather than an economic strategy. Although it will have little impact on the corporate bottom line, it does directly challenge the reputation and political power of the fossil fuel industry. Students in Canada and around the world are insisting that it is both socially and morally unacceptable for public institutions — including institutions of higher learning — to be financing fossil fuel extraction. At the heart of their struggle for a new economy is that public universities have a responsibility to use whatever moral authority they have left to counter the growing climate change threat.

In some ways, the growing militancy of student resistance today is reminiscent of the student movements of the 1960s. Like the 1960s movements, students are directly addressing the "student condition" on campus while simultaneously integrating with — and in some cases spearheading — broader movements for change. These developments may be in their early stages, but the fact that students around the world are explicitly linking the state of public education to larger issues of neoliberalism, class inequality, attacks on the public sector and environmental destruction is an important development. It highlights that, despite efforts to render corporate influences invisible or explain them in positive terms, students are aware of the current threat they pose to higher education and to society at large. It also demonstrates the new forms of solidarity that are beginning to emerge across social movements. In many respects, student organizing against educational restructuring and broader sociopolitical developments is at the forefront of issues that the wider society is going to have to confront in the years ahead.

ACADEMIC INTELLECTUALS OPPOSING CORPORATIZATION

Much critical scholarship has focused on the role that intellectuals play in perpetuating systems of power and domination. While many intellectuals — located inside and outside of the academy — have dedicated their lives to a kind of calling to advance social justice, evidence suggests that this is the exception rather than the rule. The dominant social role of intellectuals is (and has been) to serve power. This tendency has been traced over time, from the work of Karl Marx and his contemporary Antonio Gramsci (1971) to more modern thinkers and writers like Chomsky (1982, 1987a, 1987b), Mills (1959, 1963) and Said (1994, 2004).

These works underscore just how pervasive ideology and indoctrination are within educational institutions and the broader intellectual culture.

In the West today, the vast majority of intellectuals (and tenured professors in particular) work under conditions of enormous political freedom and security. So how do we account for the fact that so many assume a commissarial rather than a subversive social role? In most cases, intellectuals align their goals and activities with outside power out of their own free choice. For some, this decision reflects a desire to achieve power or to share in its rewards. For others, institutional pressures — residing in the disciplinary organization of knowledge and the professional reward structure — provide a subtle but effective screening mechanism. Academia conditions faculty to believe that social and political engagement are not part of their jobs and that academic allegiances should remain with one's discipline or professional field. Similarly, there are few professional rewards for public service; service to society is given little if any weight in professional decisions about job performance, promotion or tenure. Moreover, within the academic "cult of professionalism," as Said (1994) describes it, research that advances a strong position on social issues is not often regarded as professional scholarship in comparison with research that exhibits "balance," "moderation" and apolitical detachment. Given this context, it is not surprising that that so many important scholarly contributions come from individuals outside of the academy. In the words of Derrick Bok (1990: 105), "[w]hat Rachel Carson did for risks to the environment, Ralph Nader for consumer protection, Michael Harrington for problems of poverty, Betty Friedan for women's rights, they did as independent critics, not as members of a faculty." It is not surprising, then, that the academic community has played a role, even if it is largely a complicit one, in advancing the corporatization process.

However, this characterization of the intellectual's role is only part of the story. Like universities, intellectuals can and do play a subversive and liberating role. Few would contest that public intellectuals have had a long tradition of producing and disseminating knowledge to expand public consciousness and support practices of social liberation. Prominent scientists in the early 1900s, for example, produced popular works in physics and mathematics in the belief that this knowledge should be shared by everyone (such as Lancelot Hogben's *Mathematics for the Million* 1936). Popular education in the form of community development and worker education programs and other alternatives to formal schooling are also part of this tradition. In some cases, these movements succeeded in creating separate working class schools (see the writings of A.J. Muste in Hentoff 1967). Likewise, the U.S. Intercollegiate Socialist Society (ISS) of the early twentieth century forged important alliances between the academy and movements for industrial democracy. Founded in New York by Jack London and Upton Sinclair in 1905, the ISS was an "organizational bridge between the labor movement, working-class intellectuals, and traditional intellectuals in the university" (Barrow 1990: 178). Between 1910 and 1917, approximately 20 percent of all four-year colleges and universities in the U.S. had an official ISS chapter affiliated with the national movement. Of course, many academic intellectuals also became more socially and politically engaged during the social uprisings of the 1960s, and played an important supportive role in the student, feminist, civil-rights and anti-war movements.

The participation of faculty in challenging the corporatization process is essential, and to do so, academics need to take their subversive responsibilities seriously. In the first place, academic intellectuals should use the freedoms that remain available to them — most notably their academic freedom. Critics have focused much of their attention on the threat that corporatization poses to academic freedom. Embedded in these critiques is that academic freedom should also be a key source of resistance. Tudiver (1999), for one, claims that academic freedom is incompatible with corporatization — and a direct challenge to it — because it exists to protect professors from the influence of corporate power and the market. Similarly, educational historian Michael Katz (1986: 20) argues that tenure and academic freedom are the "great barriers to the total victory of the marketplace" because they restrict the operation of free wage labour, which in turn reduces the conversion of faculty into commodities. Intellectuals need to maintain their academic freedom to oppose corporatization, and to do so they will need public support. Generating this public support will only come through linking academic freedom explicitly to the public interest rather than as something that provides job security to elites. To make that connection, people who have academic freedom need to *use it*, prominently and in the public interest.

In my view, if academics are going to push back against corporatization, they also need to recognize the limitations of "radical scholarship." A large amount of critical research and writing is never read by anyone except other academics, and "political battles" in the scholastic universe are limited in what they can achieve. Moreover, academics should recognize the limitations of confining their audience to politicians or university administrators. As Chomsky (1997) has argued, "speaking truth to power" is not a particularly effective or honourable vocation. Those who exercise power in coercive institutions already know the truth, for the most part, and even if they can be swayed by intellectual analyses or moral arguments, they remain constrained by institutional imperatives. Rather, intellectuals should "seek out an audience that matters;" namely, groups that are able and willing to oppose corporatization in higher education and elsewhere. Further, "it should not be seen as an audience, but as a community of common concern in which one hopes to participate constructively. We should not be speaking *to*, but *with*" (61, emphasis in original).

Fortunately, evidence indicates that the public could be a remarkably effective ally in the struggle against corporatization. On almost every measure, as documented throughout the book, the Canadian public opposes a corporatization agenda. The majority of the public strongly disagrees with a "customers pay" model of university financing; is steadfast in its opposition to public funding cuts; believes that teaching — not research — is the most important factor in considering university quality; and agrees that tuition fees should be eliminated altogether. Moreover, a majority of the population believes that the best strategy to compensate for funding shortfalls in universities would be to reduce central administration costs (CAUT 2011a). And, although the opinions of university scientists have been largely ignored by our political leaders, the public believes they should be taken seriously. According to a nation-wide poll, 44 percent of Canadians said they find the opinions of university scientists to be the most trustworthy in debates over university research funding in Canada. Further, 18 percent of respondents endorsed students as the most trustworthy source; 10 percent said corporations; 9 percent said university administrators; and just 9 percent said the federal government (CAUT 2009b). Indeed, we should not merely be coveting the general population as an ally, we should be taking our cues from it.

Finally, like students, one of the most important things that faculty can do in opposing corporatization is to forge alliances with broader social struggles. Within this context, intellectuals can make important contributions by providing information and analysis to popular movements. As Mills (1959: 186) describes it, intellectuals can help people to become "self-educating" individuals, at the same time as helping society to build "self-cultivating publics." Put another way, intellectuals play a key role in helping people recognize and critique – independently and for themselves — prevailing structures of power. Their high level of workplace autonomy and access to resources also means that they have the potential to be effective organizers. It is also not unreasonable to expect that intellectuals should provide people with a means of defending themselves against the distortions and illusions of the dominant intellectual culture.

There are two concrete, relatively simple ways that academics can help to forge partnerships with social movements outside the university. First, faculty members can bring activists and community leaders into the university to participate in study programs on urban problems, environmental decay, alternative food systems, educational restructuring, corporate crime and other issues. They could even involve outside participants more directly by putting these programs into the hands of communities themselves. An example of this kind of initiative is the Labor and Working Class Studies Project at the University of Wisconsin, which is a collaboration of academics, organized labour and community activists that connects the university and the community in dialogue and action on labour related issues.

Second, intellectuals can "take the university" into the wider society by encouraging students to get practically involved with groups working for social change. In 2012, Columbia University began offering an "Occupy Wall Street" course in which students could earn full course credits by getting involved in the movement's projects outside of the classroom. In Canada, there have also been promising efforts to align university teachers, students, citizens and social movements into programs of liberatory education. In the early 2000s, for instance, the People's Free University of Saskatchewan (PFU) began offering a wide variety of courses to members of the public, which were all provided free of charge. Many of those involved with the PFU worked and studied at the University of Saskatchewan. PFU incorporated a democratic and inclusive community-based model of education that combined practical and theoretical subjects. Faculty, staff and students worked with community leaders and activists to break down the barriers between school and community and disseminate knowledge in the public interest (see Woodhouse 2009). Toronto's "Anarchist University" (Antliff 2007) and "Critical U" in Vancouver (Coté, Day and de Peuter 2007) are other notable examples of community-based education projects that have created alliances between formal education systems and movements of civil society. The educational value of these alliances and partnerships cannot be overestimated. As Chomsky (2002: 187) notes, awareness and understanding of oppressive power systems arise primarily "through practice and experience with the world ... you can hear all the lectures you like about the way that power works, but you learn it very fast when you actually confront it, without the lectures." This insight was not lost on Gabriel Nadeau-Dubois, leader of the Quebec student movement, who attributed the success of the movement, in part, to its radicalization, a process that occurred "in the struggle, not through beautiful speeches" (cited in Fidler 2013).

Universities in Canada and elsewhere remain heavily dependent on external power. The major institutions in capitalist society would never tolerate (and could easily thwart) radical or other educational reforms that are isolated from broader struggles. Moreover, the use of universities to sort individuals into occupational hierarchies and support capitalist objectives has become so deeply rooted under neoliberalism that it could not be altered without a more thorough social and political transformation. It is for this reason that connecting educational struggles with broader movements of civil society is critical for students and intellectuals. Ironically, the corporatization of the university may have created additional space for these necessary alliances to grow. As Nick Dyer-Witheford (2007: 52) explains:

> The revolts of forty years ago were resisting capital's tendency to make the university a 'knowledge factory.' But because this assimilation was only partially complete, these uprisings had a certain isolation ... Today, the much tighter fusion of academia with business, and the manifest

subordination of education to the job market has ended this relative isolation and has opened other possibilities. The conventional distinction between university and the 'real world' — at once self-deprecating and self-protective — is becoming less and less relevant. If students and teachers have lost some of the latitude of action and relative privilege that universities once afforded, they have also become connected to and potential participants in movements outside the university.

RELEVANCE REVISITED

The university plays a relevant role in the lives of people and communities and in the wider society. But there are differences in how relevance is understood. Some see universities as relevant to the extent that they prepare people for employment in the capitalist economy and support economic competitiveness. Others view relevance in terms of intellectual inquiry for its own sake, where knowledge acquisition and scholarly engagement are meaningful in and of themselves. Still others locate the university's relevance in its ongoing contributions to social justice and social change. Under corporatization, however, "relevance" has largely become a euphemism for service to the state and to the market. Is education a worthwhile investment? How can higher education better contribute to corporate profitability and national competitiveness? Can it create enough "human capital" to facilitate economic growth? Needless to say, this version of relevance offers a distorted and dehumanized view of the value and purpose of education.

In my view, university should be a place where all people have the opportunity to develop their independence, their capacity to discover and be creative, and their ability to work with others to achieve socially desirable ends. Higher education has a responsibility to equip people to fight for issues of social concern. Today, the most pressing of these include tackling poverty, chronic unemployment and growing inequality; rebuilding economies devastated by neoliberal policies; halting the poisoning of our land, air and water; mitigating the potentially disastrous effects of climate change; reducing the threats of militarism and war; and designing a new global economic system that serves the interests of the global population. The causes of these complex, and often related, challenges are rooted in society's major institutions and structures of power. Therefore, it is vital that these institutions and their supporting ideologies be subject to critical analysis, and ultimately to direct challenge. Universities should be subject to such analysis and, just as importantly, they should provide a venue — an institutional position of authority and influence — within and through which this analysis and activism takes place. It is this definition of "relevance" — emphasizing the university's role in social justice — that principally motivated this book. It was also the entry point for student protests in the 1960s, which emphasized that insofar as the "ivory tower" meant isolation from or a refusal to engage with critical social issues, it played a largely irrelevant role. According to Students for a Democratic Society (1962) activists:

> The university is located in a permanent position of social influence. Its educational function makes it indispensable and automatically makes it a crucial institution in the formation of social attitudes ... in an unbelievably complicated world, it is the central institution for organizing, evaluating, and transmitting knowledge ... the university is the only mainstream institution that is open to participation by individuals of nearly every viewpoint ... these together make the university a potential base and agency in a movement of social change.

As these students recognized, and as many students and educators recognize today, there is something distinctive about the university that cannot be found elsewhere in society. The university's subversive function and its commitment to the development of new social visions is why universities have always been connected with broader movements for change. In the past half century, the university has been deeply implicated in 1960s student power, anti-war and civil rights movements, the 1970s feminist, anti-nuclear, gay liberation and environmental movements, and the more recent "anti-globalization" and social justice movements. To this list one could add the international movement against growing corporate power, climate change, Occupy Wall Street and countless other democratization struggles taking place around the world. The problems facing humanity are of such a magnitude that universities will only be relevant to the extent that they provide an institutional forum in which to meaningfully challenge current social and economic arrangements and bring about radical social change.

NOTE
1   For a useful discussion of contract faculty organizing in the U.S., see Berry (2005). U.S. initiatives, like The New Faculty Majority and The Adjunct Project, provide models on which to educate and mobilize contract faculty in Canada.

APPENDIX A

CHARACTERIZATIONS OF MODERN UNIVERSITIES

- **The Corporate University**: A broad concept that refers to private, for-profit universities and non-profit (usually public) institutions that increasingly operate like for-profit firms. In the case of non-profit institutions, the corporate university accentuates many of the features of the corporatization process, including the university's enhanced revenue-generating capacity, the infusion of corporate values into higher education, the commercialization of academic research and the presence of managerial and academic labour practices that resemble those of private companies (see, for example, Aronowitz 2000; Côté and Allahar 2011; Donoghue 2008; Johnson, Kavanagh and Mattson 2003; Tuchman 2009; Tudiver 1999).
- **The Entrepreneurial University**: Popularized by the work of Burton Clarke (1998), the entrepreneurial university concept incorporates a wide international literature that addresses both the causes (for example, reductions in public funding, "innovation" agendas and economic competition) and the consequences (for example, market-led curriculum reform and the expansion of university-state-corporate research ties) of university restructuring. Many of the most prominent studies on the entrepreneurial university analyze institutional/academic entrepreneurship in the areas of intellectual property and technology transfer (see, for example, Etzkowitz 2004; Etzkowitz, Webster and Healy 1998). For an overview, see Gibb, Haskins and Robertson (2009).
- **The Enterprise University**: Focusing on university restructuring in Australia, the work of Simon Marginson and Mark Considine (2000) on the enterprise university highlights the process whereby university missions and governing bodies assume a distinctly corporate character. As part of this process, universities are defined by strong executive control and man-

agerial governance, with an emphasis on marketing, performance targets and greater competition for resources.
- **The Service University**: Within the service university paradigm, the delivery of contract research and instructional/training programs are designed to satisfy the needs of external clients, most notably those in the corporate sector. Internally, service-oriented fields and applied/commercial disciplines are prioritized over the university's traditional emphasis on the liberal arts and sciences (Buchbinder 1993; Cummings 1998, 1999; Newson and Buchbinder 1988).
- **The Exchange University**: The concept of the exchange university locates corporatization as the extension of market ideology and market relations into higher education. Here, research products, educational credentials and even knowledge itself become commodities valued more for their "exchange" value than their "use" value (Chan and Fisher 2008).
- **The Hybrid University**: Framed within the context of reduced public funding, the concept of the hybrid university is used to describe institutions that receive a substantial (and growing) portion of their income from private sources, including student fees, corporate sponsorships and contract research. The term also highlights strategies used by university mangers to facilitate a "successful" coexistence of traditional academic and modern market cultures (Mouwen 2000).
- **The Innovative University**: The notion of the innovative university is centered on the idea that existing models of higher education are unsustainable and that modern universities must find less costly ways of performing their unique functions. The emphasis is on new institutional strategies driven by information technology and online and distance education. Curriculum specialization and reformed systems of tenure and promotion are also features of the innovative university (Christensen and Eyring 2011).
- **The McUniversity**: This concept refers to universities that rely more on quantifiable measures — such as standardized instruction, performance indicators and institutional rankings — as markers of "quality" and "efficiency." In these configurations, cost accounting principles redefine the meaning and purpose of higher education along corporate lines, and administrators and students adopt a more consumer-driven orientation to higher learning (Rinne 1999; Ritzer, 2002).

REFERENCES

Allen, Kate. 2013. "National Research Council 'Open for Business,' Conservative Government Says." *Toronto Star*, May 7.

Altbach, Philip, Liz Reisberg, Maria Yudkevich, Gregory Androushchak and Iván Pacheco (eds.). 2012. *Paying the Professoriate: A Global Comparison of Compensation and Contracts*. New York: Routledge.

American Association of University Professors. 2014. "Summary of Recommendations: 56 Principles to Guide Academy-Industry Engagement." Available at <aaup.org/sites/default/files/files/Principles-summary.pdf>.

____. 2010. "Selected References on Contingent Faculty and Student Success." At <aacu.org/meetings/annualmeetingAM10/documents/AAUPHandout.pdf>.

____. 2003. "Contingent Appointments and the Academic Profession." At <aaup.org/AAUP/pubsres/policydocs/contents/conting-stmt.htm>.

Anderson, Erin. 2012. "Can Canada's Schools Pass the Next Great Intelligence Test?" *Globe and Mail*, October 5.

Angulo, Fernando, Albena Pergelova and Josep Rialp. 2010. "A Market Segmentation Approach for Higher Education Based on Rational and Emotional Factors." *Journal of Marketing for Higher Education* 20, 1.

Angus, Ian. 2009. *Love the Questions: University Education and Enlightenment*. Winnipeg: Arbeiter Ring Publishing.

Annis, Roger. 2012. "Government Repression of Quebec Student Movement Sparks Massive Protest." *The Bullet*, Socialist Project E-Bulletin 641 (May 28).

Antliff, Alan. 2007. "Breaking Free: Anarchist Pedagogy." In M. Coté, R. Day and G. de Peuter (eds.), *Utopian Pedagogy: Radical Experiments Against Neoliberal Globalization*. Toronto: University of Toronto Press.

Aronowitz, Stanley. 2001. *The Last Good Job in America: Work and Education in the New Global Technoculture*. Lanham, MD: Rowman & Littlefield.

____. 2000. *The Knowledge Factory: Dismantling the Corporate University and Creating True Higher Learning*. Boston: Beacon Press.

Arsenault, Chris. 2007. *A New Paradigm for Paying the Piper: Access, Control and Commercialization at Halifax Universities*. Halifax: Nova Scotia Public Interest Research Group.

Association of Part-Time Professors of the University of Ottawa. 2011. "Rocky Road Ahead for Canada's University's Part-Time Professors." At <APTPUO-PrRel-20110426-main.pdf>.

Astin, Alexander. 2000. *The American Freshman: National Norms for Fall 2000*. California: American Council on Education.
___. 1998. "The Changing American College Student: Thirty-Year Trends, 1966–1996." *The Review of Higher Education* 21, 2.
Atkinson-Grosjean, Janet. 2006. *Public Science, Private Interests: Culture and Commerce in Canada's Networks of Centres of Excellence*. Toronto: University of Toronto Press.
Atkinson-Grosjean, Janet, and Cory Fairly. 2009. "Moral Economies in Science: From Ideal to Pragmatic." *Minerva* 47, 2.
AUCC (Association of Universities and Colleges of Canada). 2012. "Back to School Quick Facts." Ottawa.
___. 2011a. *Trends in Higher Education: Volume 1 – Enrolment*. Ottawa.
___. 2011b. "Statement on Academic Freedom." At <aucc.ca/media-room/news-and-commentary/canadas-universities-adopt-new-statement-on-academic-freedom>.
___. 2011c. "The Revitalization of Undergraduate Education in Canada." Ottawa.
___. 2010a. "The Value of a University Degree." Ottawa.
___. 2010b. "Value of a Degree in a Global Marketplace." Ottawa.
___. 2008a. *Trends in Higher Education: Volume 3 — Finance*. Ottawa.
___. 2008b. "Momentum: The 2008 Report on University Research and Knowledge Mobilization." Ottawa.
___. 2007a. *Trends in Higher Education: Volume 2 – Faculty*. Ottawa.
___. 2007b. "Canadian Universities and International Student Mobility." Ottawa.
___. 2002. "Framework of Agreed Principles on Federally Funded University Research." Ottawa.
Axelrod, Paul. 2008. "Public Policy in Ontario Higher Education: From Frost to Harris." In A. Chan and D. Fisher (eds.), *The Exchange University: Corporatization of Academic Culture*. Vancouver: UBC Press.
___. 2002. *Values in Conflict: The University, the Marketplace, and the Trials of Liberal Education*. Montreal: McGill-Queen's University Press.
___. 1998. "Challenges to Liberal Education in an Age of Uncertainty." *Historical Studies in Education* 10, 1/2.
___. 1986. "Service or Captivity? Business-University Relations in the Twentieth Century." In W. Neilson and C. Gaffield (eds.), *Universities in Crisis: A Mediaeval Institution in the Twenty-First Century*. Montreal: The Institute for Research on Public Policy.
___. 1982a. *Scholars and Dollars: Politics, Economics, and the Universities of Ontario 1945–1980*. Toronto: University of Toronto Press.
___. 1982b. "Businessmen and the Building of Canadian Universities: A Case Study." *Canadian Historical Review* 68, 2.
Barkans, John, and Norene Pupo. 1978. "Canadian Universities and the Economic Order." In R. Nelsen and D. Nock (eds.), *Reading, Writing, and Riches: Education and the Socio-Economic Order in North America*. Toronto: Between the Lines.
___. 1974. "The Board of Governors and the Power Elite: A Case Study of Eight Canadian Universities." *Sociological Focus* 7, 3.
Barlow, Maude, and Heather-Jane Robertson. 1994. *Class Warfare: The Assault on Canada's Schools*. Toronto: Key Porter Books.
Barnes, Deborah, and Lisa Bero. 1998. "Why Review Articles on the Health Effects

of Passive Smoking Reach Different Conclusions." *Journal of the American Medical Association* 279, 19.

Barnetson, Bob, and Alice Boberg. 2000. "Resource Allocation and Public Policy in Alberta's Postsecondary System." *The Canadian Journal of Higher Education* 30, 2.

Barr-Telford, Lynn, Fernando Cartwright, Sandrine Prasil and Kristina Shimmons. 2003. "Access, Persistence and Financing: First Results from the Postsecondary Education Participation Survey (PEPS)" Statistics Canada, Catalogue No. 81-595-MIE2003007.

Barrett, David. 2011. "The Cheating Epidemic at Britain's Universities." *The Telegraph*, March 5.

Barrow, Clyde. 1990. *Universities and the Capitalist State: Corporate Liberalism and the Reconstruction of American Higher Education, 1894–1928*. Madison, Wisconsin: University of Wisconsin Press.

Barzun, Jacques. 1993. *The American University: How it Runs, Where it Is Going*. Second edition. Chicago: University of Chicago Press.

Basen, Ira. 2014. "Most University Undergrads Now Taught by Poorly Paid Part-Timers." *CBC News*, September 7.

Basken, Paul. 2009. "'Ghostwriting' Is Still a Common Practice, Study Shows." *Chronicle of Higher Education*, September 10.

Bauder, Harald. 2006. "The Segmentation of Academic Labour: A Canadian Example." *ACME – An International E-Journal for Critical Geographies* 4, 2.

Bauer, Louise. 2011. "Permanently Precarious? Contingent Academic Faculty Members, Professional Identity and Institutional Change in Quebec Universities." Unpublished Master's of Arts thesis. At <spectrum.library.concordia.ca/7285/1/BirdsellBauer_MA_ S2011.pdf>.

Beeston, Laura. 2012. "Liberal Budget Could Seriously Affect Quebec University Funding." *Montreal Gazette*, July 19.

Bekelman, Justin, Yan Li and Cary Gross. 2003. "Scope and Impact of Financial Conflicts of Interest in Biomedical Research: A Systematic Review." *Journal of the American Medical Association* 289, 4.

Benjamin, Ernst. 2003. "Reappraisal and Implications for Policy and Research." *New Directions for Higher Education* 123.

Bennett, Roger, and Rehnuma Ali-Choudhury. 2009. "Prospective Students' Perceptions of University Brands: An Empirical Study." *Journal of Marketing for Higher Education* 19, 1.

Bennett, William. 1984. *To Reclaim a Legacy: A Report on the Humanities in Higher Education*. Washington: National Endowment for the Humanities.

Bercuson, David, Robert Bothwell and J.L. Granatstein. 1997. *Petrified Campus: The Crisis in Canada's Universities*. Toronto: Random House.

____. 1984. *The Great Brain Robbery: Canada's Universities on the Road to Ruin*. Toronto: McClelland and Stewart.

Berger, Joseph. 2009. "Student Debt in Canada." In J. Berger, A. Motte and A. Parkin (eds.), *The Price of Knowledge: Access and Student Finance in Canada*. Montreal: Canada Millennium Scholarship Foundation.

Bernasconi, Andrés. 2012. "Not Another Brick in the Wall: Capitalism and Student Protests in Chile." *Academic Matters*, November.

Berry, Joe. 2005. *Reclaiming the Ivory Tower: Organizing Adjuncts to Change Higher Education*.

New York: Monthly Review Press.
Bissell, Claude. 1968. *The Strength of the University*. Toronto: University of Toronto Press.
Bloom, Alan. 1987. *The Closing of the American Mind*. New York: Simon and Schuster.
Bloom, Michael (ed.). 1990. *Reaching for Success: Business and Education Working Together. First National Conference on Business-Education Partnerships*. Ottawa: Conference Board of Canada.
Bok, Derek. 2004. "The Benefits and Costs of Commercialization of the Academy." In D. Stein (ed.), *Buying In or Selling Out? The Commercialization of the American Research University*. New Brunswick, NJ: Rutgers University Press.
____. 2003. *Universities in the Marketplace: The Commercialization of Higher Education*. Princeton, NJ: Princeton University Press.
____. 1990. *Universities and the Future of America*. Durham: Duke University Press.
Bollier, David. 2002. *Silent Theft: The Private Plunder of our Common Wealth*. New York: Routledge.
Bourdieu, Pierre. 1988. *Homo Academicus*. Cambridge: Polity Press.
Bousquet, Marc. 2008. *How the University Works: Higher Education and the Low-Wage Nation*. New York: New York University Press.
Bowie, Norman. 1994. *University-Business Partnerships: An Assessment*. Lanham, MD: Rowman and Littlefield.
Boyer, Ernest. 1990. *Scholarship Reconsidered: Priorities of the Professoriate*. Princeton: Carnegie Foundation for the Advancement of Teaching.
Bradshaw, James. 2012. "No Department Is Safe as Universities Employ U.S. Cost-Cutting Strategy." *Globe and Mail*, December 25.
____. 2011. "For Undergrads at Canada's Universities, a New Way of Learning." *Globe and Mail*, September 14.
Brainard, Jeffrey. 2006. "Study Finds Conflicts of Interest on Many Research-Review Boards." *Chronicle of Higher Education*, December 8.
Bramwell, Allison, and David Wolfe. 2008. "Universities and Regional Economic Development: The Entrepreneurial University of Waterloo." *Research Policy* 37, 8.
Breslauer, Helen. 1985. "Women in the Professoriate — The Case of Multiple Disadvantage." In In C. Watson (ed.), *The Professoriate — Occupation in Crisis*. Toronto: Ontario Institute for Studies in Education.
Brock University. 2009. "Brock 2014: Knowledge, Engagement, Transformation." At <brocku.ca/webfm_send/425>.
Brotheridge, Céleste, and Raymond Lee. 2005. "Correlates and Consequences of Degree Purchasing among Canadian University Students." *The Canadian Journal of Higher Education* 35, 2.
Brown, Louise. 2012. "Why Canada's Professors Are the Best (Best-Paid, That Is)." *Toronto Star*, March 22.
Brownlee, Jamie. 2015a. "Exposing the Transformation of Academic Labour Using Access to Information Requests." In *Casualization of the Academy*. Toronto: Lorimer (forthcoming).
____. 2015b. "Contract Faculty in Canada: Using Access to Information Requests to Uncover Hidden Academics in Canadian Universities." *Higher Education* (forthcoming).
____. 2005. *Ruling Canada: Corporate Cohesion and Democracy*. Halifax: Fernwood

Publishing.
Bruneau, William, and Donald Savage. 2002. *Counting Out the Scholars: How Performance Indicators Undermine Universities and Colleges*. Toronto: Lorimer.
Bubela, Tania, and Timothy Caulfield. 2010. "Role and Reality: Technology Transfer at Canadian Universities." *Trends in Biotechnology* 28, 9.
Buchbinder, Howard. 1993. "The Market Oriented University and the Changing Role of Knowledge." *Higher Education* 26, 3.
Buchbinder, Howard, and Janice Newson. 1990. "Corporate-University Linkages in Canada: Transforming a Public Institution." *Higher Education* 20, 4.
Budros, Art. 2002. "Do University Presidents Make a Difference? A Strategic Leadership Theory of University Retrenchment." *The Canadian Journal of Higher Education* 32, 1.
Burgan, Mary. 2008. "Production in the Humanities." In J. Turk (ed.), *Universities at Risk: How Politics, Special Interests and Corporatization Threaten Academic Integrity*. Toronto: Lorimer.
Burke, Mike, and Joanne Naiman. 2003. "Dueling Identities and Faculty Unions: A Canadian Case Study." In D. Herman and J. Schmid (eds.), *Cogs in the Classroom Factory: The Changing Identity of Academic Labor*. Westport, CT: Praeger.
Business Council on National Issues. 1993. *Building a New Century Economy: The Canadian Challenge*. Ottawa.
Business-Higher Education Forum. 2001. *Working Together, Creating Knowledge*. The University-Industry Research Collaboration Initiative. Washington, DC: American Council on Education.
Calgary Herald. 2008. "University Presidents' Pay Cracks $500,000." April 4.
Calhoun, Craig. 2006. "The University and the Public Good." *Thesis Eleven* 84.
Callender, Claire. 2008. "The Impact of Term-Time Employment on Higher Education Students' Academic Attainment and Achievement." *Journal of Education Policy* 23, 4.
Cameron, David. 1991. *More Than an Academic Question: Universities, Government, and Public Policy in Canada*. Halifax: Institute for Research on Public Policy.
Cameron, James. 1978. *On the Idea of a University*. Toronto: University of Toronto Press.
Camfield, David. 2012. "Quebec's 'Red Square' Movement: The Story so Far." *The Bullet*, Socialist Project E-Bulletin No. 680, August 13.
Campbell, Eric, Russell Gruen, James Mountford, Lawrence Miller, Paul Cleary and David Blumenthal. "A National Survey of Physician-Industry Relationships." 2007. *New England Journal of Medicine* 356, 17.
Campbell, Eric, Joel Weissman, Brian Clarridge, Recai Yucel, Nancyanne Causino and David Blumenthal. 2003. "Characteristics of Medical School Faculty Members Serving on Institutional Review Boards: Results of a National Survey. *Academic Medicine* 78, 8.
Canadian Bar Association. 2003. "Response to the Provost Study of Accessibility and Career Choice in the University of Toronto Faculty of Law." At <cba.org/cba/submissions/pdf/03-13-eng.pdf>.
Canadian Council on Learning. 2010a. "Tallying the Costs of Post-Secondary Education: The Challenge of Managing Student Debt and Loan Repayment in Canada." Ottawa.
____. 2010b. "State of Learning in Canada: A Year in Review." Ottawa.
____. 2009a. "2008 Survey of Canadian Attitudes Toward Learning: Results for Learning Throughout the Lifespan." Ottawa.

____. 2009b. "Where Did They Go? Post-Secondary Experiences, Attitudes & Intentions of 2005/06 BC High School Graduates Who Did Not Pursue Public Post-Secondary Education in British Columbia by Fall 2007." Vancouver: British Columbia Council on Admissions and Transfer.
____. 2009c. "Post-Secondary Education in Canada: Meeting Our Needs?" Ottawa.
Canadian Health Coalition. 2011. "Funding Decisions for B.C.'s Drug Formulary to be Based on Industry Marketing instead of Independent Drug Assessment." At <healthcoalition. ca/wp-content/uploads/2011/03/TI-BN.pdf>.
Carnegie Commission on Higher Education. 1973. *Priorities for Action: Final Report of the Carnegie Commission on Higher Education*. New York: McGraw-Hill.
Carroll, William. 2004. *Corporate Power in a Globalizing World: A Study in Elite Social Organization*. Don Mills: Oxford University Press.
Carroll, William, Linda Christiansen-Ruffman, Raymond Currie and Deborah Harrison (eds.). 1992. *Fragile Truths: Twenty-Five Years of Sociology and Anthropology in Canada*. Ottawa: Carleton University Press.
Carvalho, Sergio, and Márcio de Oliveira Mota. 2010. "The Role of Trust in Creating Value and Student Loyalty in Relational Exchanges between Higher Education Institutions and their Students." *Journal of Marketing for Higher Education* 20, 1.
CAUT (Canadian Association of University Teachers). 2014. CAUT *Almanac of Post-Secondary Education in Canada* 2014–2015. Ottawa.
____. 2013. "Open for Business on What Terms? An Analysis of 12 Collaborations between Canadian Universities and Corporations, Donors and Governments." Ottawa.
____. 2012. CAUT *Almanac of Post-Secondary Education in Canada* 2012–2013. Ottawa.
____. 2011a. "Decima Summary: Public Opinion and Post-Secondary Education." At <caut. ca/uploads/DecimaSummary_Fall2011.pdf>.
____. 2011b. CAUT *Almanac of Post-Secondary Education in Canada* 2011–2012. Ottawa.
____. 2010a. "The Changing Academy?" CAUT *Education Review* 12, 1.
____. 2010b. "Fight Brewing over Ottawa U's Proposed Cuts." CAUT *Bulletin* 57, 4. Ottawa.
____. 2010c. "NSERC Discovery Grants Spiral Downward." CAUT *Bulletin* 57, 8. Ottawa.
____. 2009a. "University Finances, 2007–2008." CAUT *Education Review* 11, 1.
____. 2009b. "Public Opinion of Post-Secondary Education Issues." At <caut.ca/uploads/ Summary_Spring_2009.pdf>.
____. 2009c. "Knowledge Infrastructure Program Funding Going Mostly to Repairs, Not Research." At <caut.ca/pages.asp?page=836&lang=1>.
____. 2007. "CAUT's Submission to the Review of the Canada Student Loan Program." At <caut.ca/pages.asp?page=620&lang=1>.
____. 2006. CAUT *Almanac of Post-Secondary Education in Canada 2006*. Ottawa.
____. 2003. "University Tuition Fees in Canada, 2003." CAUT *Education Review* 5, 1.
CBC News. 2011. "Canadians Save Too Little for Children's Schooling, TD Says." July 19. At <cbc.ca/news/business/story/2011/07/19/td-survey-education-finances.html>.
CCPA (Canadian Centre for Policy Alternatives). 2014. "Tuition in Canada: 1975 to 2013." Ottawa: Canadian Centre for Policy Alternatives Monitor, July/August.
____. 2013a. "Not Your Parents Education: Ontario Tuition Fact Sheet." Ottawa.
____. 2013b. *Alternative Federal Budget 2013: Doing Better Together*. Ottawa.
____. 2005. *Challenging McWorld*. Second edition. Ottawa.

CFS (Canadian Federation of Students). 2012. "Public Education for the Public Good: A National Vision for Canada's Post-Secondary Education System." Ottawa.

____. 2011. "83% of Nova Scotians Support Reducing Tuition Fees." At <cfs-fcee.ca/html/english/media/mediapage.php?release_id=1196>.

____. 2010. "The Racialised Impact of Tuition Fees: Assessing the Social Cost of Post-Secondary Education." Ottawa.

____. 2009. "Canada's Education Action Plan." Ottawa.

____. 2007a. "Strategy for Change: Money Does Matter." Ottawa.

____. 2007b. "Millennium Scholarship Foundation: A Failed Experiment in Student Financial Aid." Ottawa.

Chan, Adrienne, and Donald Fisher. 2008a. *The Exchange University: Corporatization of Academic Culture*. Vancouver: UBC Press.

____. 2008b. "Academic Culture and the Research-Intensive University: The Impact of Commercialism and Scientism." In A. Chan and D. Fisher (eds.), *The Exchange University: Corporatization of Academic Culture*. Vancouver: UBC Press.

Chapin, Angelina. 2010. "Lansbridge University Gets a Permanent Black Mark." *Canadian Business* 83, 18.

Cheadle, Bruce. 2012. "Carleton University Rewrites Controversial $15-Million Donor Deal." *Globe and Mail*, August 28.

Chernomas, Robert, and Errol Black. 2004. "Fast Facts: Should University Students Pay More?" Winnipeg: Canadian Centre for Policy Alternatives.

Cho, Mildred, and Lisa Bero. 1996. "The Quality of Drug Studies Published in Symposium Proceedings." *Annals of Internal Medicine* 124, 5.

Chomsky, Noam. 2009. "An Email from Noam Chomsky." At <chomsky.info/letters/20091130htm>.

____. 2003. *Chomsky on Democracy and Education*. New York: RoutledgeFalmer.

____. 1997. *Perspectives on Power: Reflections on Human Nature and the Social Order*. New York: Black Rose Books.

____. 1987a. "The Responsibility of Intellectuals." In J. Peck (ed.), *The Chomsky Reader*. New York: Pantheon.

____. 1987b. "Objectivity and Liberal Scholarship." In J. Peck (ed.), *The Chomsky Reader*. New York: Pantheon.

____. 1982. "Intellectuals and the State." In *Towards a New Cold War*. New York: Pantheon.

Christensen, Clayton, and Henry Eyring. 2011. *The Innovative University: Changing the DNA of Higher Education from the Inside Out*. San Francisco: Jossey-Bass.

Clark, Ian, Greg Moran, Michael Skolnik and David Trick. 2009. *Academic Transformation: The Forces Reshaping Higher Education in Ontario*. Montreal: McGill-Queen's University Press.

Clark, Ian, David Trick and Richard Van Loon. 2011. *Academic Reform: Policy Options for Improving the Quality and Cost-Effectiveness of Undergraduate Education in Ontario*. Kingston: McGill-Queen's University Press.

Clarke, Burton. 1998. *Creating Entrepreneurial Universities: Organizational Pathways of Transition*. Oxford: Pergamon Press.

CLASSÉ. 2012. "Share Our Future — The CLASSÉ Manifesto." At <http://www.stopthehike.ca/2012/07/share-our-future-the-classe-manifesto/>.

Clement, Wallace. 1975. *The Canadian Corporate Elite: An Analysis of Economic Power.* Toronto: McClelland and Stewart.

Coalition on the Academic Workforce. 2012. "A Portrait of Part-Time Faculty Members: A Summary of Findings on Part-Time Faculty Respondents to the Coalition on the Academic Workforce Survey of Contingent Faculty Members and Instructors." At <academicworkforce.org/survey.html>.

Coates, Ken, and Bill Morrison. 2011. *Campus Confidential: 100 Startling Things You Don't Know about Canadian Universities.* Toronto: James Lorimer.

Cockburn, Alexander. 2012. "When Half a Million Americans Died and Nobody Noticed." *The Week,* May 9. At <theweek.co.uk/us/46535/when-half-million-americans-died-and-nobody-noticed>.

Coelli, Michael. 2009. "Tuition Fees and Equality of University Enrolment." *Canadian Journal of Economics* 42, 3.

____. 2005. "Tuition, Rationing and Inequality in Post-Secondary Education Attendance." University of British Columbia Working Paper.

Cohen, Joanna. 2008. "Principles and Interest: Is the Academy an Accomplice in a Corporate-Caused Pandemic?" In J. Turk (ed.), *Universities at Risk: How Politics, Special Interests and Corporatization Threaten Academic Integrity.* Toronto: James Lorimer.

Cohen, Patricia. 2009. "In Tough Times, the Humanities Must Justify Their Worth." *New York Times,* February 24.

Conlon, Michael. 2006. "The Politics of Access: Measuring the Social Returns on Post-Secondary Education." *Higher Education Management and Policy* 18, 2.

____. 2004. "Performance Indicators: Accountable to Whom?" *Higher Education Management and Policy* 16, 1.

Conway, John. 2004. "Improving Access to Affordable University Education in Saskatchewan." Regina: Canadian Centre for Policy Alternatives.

Corry, James Alexander. 1970. *Farewell the Ivory Tower: Universities in Transition.* Montreal: McGill-Queen's University Press.

Côté, James, and Anton Allahar. 2011. *Lowering Higher Education: The Rise of Corporate Universities and the Fall of Liberal Education.* Toronto: University of Toronto Press.

____. 2007. *Ivory Tower Blues: A University System in Crisis.* Toronto: University of Toronto Press.

Coté, Mark, Richard Day and Greig de Peuter. 2007. "Academicus Affinitatus: Academic Dissent, Community Education, and Critical U." In M. Coté, R. Day and G. de Peuter (eds.), *Utopian Pedagogy: Radical Experiments Against Neoliberal Globalization.* Toronto: University of Toronto Press.

Coughlan, Sean. 2010. "Students Stage Day of Protests over Tuition Fee Rises." *BBC News,* November 24.

Council of Canadian Academies. 2012a. "Strengthening Canada's Research Capacity: The Gender Dimension." Ottawa.

____. 2012b. "The State of Science and Technology in Canada, 2012." Ottawa.

____. 2006. "The State of Science and Technology in Canada: Summary and Main Findings." Ottawa.

Council of Ontario Universities. 2012. "Employment Outcomes of 2009 Graduates of Ontario University Undergraduate Programs: 2011 Survey Highlights." Toronto.

____. 2011a. "Innovative Ideas: Improving Efficiency at Ontario Universities." Toronto.
____. 2011b. "Employment Outcomes of 2008 Graduates of Ontario University Undergraduate Programs: 2010 Survey Highlights." Toronto.
____. 2010. "Inventory of Physical Facilities of Ontario Universities 2007–08." Toronto.
Cox, Ana Marie. 2000. "Study Shows Colleges' Dependence on their Part-Time Instructors." *Chronicle of Higher Education*, December 1.
Crespo, Manuel, and Houssine Dridi. 2007 "Intensification of University-Industry Relationships and its Impact on Academic Research." *Higher Education* 54, 1.
Crocker, Robert, and Alex Usher. 2006. "Innovation and Differentiation in Canada's Post-Secondary Institutions." Ottawa: Canadian Policy Research Networks.
Cross, Allison. 2010. "Report Reveals Gender Gap in University Professor Salaries." *Montreal Gazette*, August 13.
Crozier, Michel, Samuel Huntington and Joji Watanuki. 1975. *The Crisis of Democracy: Report on the Governability of Democracies to the Trilateral Commission*. New York: New York University Press.
Cummings, W.K. 1999. "The Service Orientation in Academia, or Who Serves in Comparative Perspective." In I. Fägerlind, I. Holmesland and G. Strömqvist (eds.), *Higher Education at the Crossroads*. Stockholm: Institute of International Education, Stockholm University.
____. 1998. "The Service University in Comparative Perspective." *Higher Education* 35, 1.
CUPE (Canadian Union of Public Employees). 2010. "'Resource Optimization' in Canadian Universities Threatens Education, Job Security." At <cupe.ca/education/resource-optimization-canadian>.
Curtis, John. 2014. "The Employment Status of Instructional Staff Members in Higher Education, Fall 2011." Washington, DC: American Association of University Professors.
D'Aquino, Thomas, and David Stewart-Patterson. 2001. *Northern Edge: How Canadian Can Triumph in the Global Economy*. Toronto: Stoddart.
D'Souza, Dinesh. 1991. *Illiberal Education: The Politics of Race and Sex on Campus*. New York: Free Press.
de Broucker. Patrice. 2005. "Getting There and Staying There: Low-Income Students and Post-Secondary Education." Ottawa: Canadian Policy Research Networks.
Deem, Rosemary. 2008. "Unravelling the Fabric of Academe: The Managerialist University and its Implications for the Integrity of Academic Work." In J. Turk (ed.), *Universities at Risk: How Politics, Special Interests and Corporatization Threaten Academic Integrity*. Toronto: James Lorimer.
Denholm, Andrew. 2012a. "Universities Oppose Plan to Set Recruitment Targets." *Scotland Herald*, March 1.
____. 2012b. "Universities Ordered to Admit Deprived Students." *Scotland Herald*, October 5.
Deresiewicz, William. 2011. "Faulty Towers: The Crisis in Higher Education." *The Nation*, May 4. At <thenation.com/article/160410/faulty-towers-crisis-higher-education>.
Desjardins, Louise. 2012. "Profile and Labour Market Outcomes of Doctoral Graduates from Ontario Universities." Statistics Canada, Catalogue No. 81-595-M.
Dewey, John. 1966 [1916]. *Democracy and Education: An Introduction to the Philosophy of Education*. New York: Free Press.

___. 1964. *John Dewey on Education: Selected Writings.* New York: Modern Library.
Diallo, Bayero, Claude Trottier and Pierre Doray. 2009. "What Do We Know About the Pathways and Transitions of Canadian Students in Post-Secondary Education?" Montreal: Canada Millennium Scholarship Foundation.
Dobbie, David, and Ian Robinson. 2008. "Reorganizing Higher Education in the United States and Canada: The Erosion of Tenure and the Unionization of Contingent Faculty." *Labor Studies Journal* 33, 2.
Dodge, David. 1981. *Labour Market Development in the 1980s.* Ottawa: Minister of Supply and Services.
Doherty-Delorme, Denise, and Erika Shaker. 2004. "'Accessive' Policies or Excessive Debt: Who's Paying for Higher Education?" In D. Doherty-Delorme and E. Shaker (eds.), *Missing Pieces V: An Alternative Guide to Canadian Post-Secondary Education.* Ottawa: Canadian Centre for Policy Alternatives.
Donoghue, Frank. 2008. *The Last Professors: The Corporate University and the Fate of the Humanities.* New York: Fordham University Press.
Duderstadt, James. 2004. "Delicate Balance: Market Forces Versus the Public Interest." In D. Stein (ed.), *Buying In or Selling Out? The Commercialization of the American Research University.* New Brunswick, NJ: Rutgers University Press.
Duff, James, and Robert Berdahl. 1966. "University Government in Canada: Report of a Commission Sponsored by the Canadian Association of University Teachers and the Association of Universities and Colleges of Canada." Toronto: University of Toronto Press.
Dyer-Witheford, Nick. 2007. "Teaching and Tear Gas: The University in the Era of General Intellect." In M. Coté, R. Day and G. de Peuter (eds.), *Utopian Pedagogy: Radical Experiments Against Neoliberal Globalization.* Toronto: University of Toronto Press.
Economic Council of Canada. 1964. *First Annual Review: Economic Goals for Canada to 1970.* Ottawa.
___. 1965. *Second Annual Review: Towards Sustained and Balanced Economic Growth.* Ottawa.
Ehrenreich, Barbara. 1997. "What Yale Is Teaching Us." In C. Nelson (ed.), *Will Teach for Food: Academic Labor in Crisis.* Minneapolis: University of Minnesota Press.
Ekos Research Associates. 2006. "Investing in Their Future: A Survey of Student and Parental Support for Learning." Montreal: Canada Millennium Scholarship Foundation.
___. 2005. "Ontario Universities: Public Perceptions of Tuition and Funding." Ottawa: Council of Ontario Universities.
___. 2003. "Public Perceptions on Quality: Final Report." Ottawa: Council of Ontario Universities.
Elliot, Carl. 2010. *White Coat Black Hat: Adventures on the Dark Side of Medicine.* Boston: Beacon Press.
Enros, Philip. 1991. "The 'Bureau of Scientific and Industrial Research and School of Specific Industries': The Royal Canadian Institute's Attempt at Organizing Industrial Research in Toronto, 1914–1918." In R. Jarrell and J. Hull (eds.), *Science, Technology and Medicine in Canada's Past: Selections from Scientia Canadensis.* Thornhill, ON: Scientia Press.
___. 1983. "The University of Toronto and Industrial Research in the Early Twentieth Century." In R. Jarrell and A. Roos (eds.), *Critical Issues in the History of Canadian Science, Technology and Medicine.* Ottawa: HSTC Publications.

Enros, Philip, and Michael Farley. 1986. "University Offices for Technology Transfer: Toward the Service University." Ottawa: Science Council of Canada.

Essaji, Azim, and Sue Horton. 2010. "Silent Escalation: Salaries of Senior University Administrators in Ontario, 1996–2006." *Higher Education* 59, 3.

Etzkowitz, Henry. 2004. "The Evolution of the Entrepreneurial University." *International Journal of Technology and Globalisation* 1, 1.

Etzkowitz, Henry, Andrew Webster and Peter Healy (eds.). 1998. *Capitalizing Knowledge: New Intersections of Industry and Academia*. Albany: State University of New York Press.

Falvo, Nick. 2012. "Canada's Self-Imposed Crisis in Post-Secondary Education." The Progressive Economics Forum. At <progressive-economics.ca/2012/06/07/canadas-self-imposed-crisis-in-post-secondary-education/>.

Fang, Ferric, Grant Steen and Arturo Casadevall. 2012. "Misconduct Accounts for the Majority of Retracted Scientific Publications." *Proceedings of the National Academy of Sciences* 109, 42.

Fanelli, Daniele. 2009. "How Many Scientists Fabricate and Falsify Research? A Systematic Review and Meta-Analysis of Survey Data." *PLoS ONE* 4, 5.

Fekete, John. 1994. *Moral Panic: Biopolitics Rising*. Montreal: Robert Davies Publishing.

Ferguson, Charles. 2010. "Larry Summers and the Subversion of Economics." *Chronicle of Higher Education*, October 3.

Ferretti, Dustin. 2013. "Chileans for Free Education" *Canadian Dimension* 47, 5.

Ferrie, Helke. 2013. *Creative Outrage*. Caledon, ON: KOS Publishing.

_____. 2009. "Deadly Side-Effects of Prescription Drugs Spark Lawsuits." Ottawa: Canadian Centre for Policy Alternatives Monitor, June.

Fidler, Richard. 2013. "Whither the Quebec Left and Student Movement after the 'Maple Spring'?" *Canadian Dimension*, January 29.

Field, Cynthia, Glen Jones, Grace Karram Stephenson and Artur Khoyetsyan. 2014. "The 'Other' University Teachers: Non-Full-Time Instructors at Ontario Universities." Toronto: Higher Education Quality Council of Ontario.

Field, Erica. 2009. "Educational Debt Burden and Career Choice: Evidence from a Financial Aid Experiment at NYU Law School." *American Economic Journal: Applied Economics* 1, 1.

Findlay, Len. 2010. "Report: Investigation into the Termination of Dr. Ramesh Thakur as Director of the Balsillie School of International Affairs." Ottawa: Canadian Association of University Teachers. At<caut.ca/uploads/Findlay_Report_Final.pdf>.

Fine, Philip. 2010. "Canadian Presidents Stress Partnerships." *University World News* 148, November 21.

_____. 2009. "PhD Offers Little Salary Difference." *University World News* 77, May 24.

Finnie, Ross, Stephen Childs, Dejan Pavlic and Nemanja Jevtovic. 2014. "How Much Do University Graduates Earn?" Ottawa: Education Policy Research Initiative.

Finnie, Ross, Stephen Childs and Andrew Wismer. 2011. "Access to Postsecondary Education: How Ontario Compares." Toronto: Higher Education Quality Council of Ontario.

Fisher, Donald, and Janet Atkinson-Grosjean. 2002. "Brokers on the Boundary: Academy-Industry Liaison in Canadian Universities." *Higher Education* 44, 3–4.

Fisher, Donald, Kjell Rubenson, Jean Bernatchez, Robert Clift, Glen Jones, Jacy Lee, Madeleine MacIvor, John Meredith, Theresa Shanahan and Claude Trottier. 2006.

Canadian Federal Policy and Postsecondary Education. University of British Columbia: Centre for Policy Studies in Higher Education and Training.
Fisher, Donald, Kjell Rubenson, Glen Jones and Theresa Shanahan. 2009. "The Political Economy of Post-Secondary Education: A Comparison of British Columbia, Ontario and Quebec." *Higher Education* 57, 5.
Flanagan, Tom. 2007. "A Conservative Look at the Liberal Arts." *Academic Matters*, April.
Fowke, Vernon. 1959. "Who Should Determine University Policy?" CAUT *Bulletin* 7, 4.
Franklin, Ursula. 2000. "What Is at Stake? Universities in Context." In J. Turk (ed.), *The Corporate Campus: Commercialization and the Dangers to Canada's Colleges and Universities*. Toronto: James Lorimer.
Freire, Paulo, Miguel Escobar, Alfredo Fernández and Gilberto Guevara-Niebla. 1994. *Paulo Freire on Higher Education: A Dialogue at the National University of Mexico*. New York: State University of New York Press.
Frenette, Marc. 2008. "University Access amid Tuition Fee Deregulation: Evidence from Ontario Professional Programs." *Canadian Public Policy* 34, 1.
Freudenburg, William. 2005. "Seeding Science, Courting Conclusions: Reexamining the Intersection of Science, Corporate Cash, and the Law." *Sociological Forum* 20, 1.
Friedberg, Mark, Bernard Saffran, Tammy Stinson, Wendy Nelson and Charles Bennett. 1999. "Evaluation of Conflict of Interest in Economic Analysis of New Drugs Used in Oncology." *Journal of the American Medical Association* 282, 15.
Fulton, E. Margaret. 1986. "Historical Commitments in New Times: The Restructuring and Reorientation of Teaching and Research." In W. Neilson and C. Gaffield (eds.), *Universities in Crisis: A Mediaeval Institution in the Twenty-First Century*. Montreal: Institute for Research on Public Policy.
Gallagher, Paul. 2012. "Revealed: How the Cost of a Degree is Now £100,000." *The Independent*, December 9.
Gatto, John Taylor. 2003. *The Underground History of American Education*. New York: Oxford Village Press.
Gauthier, Michelle. 2004. "Incentives and Accountability: The Canadian Context." *Higher Education Management and Policy* 16, 2.
Geiger, Roger. 2004. *Knowledge and Money: Research Universities and the Paradox of the Marketplace*. Stanford, CA: Stanford University Press.
Gergin, Maria. 2011. *Silencing Dissent: The Conservative Record*. Ottawa: Canadian Centre for Policy Alternatives.
Ghabrial, Sarah. 2009. "Getting a (Neo-)Liberal Arts Education in Canada." *Rabble.ca*, March 25. At <rabble.ca/news/getting-neo-liberal-arts-education-canada>.
Gibb, Allan, Gay Haskins and Ian Robertson. 2009. *Leading the Entrepreneurial University: Meeting the Entrepreneurial Development Needs of Higher Education Institutions*. At <ncge.org.uk/publication/leading_the_entrepreneurial_university.pdf>.
Gilbert, Sid, Judy Chapman, Peter Dietsche, Paul Grayson and John Gardner. 1997. *From Best Intentions to Best Practices: The First Year Experience in Canadian Postsecondary Education*. Columbia, SC: National Resource Centre for the Freshman Experience, University of South Carolina.
Gingrich, Paul. 2011. "After the Freeze: Restoring University Affordability in Saskatchewan." Saskatchewan: Canadian Centre for Policy Alternatives.

____. 2009. "A Reappraisal of University Access and Affordability 2009." Saskatchewan: Canadian Centre for Policy Alternatives.
Ginsberg, Benjamin. 2011. *The Fall of the Faculty: The Rise of the All-Administrative University and Why It Matters.* New York: Oxford University Press.
Giroux, Henry. 2014. *Neoliberalism's War on Higher Education.* Toronto: Between the Lines.
____. 2008. "Marketing the University: Corporate Power and the Academic Factory." *Our Schools, Our Selves* 17, 3.
____. 2007. *The University in Chains: Confronting the Military-Industrial-Academic Complex.* Boulder, CO: Paradigm Publishers.
____. 2003. "Public Time and Educated Hope: Educational Leadership and the War Against Youth." At <units.muohio.edu/eduleadership/anthology/OA/OA03001.html#_edn32>.
____. 2002. "Neoliberalism, Corporate Culture, and the Promise of Higher Education: The University as a Democratic Public Sphere." *Harvard Educational Review* 72, 4.
Giroux, Henry, and Susan Searls Giroux. 2004. *Take Back Higher Education: Race, Youth, and the Crisis of Democracy in the Post-Civil Rights Era.* New York: Palgrave Macmillan.
Goodman, Paul. 1959. *Growing Up Absurd.* New York: Random House.
Gould, Eric. 2003. *The University in a Corporate Culture.* New Haven: Yale University Press.
Government of Canada. 2014. "Canada's International Education Strategy: Harnessing Our Knowledge Advantage to Drive Innovation and Prosperity." Ottawa: Foreign Affairs, Trade and Development Canada.
____. 2009. "Formative Evaluation: Additional Canada Education Savings Grant and Canada Learning Bond, November 2009." Ottawa: Employment and Social Development Canada.
____. 2007a. "Mobilizing Science and Technology to Canada's Advantage." Ottawa: Minister of Public Works and Government Services Canada.
____. 2007b. "Budget Plan 2007: Aspire to a Stronger, Safer, Better Canada." Ottawa: Department of Finance.
Gramsci, Antonio. 1971. *Selections from the Prison Notebooks.* London: Lawrence and Wishart.
Grant, Karen. 2002. "A Conversation on the Future of the Academy with James Turk, PhD, Executive Director, Canadian Association of University Teachers." *Canadian Review of Sociology and Anthropology* 39, 3.
Greenberg, Milton. 2004. "The University Is Not a Business (and Other Fantasies)." *Educause* 39, 2.
Guard, Julie, Rachel Gotthilf, Rachel Heinrichs, Brian Latour, Kyle Mytruk, Kim Parry, Zachery Saltis and Chris Rigaux. 2007. "Where Does the Money Go? University of Manitoba Senior Administrators Get Big Pay Hikes but Faculty and Staff Morale Remains Low." Winnipeg: Canadian Centre for Policy Alternatives.
Guppy, Neil, Edward Grabb and Clayton Mollica. 2013. "The Canada Foundation for Innovation, Sociology of Knowledge, and the Re-engineering of the University." *Canadian Public Policy* 39, 1.
Gutstein, Donald. 2014. "Follow the Money, Part 3: Big Oil and Calgary's School of Public Policy." *Rabble.ca,* April 8.
____. 2009. *Not a Conspiracy Theory: How Business Propaganda Hijacks Democracy.* Toronto:

Key Porter Books.
Hardy, Cynthia. 1984. "The Management of University Cutbacks: Politics, Planning and Participation." *The Canadian Journal of Higher Education* 14, 1.
Harris, Robin. 1976. *A History of Higher Education in Canada, 1663–1960*. Toronto: University of Toronto Press.
Harvey, Lee. 2008. "Ranking of Higher Education Institutions: A Critical Review." *Quality in Higher Education* 14, 3.
Hatt, Kayle. 2014. "Help Not Wanted: Federal Public Service Cuts Have Hit Student Hiring Hard." Ottawa: Canadian Centre for Policy Alternatives.
Healy, David. 2012. *Pharmageddon*. Los Angeles: University of California Press.
____. 2008. "Academic Stalking and Brand Fascism." In J. Turk (ed.), *Universities at Risk: How Politics, Special Interests and Corporatization Threaten Academic Integrity*. Toronto: James Lorimer.
Healy, David, and Dinah Cattell. 2003. "The Interface between Authorship, Industry and Science in the Domain of Therapeutics." *British Journal of Psychiatry* 182.
Hearn, Alison. 2010. "Exploits in the Undercommons." In J. Newson and C. Polster (eds.), *Academic Callings: The University We Have Had, Now Have, and Could Have*. Toronto: Canadian Scholars' Press.
Henderson, Peter. 2012. "Carleton University Renegotiation over $15M Politics School Blindsides Donor." *Ottawa Citizen*, July 12.
Henry, Julie. 2010. "Half of University Students Willing to Cheat, Study Finds." *Telegraph*, June 20.
Hentoff, Nat. 1967. *The Essays of A.J. Muste*. Indianapolis: Bobbs-Merrill.
Hogben, Lancelot. 1936. *Mathematics for the Million*. London: Allen and Unwin.
Holden, Constance. 2006. "Professional Practice: Scientists Keep Some Data to Themselves." *Science* 311 (5760).
Horowitz, David. 2006. *The Professors: The 101 Most Dangerous Academics in America*. Washington, DC: Regnery Publishing.
Horowitz, David, and Jacob Laksin. 2009. *One-Party Classroom: How Radical Professors at America's Top Colleges Indoctrinate Students and Undermine Our Democracy*. New York: Crown Forum Publishing Group.
Human Resources Development Canada. 2002. *Knowledge Matters: Skills and Learning for Canadians: Canada's Innovation Strategy*. Ottawa
Impact Group. 2008. "The Economic Role and Influence of the Social Sciences and Humanities: A Conjecture." Toronto.
Industry Canada. 2012. "Knowledge Infrastructure Program Finale." Ottawa.
____. 2002. *Achieving Excellence: Investing in People, Knowledge and Opportunity*. Ottawa.
Innis, Harold. 1946. *Political Economy in the Modern State*. Toronto: Ryerson Press.
Ipsos Reid. 2012. "Imagine Education au/in Canada: Executive Summary of Qualitative Research." Ottawa: Department of Foreign Affairs and International Trade. At <epe.lac-bac.gc.ca/100/200/301/pwgsc-tpsgc/por ef/foreign_affairs_intl_ trade/2012/064-11/summary.pdf>.
____. 2004. "Canadians Attitudes Towards Financing Post-Secondary Education: Who Should Pay and How?" Montreal: Canada Millennium Scholarship Foundation.
Ivanova, Iglika. 2012. "Paid in Full Update: Who Pays for University Education in BC?"

Vancouver: Canadian Centre for Policy Alternatives.
Jaeger, Audrey. 2008. "Contingent Faculty and Student Outcomes." *Academe* 94, 6.
Jamrisko, Michelle, and Ilan Kolet. 2012. "Cost of College Degree in U.S. Soars 12 Fold: Chart of the Day." *Bloomberg*, August 15. At <bloomberg.com/news/2012-08-15/cost-of-college-degree-in-u-s-soars-12-fold-chart-of-the-day.html>.
Jaschik, Scott. 2011. "Ethos Matters." *Inside Higher Ed*, February 1.
____. 2010. "He Won't Censor Himself." *Inside Higher Ed*, December 16.
Johnson, Andy. 2012. "Student Suing Concordia University over Grade." CTV *News*, November 12.
Johnson, Benjamin. 2003. "The Drain-O of Higher Education: Casual Labor and University Teaching." In B. Johnson, P. Kavanagh and K. Mattson (eds.), *Steal This University: The Rise of the Corporate University and the Academic Labor Movement*. New York: Routledge.
Johnson, Benjamin, Patrick Kavanagh and Kevin Mattson (eds.). 2003. *Steal This University: The Rise of the Corporate University and the Academic Labor Movement*. New York: Routledge.
Johnstone, Bruce D. 1998. *The Financing and Management of Higher Education: A Status Report on Worldwide Reforms*. Paper submitted to the UNESCO World Conference on Higher Education, Paris, France.
Jones, Glen. 1998. "The Idea of a Canadian University." *Interchange* 29, 1.
____. 1990. "Imminent Disaster Revisited, Again: The Crisis Literature of Canadian Higher Education." *The Canadian Journal of Higher Education* 20, 2.
Jones, Glen, Theresa Shanahan and Paul Goyan. 2004. "The Academic Senate and University Governance in Canada." *The Canadian Journal of Higher Education* 34, 2.
Jones, Glen, Julian Weinrib, Amy Scott Metcalfe, Don Fisher, Kjell Rubenson and Iain Snee. 2012. "Academic Work in Canada: The Perceptions of Early-Career Academics." *Higher Education Quarterly* 66, 2.
Jones, Glen, and Stacey Young. 2004. "'Madly off in All Directions': Higher Education, Marketisation and Canadian Federalism." In P. Teixeira, B. Jongbloed, D. Dill and A. Amaral (eds.), *Markets in Higher Education: Rhetoric or Reality?* Dordrecht: Kluwer.
Kachur, Jerrold. 2003. "Whose Intellectual Property? Whose Rights? GATS, TRIPS and Education in Canada." *Globalisation, Societies and Education* 1, 3.
Katz, Michael. 1986. "The Moral Crisis of the University, Or, the Tension Between Marketplace and Community in Higher Learning." In W. Neilson and C. Gaffield (eds.), *Universities in Crisis: A Mediaeval Institution in the Twenty-First Century*. Montreal: The Institute for Research on Public Policy.
Keeney, Patrick. 2011. "Don't Turn Universities into Trade Schools." *National Post*, August 18.
Kennedy, Kaley. 2010. "Sweatshop U: Part-Time, Precarious Work Becoming the Norm at Canadian Universities." At <halifax.mediacoop.ca/story/sweatshop-u/4634>.
Kerr, Clark. 1963. *The Uses of the University*. Cambridge: Harvard University Press.
____. 2001. *The Uses of the University*. Cambridge: Harvard University Press.
Kimball, Roger. 1990. *Tenured Radicals: How Politics Has Corrupted Our Higher Education*. New York: Harper and Row.
King, Ralph. 1999. "Medical Journals Rarely Disclose Researchers' Ties, Drawing Ire." *The Wall Street Journal*, February 2.

Kirp, David. 2003. *Shakespeare, Einstein, and the Bottom Line: The Marketing of Higher Education*. Cambridge: Harvard University Press.

Kirsch, Irving. 2010. *The Emperor's New Drugs: Exploding the Antidepressant Myth*. New York: Basic Books.

Klein, Naomi. 2014. *This Changes Everything: Capitalism vs. the Climate*. Toronto: Knopf Canada.

Klein, Seth. 2006. "The Importance of Public Post-Secondary Education." Vancouver: Canadian Centre for Policy Alternatives.

Kleinman, Daniel, and Steven Vallas. 2001. "Science, Capitalism, and the Rise of the 'Knowledge Worker': The Changing Structure of Knowledge Production in the United States." *Theory and Society* 30, 4.

Krimsky, Sheldon. 2013. "Do Financial Conflicts of Interest Bias Research? An Inquiry into the 'Funding Effect' Hypothesis." *Science, Technology and Human Values* 38, 4.

____. 2008. "When Sponsored Research Fails the Admissions Test: A Normative Framework." In J. Turk (ed.), *Universities at Risk: How Politics, Special Interests and Corporatization Threaten Academic Integrity*. Toronto: James Lorimer.

____. 2003. *Science in the Private Interest: Has the Lure of Profits Corrupted Biomedical Research?* New York: Rowman and Littlefield.

Krimsky S., L.S. Rothenberg, P. Stott and G. Kyle. 1996. "Financial Interests of Authors in Scientific Journals: A Pilot Study of 14 Publications." *Science and Engineering Ethics* 2, 3.

Lacasse, Jeffrey, and Jonathan Leo. 2010. "Ghostwriting at Elite Academic Medical Centers in the United States." *PLoS Medicine* 7, 2.

Lafrance, Xavier. 2010. "The Battle of York." *New Socialist*, September 1. At <newsocialist.org/webzine/analysis/264-the-battle-of-york>.

Larrabure, Manuel, and Carlos Torchia. 2011. "'Our Future Is Not for Sale': The Chilean Student Movement Against Neoliberalism." *The Bullet*, Socialist Project E-Bulletin No. 542, September 6.

Larsen, Mike, and Kevin Walby. 2012. "Introduction: On the Politics of Access to Information." In M. Larsen and K. Walby (eds.), *Brokering Access: Power, Politics, and Freedom of Information Process in Canada*. Vancouver: UBC Press.

Lavars, Nick. 2012. "Students Propose Another Plan for Free Education in Chile." *The Santiago Times*, March 5.

Lea, Russ. 2010. "BP, Corporate R&D, and the University." *Academe* 96, 6.

Leblanc, Daniel. 2014. "Former Harper Advisor Bruce Carson Facing New Charges." *Globe and Mail*, May 12.

Lee, Jenny, and Robert Rhoads. 2004. "Faculty Entrepreneurialism and the Challenge to Undergraduate Education at Research Universities." *Research in Higher Education* 45, 7.

Lesser, Lenard, Cara Ebbeling, Merrill Goozner, David Wypij and David Ludwig. 2007. "Relationship between Funding Source and Conclusion among Nutrition-Related Scientific Articles." *PLoS Medicine* 4, 1.

Levine, Arthur, and Diane Dean. 2012. *Generation on a Tightrope: A Portrait of Today's College Student*. San Francisco: Jossey-Bass.

Levy, Sheldon. 2011. "Innovation and Entrepreneurship: A New Direction for Universities." Speech to the Economic Club of Canada, November 2.

Lexchin, Joel. 2010. "Ontario's Big Pharma Drug War." *The Bullet*, Socialist Project E-Bulletin

No. 342, April 19.

Lexchin, Joel, Lisa Bero, Benjamin Djulbegovic and Otavio Clark. 2003. "Pharmaceutical Industry Sponsorship and Research Outcome and Quality: Systematic Review." *British Medical Journal* 326.

Liu, Shuping, Ursula McCloy and Lindsay DeClou. 2012. "Early Labour Market Outcomes of Ontario College and University Graduates, 1982–2005." Toronto: Higher Education Quality Council of Ontario.

Livingstone, D.W. 1999. *The Education-Jobs Gap: Underemployment or Economic Democracy.* Toronto: Garamond Press.

Loveys, Kate. 2011. "Universities Axe 5,000 'Soft-Degree Courses' as Funding Cuts Sink In." *Daily Mail*, November 21.

Loxley, John. 2010. *Public Service, Private Profits: The Political Economy of Public-Private Partnerships in Canada.* Halifax: Fernwood Publishing.

Luong, May. 2010. "The Financial Impact of Student Loans." Statistics Canada, *Perspectives on Labour and Income* 11, 1. Catalogue No. 75-001-X.

MacAulay, James. 1984. *The Machine in the Garden: The Advent of Industrial Research Infrastructure in the Academic Milieu.* Ottawa: Science Council of Canada.

Macdonald, David, and Erika Shaker. 2012. "Eduflation and the High Cost of Learning." Ottawa: Canadian Centre for Policy Alternatives.

———. 2011. "Under Pressure: The Impact of Rising Tuition Fees on Ontario Families." Ottawa: Canadian Centre for Policy Alternatives.

MacDonald, Moira. 2013. "Sessionals, Up Close." *University Affairs*, January 9.

Mackenzie, Hugh. 2013. "Learning and Earning: The Impact of Taxation in the Higher Education Debates." Ottawa: Canadian Centre for Policy Alternatives.

MacLaren, Jordan. 2014. "It's Complicated: An Interprovincial Comparison of Student Financial Aid. Ottawa: Canadian Centre for Policy Alternatives.

Malcolmson, John, and Marc Lee. 2004. "Financing Higher Learning: Post-Secondary Education Funding in BC." Vancouver: Canadian Centre for Policy Alternatives.

Mangan, Katherine. 2007. "Medical Schools See Many Ties to Industry." *Chronicle of Higher Education*, October 26.

Mangaroo, Kelvin. 2012. "Back to School Reality CHEQUE." At <ratesupermarket.ca/blog/back-to-school-reality-cheque/>.

Marcucci, Pamela, and Alex Usher. 2012. *2011 Year in Review: Global Changes in Tuition Fee Policies and Student Financial Assistance.* Toronto: Higher Education Strategy Associates.

Marcuse, Herbert. 1964. *One-Dimensional Man.* Boston: Beacon Press.

Marginson, Simon, and Mark Considine. 2000. *The Enterprise University: Power, Governance and Reinvention in Australia.* New York: Cambridge University Press.

Maritime Provinces Higher Education Commission. 2008. "Intentions of Maritime University Students Following Graduation." Fredericton, NB: Maritime Provinces Higher Education Commission

———. 2007. "Two Years On: A Survey of Class 2003 Maritime University Graduates." Fredericton, NB: Maritime Provinces Higher Education Commission.

Market Quest Research Group. 2005. "Survey of 2002 New Brunswick High School Graduates." Fredericton: Department of Training and Employment Development and the Department of Education.

Marseilles, Makki. 2011. "Protests Erupt Over Higher Education Reforms." *University World News* 187, September 4.

Marshall, Dave. 2008. "Differentiation by Degrees: System Design and the Changing Undergraduate Environment in Canada." *The Canadian Journal of Higher Education* 38, 3.

Martin, Eric, and Simon Tremblay-Pepin. 2011. "Do We Really Need to Raise Tuition Fees? Eight Misleading Arguments for the Hikes." Montreal: IRIS. At <iris-recherche.qc.ca/wp-content/uploads/2011/09/Brochure-English-web.pdf>.

Maxwell, Judith, and Stephanie Currie. 1984. *Partnership for Growth: Corporate-University Cooperation in Canada*. Montreal: Corporate-Higher Education Forum.

Mazurkewich, Karen. 2011. "Confronting Canada's Innovation Gap." At <opencanada.org/news/op-eds/confronting-canadas-innovation-gap/>.

McAlexander, Harry, and Harold Koenig. 2010. "Contextual Influences: Building Brand Community in Large and Small Colleges." *Journal of Marketing for Higher Education* 20, 1.

McDaniel, Susan, Bonnie Watt-Malcolm and Lloyd Wong. 2013. "Is the Math Sufficient? Aging Workforce and the Future Labour Market in Canada." Available at <uleth.ca/prenticeinstitute/sites/prenticeinstitute/files/KnowledgeSynthesis%20full%20report%20--McDaniel%20Watt-Malcolm%20Wong.pdf>.

McElroy, Lori. 2005. "Student Aid and University Persistence: Does Debt Matter?" Montreal: Canada Millennium Scholarship Foundation.

McGrath, Earl. 1936. "The Control of Higher Education in America." *Educational Record* 17.

McKibben, Bill. 2012. "Global Warming's Terrifying New Math." *Rolling Stone*, July 19.

McMahon, Walter. 2009. *Higher Learning, Greater Good: The Private and Social Benefits of Higher Education*. Baltimore: Johns Hopkins University Press.

McMurtry, John. 2010. "Beyond Market Self-Serving: Recovering the Academy's Vocation." In J. Newson and C. Polster (eds.), *Academic Callings: The University We Have Had, Now Have, and Could Have*. Toronto: Canadian Scholars' Press.

____. 2009. "The Corporate Administration vs. the Vocation of Learning." Ottawa: Canadian Centre for Policy Alternatives *Monitor*, July/August.

____. 2004. "Reclaiming the Teaching Profession: From Corporate Hierarchy to the Authority of Learning." In D. Doherty-Delorme and E. Shaker (eds.), *Missing Pieces V: An Alternative Guide to Canadian Post-Secondary Education*. Ottawa: Canadian Centre for Policy Alternatives.

____. 1991. "Education and the Market Model." *Journal of Philosophy of Education* 25, 2.

McQuaig, Linda, and Neil Brooks. 2010. *The Trouble With Billionaires*. Toronto: Viking Canada.

Mennie, James, Katherine Wilton, Andy Riga, Chris Curtis, Max Harrold, Roberto Rocha and Jan Ravensbergen. 2012. "Peaceful Day March, Heated Night Demo." *Montreal Gazette*, May 23.

Merton, Robert. 1973. *The Sociology of Science*. Chicago: University of Chicago Press.

Messer, Ellen. 1993. "Manufacturing the Attack on Liberalized Higher Education." *Social Text* 36.

Metcalfe, Amy Scott. 2010. "Revisiting Academic Capitalism in Canada: No Longer the Exception." *Journal of Higher Education* 81, 4.

Migdal, Alex. 2013. "University of Alberta Suspends Admission to 20 Arts Programs." *Edmonton Journal*, August 19.

Mignolo, Walter. 2003. "Globalization and the Geopolitics of Knowledge: The Role of the Humanities in the Corporate University." *Views from South* 4, 1.

Mills, C. Wright. 1963. "The Social Role of the Intellectual." In I. Horowitz (ed.), *Power, Politics and People: The Collected Essays of C. Wright Mills*. New York: Oxford University Press.

———. 1959. *The Sociological Imagination*. London: Oxford University Press.

———. 1956. *The Power Elite*. New York: Oxford University Press.

Milway, James. 2005. "Post-Secondary Education and Ontario's Prosperity." In F. Iacobucci and C. Tuohy (eds.), *Taking Public Universities Seriously*. Toronto: University of Toronto Press.

Miner, Rick. 2010. *People Without Jobs, Jobs Without People: Ontario's Labour Market Future*. Toronto: Miner Management Consultants.

Minsky, Leonard. 2000. "Dead Souls: The Aftermath of Bayh-Dole." In G. White (ed.), *Campus, Inc: Corporate Power in the Ivory Tower*. New York: Prometheus Books.

Mirowski, Philip, and Robert Van Horn. 2005. "The Contract Research Organization and the Commercialization of Scientific Research." *Social Studies of Science* 35, 4.

Molesworth, Mike, Elizabeth Nixon and Richard Scullion. 2009. "Having, Being and Higher Education: The Marketisation of the University and the Transformation of the Student into Consumer." *Teaching in Higher Education* 14, 3.

Moon, Richard. 2014. "Demonstrations on Campus and the Case of Israeli Apartheid Week." In J. Turk (ed.), *Academic Freedom in Conflict: The Struggle Over Free Speech Rights in the University*. Toronto: James Lorimer.

Moore, Holly. 2014. "Cheating Students Punished by the 1000s, But Many More Go Undetected." CBC *News*, February 25.

Morgan, Matthew. 2010. "University of Ottawa Spied on Leading Burmese Activist." *Rabble.ca*, May 14. At <rabble.ca/news/2010/05/university-ottawa-spied-leading-burmese-activist>.

Motte, Anne, Joseph Berger and Andrew Parkin. 2009. "Paying for Post-Secondary Education." In J. Berger, A. Motte and A. Parkin (eds.), *The Price of Knowledge: Access and Student Finance in Canada*. Montreal: Canada Millennium Scholarship Foundation.

Motte, Anne, and Saul Schwartz. 2009. "Are Student Employment and Academic Success Linked?" Montreal: Canada Millennium Scholarship Foundation.

Mount, Joan, and Charles Bélanger. 2001. "'Academic Inc.': The Perspective of University Presidents." *The Canadian Journal of Higher Education* 31, 2.

Mouwen, Kees. 2000. "Strategy, Structure and Culture of the Hybrid University: Toward the University of the 21st Century." *Tertiary Education and Management* 6, 1.

Munro, Daniel. 2014. "Developing Skills: Where Are Canada's Employers?" Ottawa: Conference Board of Canada.

Munro, Margaret. 2009. "Scientists Protest Appointment of Pfizer Boss to Health Panel." *Montreal Gazette*, December 7

Murray, Fiona, and Scott Stern. 2007. "Do Formal Intellectual Property Rights Hinder the Free Flow of Scientific Knowledge? An Empirical Test of the Anti-Commons Hypothesis." *Journal of Economic Behaviour & Organization* 63.

Muzzin, Linda, 2008. "How Fares Equity in an Era of Academic Capitalism? The Role of Continent Faculty." In A. Chan and D. Fisher (eds.), *The Exchange University:*

Corporatization of Academic Culture. Vancouver: UBC Press.
Nadeau, Mary-Jo, and Alan Sears. 2011. "This Is What Complicity Looks Like: Palestine and the Silencing Campaign on Campus." *The Bullet*, Socialist Project E-Bulletin No. 475, March 5.
Nature. 1997. "Avoid Financial 'Correctness.'" *Nature* 385 (6616).
Naylor, David. 2006. "The Trouble With Maclean's." *Ottawa Citizen*, April 22.
Nearing, Scott. 1917. "Who's Who Among College Trustees." *School and Society* 6.
Neatby, Blair. 1985. "The Academic Profession: An Historical Perspective — 'Communities of Scholars in Ontario.'" In *The Professoriate — Occupation in Crisis*. Toronto: Ontario Institute for Studies in Education.
Neill, Christine. 2013. "What You Don't Know Can't Help You: Lessons of Behavioural Economics for Tax-Based Student Aid." C.D. Howe Institute Commentary, No. 393. Toronto: C.D. Howe Institute.
_____. 2009. "Tuition Fees and the Demand for University Places." *Economics of Education Review* 28, 5.
Nelsen, Randle. 2002. *Schooling as Entertainment: Corporate Education Meets Popular Culture*. Kingston: Cedarcreek.
_____ (ed.). 1997. *Inside Canadian Universities: Another Day at the Plant*. Kingston: Cedarcreek.
Nesi, Tom. 2008. *Poison Pills: The Untold Story of the Vioxx Drug Scandal*. New York: Thomas Dunne Books.
Nestle, Marion. 2007. *Food Politics: How the Food Industry Influences Nutrition and Health*. Los Angeles: University of California Press.
Neuman, Jennifer, Deborah Korenstein, Joseph Ross and Salomeh Keyhani. 2011. "Prevalence of Financial Conflicts of Interest among Panel Members Producing Clinical Practice Guidelines in Canada and United States: Cross Sectional Study." *BMJ* 343 (7827).
Newman, John Henry. 1959 [1852]. *The Idea of a University*. New York: Doubleday.
Newson, Janice. 2010. "Recovering the University as a Collective Project." In J. Newson and C. Polster (eds.), *Academic Callings: The University We Have Had, Now Have, and Could Have*. Toronto: Canadian Scholars' Press.
_____. 1998. "The Corporate-Linked University: From Social Project to Market Force." *Canadian Journal of Communication* 23, 1.
_____. 1994. "Subordinating Democracy: The Effects of Fiscal Retrenchment and University-Business Partnerships on Knowledge Creation and Knowledge Dissemination in Universities." *Higher Education* 27, 2.
_____. 1992. "The Decline of Faculty Influence: Confronting the Effects of the Corporate Agenda." In W. Carroll, L. Christiansen-Ruffman, R. Currie and D. Harrison (eds.), *Fragile Truths: Twenty-five Years of Sociology and Anthropology in Canada*. Ottawa: Carleton University Press.
Newson, Janice, and Howard Buchbinder. 1988. *The University Means Business: Universities, Corporations and Academic Work*. Toronto: Garamond Press.
Nikiforuk, Andrew. 2013. "What's Driving Chaotic Dismantling of Canada's Science Libraries?" *The Tyee*, December 23.
Niosi, Jorge. 2006. "Success Factors in Canadian Academic Spin-Offs." *Journal of Technology*

Transfer 31.

Nisbet, Robert. 1971. *The Degradation of the Academic Dogma: The University in America, 1945–1970.* New York: Basic Books.

Noble, David. 2007. "Mamdouh's Mandate: 'Mind to Market.'" At <archive.org/details/MamdouhsMandate-ByDavidFNoble>.

———. 2005. "Private Pretensions: The Battle for Canada's Universities." *Canadian Dimension,* September/October.

———. 2001. *Digital Diploma Mills: The Automation of Higher Education.* New York: Monthly Review Press.

———. 1977. *America by Design: Science, Technology, and the Rise of Corporate Capitalism.* New York: Oxford University Press.

Novek, Joel. 1985. "University Graduates, Jobs and University-Industry Linkages." *Canadian Public Policy* 11, 2.

OCUFA (Ontario Confederation of University Faculty Associations). 2013. "Post-Secondary Education in Ontario: Managing Challenges in an Age of Austerity." At <ocufa.on.ca/wordpress/assets/OCUFA-Survey-2013-General-Results-Jan.-10-2013.pdf>.

———. 2012a. "2012 OCUFA Faculty Survey: Part 1 — Views on University Quality and Faculty Priorities." At <ocufa.on.ca/wordpress/assets/2012-OCUFA-Faculty-Survey-Part-1-Formatted-FINAL.pdf>.

———. 2012b. "2012 OCUFA Faculty Survey: Part 2 — Faculty Views on Proposed Changes to Undergraduate Education." At <ocufa.on.ca/wordpress/assets/Faculty-Survey-Part-2-Government-Proposals-FINAL.pdf>.

———. 2010a. "The Public Wisdom of Public Funding: Ontario Universities and the Recession." Toronto.

———. 2010b. "Investing in Students, Ensuring Success: Recommendations for a Meaningful Successor to Reaching Higher." Toronto.

———. 2010c. "The Decline of Quality at Ontario Universities: Shortchanging a Generation." Toronto.

———. 2009. "Ontario University Faculty Sound Warning Over Declining Quality." At <notes.ocufa.on.ca/OCUFARsrch.nsf/9da1693cdc3d700f852573db006561fc/66196466bf165ff9852576c100766ded?OpenDocument>.

———. 2004. "Restricted Entry: Access to Information at Ontario Universities." *OCUFA Research Report* 5, 4.

Ohlendorf, Pat. 1985. "Industry's New Alliance with Universities." Report on Business Magazine, *Globe and Mail,* October 25.

Olivieri, Nancy. 2000. "When Money and Truth Collide." In J. Turk (ed.), *The Corporate Campus: Commercialization and the Dangers to Canada's Colleges and Universities.* Toronto: James Lorimer.

Omiecinski, Teresa. 2003. "Hiring of Part-Time University Faculty on the Increase." Statistics Canada, *Education Quarterly Review* 9, 3.

Opoku, Robert, Magnus Hultman and Esmail Saheli-Sangari. 2008. "Positioning in Market Space: The Evaluation of Swedish Universities' Online Brand Personalities." *Journal of Marketing for Higher Education* 18, 1.

Organization for Economic Cooperation and Development. 2014. *Education at a Glance 2014: OECD Indicators.* Paris: OECD

Ornstein, Michael. 1988. "Corporate Involvement in Canadian Hospital and University Boards, 1946–1977." *Canadian Review of Sociology and Anthropology* 25, 3.
Owram, Doug. 2010. "Fundraising for Neophytes." *University Affairs*, November 8.
Page, Stewart. 2012. "Final Observations of Canadian University Rankings: A Misadventure Now Over Two Decades Long." *Academic Matters*, November.
Page, Stewart, Kenneth Cramer and Laura Page. 2010. "Canadian University Rankings: Buyer Beware Once Again." *Interchange* 41, 1.
Pakravan, Payam. 2006. "The Future Is Not What It Used to Be: Re-Examining Provincial Postsecondary Funding Mechanisms in Canada." C.D. Howe Institute Commentary, No. 227. Toronto: C.D. Howe Institute.
Paton, Graeme. 2014. "More Students Charged Maximum £9,000 Tuition Fees." *The Telegraph*, August 22.
———. 2013. "University Fee Rise Sparks Surge in Demand for 'Jobs-Based' Degrees." *The Telegraph*, August 21.
Patton, Stacey. 2012. "The PhD Now Comes with Food Stamps." *Chronicle of Higher Education*, May 6.
Paul, Ross. 2011. *Leadership Under Fire: The Challenging Role of the Canadian University President*. Montreal: McGill-Queen's University Press.
Phaneuf, Marie-Rose, Jonathan Lomas, Chris McCutcheon, John Church and Douglas Wilson. 2007. "Square Pegs in Round Holes: The Relative Importance of Traditional and Nontraditional Scholarship in Canadian Universities." *Science Communication* 28, 4.
Pocklington, Tom, and Allan Tupper. 2002. *No Place to Learn: Why Universities Aren't Working*. Vancouver: UBC Press.
Polanyi, Michael. 1969. *Knowing and Being*. Chicago: University of Chicago Press.
Polster, Claire. 2011. "Three Broken Promises: Some Consequences of Administrative Growth in Canadian Universities." *Our Schools, Our Selves* 21, 1.
———. 2010. "Are We Losing Our Minds? Unreason in Canadian Universities Today." In J. Newson and C. Polster (eds.), *Academic Callings: The University We Have Had, Now Have, and Could Have*. Toronto: Canadian Scholars' Press.
———. 2007a. "The Nature and Implications of the Growing Importance of Research Grants to Canadian Universities and Academics." *Higher Education* 53, 5.
———. 2007b. "Private Interests at Public Expense: Transforming Higher Education in Canada." In L. Samuelson and W. Antony (eds.), *Power and Resistance: Critical Thinking About Canadian Social Issues*. Halifax: Fernwood Publishing.
———. 2004. "Rethinking and Remaking Academic Freedom." In D. Doherty-Delorme and E. Shaker (eds.), *Missing Pieces V: An Alternative Guide to Canadian Post-Secondary Education*. Ottawa: Canadian Centre for Policy Alternatives.
———. 2002. "A Break from the Past: Impacts and Implications of the Canada Foundation for Innovation and the Canada Research Chairs Initiatives." *Canadian Review of Sociology and Anthropology* 39, 3.
———. 2000. "The Future of the Liberal University in the Era of the Global Knowledge Grab." *Higher Education* 39, 1.
———. 1998. "From Public Resource to Industry's Instrument: Reshaping the Production of Knowledge in Canada's Universities." *Canadian Journal of Communications* 23, 1.
Porter, John. 1965. *The Vertical Mosaic: An Analysis of Social Class and Power in Canada*.

Toronto: University of Toronto Press.
Porter, John, Marion Porter and Bernard Blishen. 1982. *Stations and Callings: Making it Through the School System.* Toronto: Methuen.
Powell, Lewis. 1971. "Confidential Memorandum: Attack on American Free Enterprise System." At <greenpeace.org/usa/en/campaigns/global-warming-and-energy/polluterwatch/The-Lewis-Powell-Memo/>.
Prairie Research Associates. 2011. "2011 Undergraduate University Student Survey: Master Report." Ottawa: Canadian University Survey Consortium.
———. 2010. "2010 First-Year University Student Survey: Master Report." Ottawa: Canadian University Survey Consortium.
———. 2007a. "First-Year University Student Survey: Master Report 2007." Ottawa: Canadian University Survey Consortium.
———. 2007b. "Report on Student Debt: Canadian College Student Survey and Canadian Undergraduate Survey Consortium." Montreal: Canada Millennium Scholarship Foundation.
———. 2002. "Survey of Undergraduate University Students: Master Report." Ottawa: Canadian University Survey Consortium.
Pritchard, Rosalind. 2005. "Relationships and Values among Students and Staff in British and German Higher Education." *Tertiary Education and Management* 11.
Professional Institute of the Public Service of Canada. 2013. "The Big Chill: Silencing Public Interest Science, A Survey." Available at <pipsc.ca/portal/page/portal/website/issues/science/pdfs/bigchill.en.pdf>.
Pryor, John, Linda DeAngelo, Laura Blake, Sylvia Hurtado and Serge Tran. 2011. *The American Freshman: National Norms Fall 2011.* Los Angeles: Higher Education Research Institute, UCLA.
Prystupa, Mychaylo. 2015. "Fossil Fuel Divestment Fever Hits UBC and other Canadian Campuses." *Vancouver Observer,* January 25.
Puplampu, Korbla. 2004. "The Restructuring of Higher Education and Part-Time Instructors: A Theoretical and Political Analysis of Undergraduate Teaching in Canada." *Teaching in Higher Education* 9, 2.
R.A. Malatest & Associates. 2007. "The Class of 2003: High School Follow-Up Survey." Montreal: Canada Millennium Scholarship Foundation.
Rajagopal, Indhu. 2004. "Tenuous Ties: The Limited-Term Full-Time Faculty in Canadian Universities." *Review of Higher Education* 28, 1.
———. 2002. *Hidden Academics: Contract Faculty in Canadian Universities.* Toronto: University of Toronto Press.
Rajagopal, Indhu, and William Farr. 1992. "Hidden Academics: The Part-Time Faculty in Canada." *Higher Education* 24, 3.
———. 1989. "The Political Economy of Part-Time Academic Work." *Higher Education* 18, 3.
Rancourt, Denis. 2011. "This Is What Targeting a Dissident Tenured Professor Looks Like in Canada." At <http://rancourt.academicfreedom.ca/component/content/article/52.html>.
Readings, Bill. 1996. *The University in Ruins.* Cambridge: Harvard University Press.
Reid, Tim, and Julyan Reid (eds.). 1969. *Student Power and the Canadian Campus.* Toronto: Peter Martin Associates.

Reimer, Marilee (ed.). 2004. *Inside Corporate U: Women in the Academy Speak Out*. Toronto: Sumach Press.
Report of the Steering Committee on Resource Optimization to the University of Ottawa Administrative Committee. 2010. *Resource Optimization*. Ottawa. At <site.uottawa.ca/school/eegsa/public_html/docs/resource-optimization-report.pdf>.
Rhoades, Gary. 1998. *Managed Professionals: Reconstructing Academic Labor in Unionized Institutions*. Albany, NY: State University of New York Press.
Rinne, Risto. 1999. "The Rise of the McUniversity." In I. Fägerlind, I. Holmesland and G. Strömqvist (eds.), *Higher Education at the Crossroads*. Stockholm: Institute of International Education, Stockholm University.
Ritzer, George. 2002. "Enchanting McUniversity: Toward a Spectacularly Irrational University Quotidian." In D. Hayes and R. Wynyard (eds.), *The McDonaldization of Higher Education*. London: Bergin and Garvey.
Robertson, Heather-Jane, David McGrane and Erika Shaker. 2003. "For Cash and Future Considerations: Ontario Universities and Public-Private Partnerships." Ottawa: Canadian Centre for Policy Alternatives.
Robin, Raizel. 2004. "Bright Ideas." *Canadian Business* 77, 3.
Robinson, David. 2006. "The GATS: What's at Stake for Higher Education?" *Education Canada* 46, 4.
Rodríguez, Victor. 2011. "Social Protest and the Future of Higher Education in Puerto Rico." *Academe* 97, 4.
Rosell, Carlos, and Ajay Agrawal. 2009. "Have University Knowledge Flows Narrowed? Evidence from Patent Data." *Research Policy* 38, 1.
Ross, Andrew. 2000. "The Mental Labor Problem." *Social Text* 18, 2.
Ross, Murray. 1966. *New Universities in the Modern World*. New York: St. Martin's Press.
Rothman, David, Walter McDonald, Carol Berkowitz, Susan Chimonas, Catherine DeAngelis, Ralph Hale, Steven Nissen, June Osborn, James Scully, Gerald Thomson and David Wofsy. 2009. "Professional Medical Associations and their Relationships with Industry: A Proposal for Controlling Conflict of Interest." *Journal of the American Medical Association* 301, 13.
Rout, Milanda. 2009. "Vioxx Maker Merck and Co Drew Up Doctor Hit List." *The Australian*, April 1.
Rowat, Donald. 1964. "The Business Analogy." In G. Whalley (ed.), *A Place of Liberty: Essays on the Government of Canadian Universities*. Toronto: Clarke and Irwin.
Russell, Bertrand. 1932. *Education and the Social Order*. London: Allen and Unwin.
Said, Edward. 2004. *Humanism and Democratic Criticism*. New York: Columbia University Press.
____. 1994. *Representations of the Intellectual*. New York: Pantheon.
Salter, Ammon, and Ben Martin. 2001. "The Economic Benefits of Publicly Funded Basic Research: A Critical Review." *Research Policy* 30, 3.
Sanders, Jim. 2005. "Monsanto, Lawyers, Lies and Videotape: Seeds of Censorship Sown at University of Manitoba." *Canadian Dimension* 39, 5.
Sanders, Leslie. 2011. "Teaching-Stream Positions: Some Implications." COU Discussion Paper, No. 849. Toronto: Council of Ontario Universities.
Schafer, Arthur. 2008. "The University as Corporate Handmaiden: Who're Ya Gonna Trust?"

In J. Turk (ed.), *Universities at Risk: How Politics, Special Interests and Corporatization Threaten Academic Integrity*. Toronto: James Lorimer.

———. 2004. "Biomedical Conflicts of Interest: A Defence of the Sequestration Thesis — Learning from the Cases of Nancy Olivieri and David Healy." *Journal of Medical Ethics* 30, 1.

Schmidt, Jeff. 2000. *Disciplined Minds: A Critical Look at Salaried Professionals and the Soul-Battering System that Shapes their Lives*. Lanham, MD: Rowman and Littlefield.

Schrecker, Ellen. 2010. *The Lost Soul of Higher Education: Corporatization, the Assault on Academic Freedom, and the End of the American University*. New York: New Press.

Schwartz, Saul. 1999. "The Dark Side of Student Loans: Debt Burden, Default, and Bankruptcy." *Osgoode Hall Law Journal* 37, 1&2.

Sears, Alan. 2003. *Retooling the Mind Factory: Education in a Lean State*. Aurora, ON: Garamond Press.

Seidman, Karen. 2014. "Academics Unimpressed with Ottawa's New Research Fund." *Montreal Gazette*, December 10.

———. 2013. "Universities Urged to Put Focus Back on Basic Research." *Montreal Gazette*, April 25.

Senate of Canada. 2011. "Opening the Door: Reducing Barriers to Post-Secondary Education in Canada." Ottawa: Standing Senate Committee on Social Affairs, Science and Technology.

Serebrin, Jacob. 2010. "It's True. Teaching Takes a Back Seat to Research." *Maclean's*, November 14.

Shaker, Erika. 2006. "Funding Issues and Universities." Presentation at CUPE National University Workers Meeting, Montreal. At <cupe.ca/research/Funding_Issues_and_U>.

———. 1999. "The Privatization of Post-Secondary Institutions." *Education, Limited* 1, 4.

Shaker, Erica, and David Macdonald. 2014. "Tier for Two: Managing the Optics of Provincial Tuition Fee Policies." Ottawa: Canadian Centre for Policy Alternatives.

Shapiro, Ben. 2004. *Brainwashed: How Universities Indoctrinate America's Youth*. Nashville, TN: Thomas Nelson.

Sharav, Vera. 2014. "Peer-Reviewed Research to Support Drug Approval Often False." *Health Impact News*. At <healthimpactnews.com/2012/peer-reviewed-research-support-drug-approval-often-false/>.

Shrimpton, Gordon. 1987. "The Crisis in Canadian Universities." In T. Wotherspoon (ed.), *The Political Economy of Canadian Schooling*. Toronto: Methuen.

Sinclair, Upton. 1923. *The Goose-Step: A Study of American Education*. Pasadena, CA: Self-Published.

Singleton, Sharon. 2010. "Parents Can't Foot University Bill." *Toronto Sun*, September 23.

Singleton-Jackson, Jill, Dennis Jackson and Jeff Reinhardt. 2010. "Students as Consumers of Knowledge: Are They Buying What We're Selling?" *Innovative Higher Education* 35, 5.

Sismondo, Sergio. 2009. "Ghosts in the Machine: Publication Planning in the Medical Sciences." *Social Studies of Science* 39, 2.

———. 2008. "Pharmaceutical Company Funding and Its Consequences: A Qualitative Systematic Review." *Contemporary Clinical Trials* 29.

———. 2007. "Ghost Management: How Much of the Medical Literature is Shaped Behind

the Scenes by the Pharmaceutical Industry?" *PLoS Medicine* 4, 9.
Skolnik, Michael. 1988. Review of The University Means Business. *The Canadian Journal of Higher Education* 18, 1.
Slaughter, Sheila, and Larry Leslie. 1997. *Academic Capitalism: Politics, Policies, and the Entrepreneurial University*. Baltimore: The Johns Hopkins University Press.
Slaughter, Sheila, and Gary Rhoades. 2008. "The Academic Capitalist Knowledge/Learning Regime." In A. Chan and D. Fisher (eds.), *The Exchange University: Corporatization of Academic Culture*. Vancouver: UBC Press.
___. 2004. *Academic Capitalism in the New Economy: Markets, State and Higher Education*. Baltimore: Johns Hopkins University Press.
Small, J.M. 1994. "Reform in Canadian Universities." *Canadian Journal of Higher Education* 24, 2.
Smith, Richard. 2005. "Medical Journals Are an Extension of the Marketing Arm of Pharmaceutical Companies." *PLoS Medicine* 2, 5.
Smith, Stuart. 1991. *Report: Commission of Inquiry on Canadian University Education*. Ottawa: Association of Universities and Colleges of Canada.
Smith, W.D. 2010. "Where All that Money Is Going." *Maclean's*, January 14.
Snider, Laureen. 2003. "Researching Corporate Crime." In S. Tombs and D. Whyte (eds.), *Unmasking the Crimes of the Powerful: Scrutinizing States and Corporations*. New York: Peter Lang.
___. 2000. "The Sociology of Corporate Crime: An Obituary." *Theoretical Criminology* 4, 2.
Solty, Ingar. 2012. "Canada's 'Maple Spring:' From the Quebec Student Strike to the Movement Against Neoliberalism." *The Bullet*, Socialist Project E-Bulletin No. 752, December 31.
Stanford, Jim. 2014. "The Myth of the Skills Shortage in Canada's Labour Market." *Rabble.ca*, January 8.
___. 2013. "It'll Take More than Window Dressing to Fix This Problem." Ottawa: Canadian Centre for Policy Alternatives Monitor, June.
Starfield, Barbara. 2000. "Is US Health Really the Best in the World?" *Journal of the American Medical Association* 284, 4.
Statistics Canada. 2012. "University Tuition Fees, 2012/2013." *The Daily*, September 12. At <statcan.gc.ca/daily-quotidien/120912/dq120912a-eng.pdf>.
___. 2010a. "University Enrolment." *The Daily*, July 14. At <www.statcan.gc.ca/daily-quotidien/100714/dq100714a-eng.htm>.
___. 2010b. *Survey of Intellectual Property Commercialization in the Higher Education Sector 2008*. Ottawa.
___. 2009a. "Transitions to the Labour Market." Ottawa. Catalogue No. 81-599-X. Issue No. 002.
___. 2009b. "Postsecondary Enrolment and Graduation, October 2009." Ottawa. Catalogue No. 81-599-X. At <statcan.gc.ca/pub/81-599-x/81-599-x2009003-eng.htm>.
___. 2005. "University Enrolment." *The Daily*, October 11. At <statcan.gc.ca/daily-Quotidien/051011/dq051011b-eng.htm>.
___. 2000. *Survey of Intellectual Property Commercialization in the Higher Education Sector 1999*. Ottawa.
Steck, Henry. 2003. "Corporatization of the University: Seeking Conceptual Clarity." *Annals*

of the American Academy of Political and Social Science 585.
Steele, Ken. 2010. "Knowing Your Undergraduates." *Academic Matters*, October/November.
Stelfox, Henry, Grace Chua, Keith O'Rourke and Allan Detsky. 1998. "Conflict of Interest in the Debate Over Calcium-Channel Antagonists." *New England Journal of Medicine* 338, 2.
Stewart, Penni. 2011. "Collaborations: Are Universities Sacrificing Integrity?" CAUT *Bulletin* 58 (5).
———. 2010. "Nothing Casual about Academic Work." CAUT *Bulletin* 57, 5.
Street, Steve, Maria Maisto, Esther Merves and Gary Rhoades. 2012. "Who Is Professor 'Staff'" *Center for the Future of Higher Education*, Policy Report #2.
Stripling, Jack. 2011. "Most Presidents Prefer No Tenure for Majority of Faculty." *Chronicle of Higher Education*, May 15.
Students for a Democratic Society. 1962. "Port Huron Statement of the Students for a Democratic Society, 1962." At <h-net.org/~hst306/documents/huron.html>.
STV News. 2014. "Scots Have Saved £1bn in University Fees, Says Holyrood Research." October 5. <news.stv.tv/politics/294601-scots-have-saved-1bn-in-university-fees-says-holyrood-research/>.
Sumner, Jennifer. 2008. "Keeping the Commons in Academic Culture: Protecting the Knowledge Commons from the Enclosure of the Knowledge Economy." In A. Chan and D. Fisher (eds.), *The Exchange University: Corporatization of Academic Culture*. Vancouver: UBC Press.
Tal, Benjamin. 2013. "Dimensions of Youth Employment in Canada." CIBC, June 20. At <research.cibcwm.com/economic_public/download/if_2013-0620.pdf>.
Tamburri, Rosanna. 2012. "Full-Time Canadian Faculty Report High Job Satisfaction." *University Affairs*, June 6.
Tandem Social Research Consulting. 2007. *Literature Review of Postsecondary Education in Canada*. Toronto: Council of Ministers of Education, Canada.
Tanguay, Denise. 2003. "Inefficient Efficiency: A Critique of Merit Pay." In B. Johnson, P. Kavanagh and K. Mattson (eds.), *Steal This University: The Rise of the Corporate University and the Academic Labor Movement*. New York: Routledge.
Tannock, Stuart. 2006. "Higher Education, Inequality, and the Public Good." *Dissent* 53, 2.
Tedesco, Theresa. 2012. "The Uneasy Ties Between Canada's Universities and Wealthy Business Magnates." *Financial Post*, March 9.
Thompson, E.P. 1970. "The Business University." *New Society* 386.
Thompson, Jon. 2011. *No Debate: The Israeli Lobby and Free Speech at Canadian Universities*. Toronto: James Lorimer.
———. 2008. "Academic Integrity and the Public Interest." In J. Turk (ed.), *Universities at Risk: How Politics, Special Interests and Corporatization Threaten Academic Integrity*. Toronto: James Lorimer.
Thompson, Paul, Philippe Constantineau and George Fallis. 2006. "Academic Citizenship." Council of Ontario Universities Working Paper Series 5 (2).
Tremblay-Pepin, Simon. 2013. "Tuition Hike and the Media between 2005 and 2010 in Quebec." Ottawa: Canadian Centre for Policy Alternatives. At <behindthenumbers.ca/2013/02/14/tuition-hike-and-the-media-between-2005-and-2010-in-quebec/>.
Tudiver, Neil. 1999. *Universities for Sale: Resisting Corporate Control over Canadian Higher Education*. Toronto: James Lorimer.

Turk, James (ed.). 2014. *Academic Freedom in Conflict: The Struggle Over Free Speech Rights in the University.* Toronto: James Lorimer.
____. 2009. "Low Blow from 'Top Five' Universities." *Toronto Star*, September 1.
____ (ed.). 2008. *Universities at Risk: How Politics, Special Interests and Corporatization Threaten Academic Integrity.* Toronto: James Lorimer.
____ (ed.). 2000. *The Corporate Campus: Commercialization and the Dangers to Canada's Colleges and Universities.* Toronto: James Lorimer.
Turner, David. 2010. "University Managers Outpace Academics." *Financial Times*, February 22.
Tyers, Mike, et al. 2005. "Problems with Co-Funding in Canada." *Science* 308 (5730).
Umbach, Paul. 2007. "How Effective Are They? Exploring the Impact of Contingent Faculty on Undergraduate Education." *The Review of Higher Education* 30, 2.
Universities Allied for Essential Medicines. 2013. "University Global Health Impact Report Card." At <globalhealthgrades.org/>.
University of Guelph. 2008. "Strategic Research Plan." At <uoguelph.ca/research/assets/policies/srp_2008/guelph_srp.pdf>.
University of Toronto. 2010. "Memorandum of Agreement Between the Peter and Melanie Munk Charitable Foundation and the Governing Council at the University of Toronto." At <individual.utoronto.ca/paul_hamel/Documents/Munk_MoA-Global_Affairs.pdf>.
Uppal, Sharanjit, and Sébastien LaRochelle-Côté. 2014a. "Changes in the Occupational Profile of Young Men and Women in Canada." Statistics Canada, Catalogue No. 75-006-X.
____. 2014b. "Overqualification Among Recent University Graduates in Canada." Statistics Canada. Catalogue No. 75-006-X.
Urback, Robyn. 2014. "University of Saskatchewan President Needs a Lesson in Free Speech 101." *National Post*, May 15.
Usher, Alex. 2014. "Who's Progressive?" Toronto: Higher Education Strategy Associates. At <http://higheredstrategy.com/whos-progressive/>.
Usher, Alex, and Patrick Duncan. 2008. "Beyond the Sticker Shock: A Closer Look at Canadian Tuition Fees." Toronto: Educational Policy Institute.
Usher, Alex, and Andrew Potter. 2006. "A State of the Field Review of Post-Secondary Education." Toronto: Canadian Council on Learning.
Vajoczki, Susan, Nancy Fenton, Karen Menard and Dawn Pollon. 2011. "Teaching Stream Faculty in Ontario Universities." Toronto: Higher Education Quality Council of Ontario.
Vallance, Elizabeth. 1983. "Hiding the Hidden Curriculum: An Interpretation of the Language of Justification in Nineteenth-Century Educational Reform." In H. Giroux and D. Purpel (eds.), *The Hidden Curriculum and Moral Education.* Berkeley: McCutchan Publishing Corporation.
Vallas, Steven, and Daniel Kleinman. 2008. "Contradiction, Convergence, and the Knowledge Economy: The Co-Evolution of Academic and Commercial Biotechnology." *Socio-Economic Review* 6, 2.
Valleau, John, and Paul Hamel. 2010. "Idea and Reality: The University or the Universities." In J. Newson and C. Polster (eds.), *Academic Callings: The University We Have Had, Now Have, and Could Have.* Toronto: Canadian Scholars' Press.

Valpy, Michael. 2010. "Universities Bowed to Pressure by Balsillie-Funded Think Tank Over Academic Freedom, Report Says." *Globe and Mail*, October 29.

Van Loon, Richard. 2005. "Universities and Living Standards in Canada." *Canadian Public Policy* 31, 4.

Veblen, Thorstein. 1918. *The Higher Learning in America: A Memorandum on the Conduct of Universities by Business Men*. New York: B.W. Huebsch.

____. 2004 (reprinted). *The Higher Learning in America: A Memorandum on the Conduct of Universities by Business Men*. Kila, Montana: Kessinger.

Vincent-Lancrin, Stéphan. 2006. "What Is Changing in Academic Research? Trends and Future Scenarios." *European Journal of Education* 41, 2.

Vojak, Colleen. 2006. "What Market Culture Teaches Students About Ethical Behavior." *Ethics and Education* 1, 2.

von Humboldt, Wilhelm.1963. *Humanist Without Portfolio: An Anthology of the Writings of Wilhelm von Humboldt*. Detroit: Wayne State University Press.

Wallerstein, Immanual. 1969. *University in Turmoil: The Politics of Change*. New York: Atheneum.

Walters, Joe. 2010. "Neo-Liberals Push University Privatisation." *University World News* 124, May 16.

Washburn, Jennifer. 2010. "Big Oil Goes to College: An Analysis of 10 Research Collaboration Contracts between Leading Energy Companies and Major U.S. Universities." Washington, DC: Center for American Progress.

____. 2005. *University Inc: The Corporate Corruption of American Higher Education*. New York: Basic Books.

Webber, Michelle. 2008. "Miss Congeniality Meets the New Managerialism: Feminism, Contingent Labour, and the New University." *Canadian Journal of Higher Education* 38, 3.

Wente, Margaret. 2012. "Quebec's Tuition Protesters are the Greeks of Canada." *Globe and Mail*, May 19.

Westhues, Kenneth. 2009. "Ottawa's Dismissal of Denis Rancourt." At <arts.uwaterloo.ca/~kwesthue/Rancourt09.htm>.

____. 2004. *Administrative Mobbing at the University of Toronto: The Trial, Degradation, and Dismissal of a Professor during the Presidency of J. Robert S. Prichard*. Queenston, ON: Edwin Mellen Press.

Weston, Greg. 2013. "Peeved Harper Aims at 'Remaking Canadian Labour Force.'" CBC *News*, March 18.

Whitaker, Robert. 2010. *Anatomy of an Epidemic: Magic Bullets, Psychiatric Drugs, and the Astonishing Rise of Mental Illness in America*. New York: Crown Publishers.

Whitehead, Alfred North. 1967 [1929]. *The Aims of Education*. New York: Basic Books.

Williams, Jeffrey. 2012. "Academic Freedom and Indentured Students." *Academe* 98, 1.

Willinsky, John, Sally Murray, Claire Kendall and Anita Palepu. 2007. "Doing Medical Journals Differently: *Open Medicine*, Open Access, and Academic Freedom." *Canadian Journal of Communication* 32.

Wilson, Duff. 2010. "Drug Maker Hired Writing Company for Doctor' Book, Documents Say." *New York Times*, November 29.

____. 2009. "Harvard Medical School in Ethics Quandary." *New York Times*, March 2.

Wolff, Robert. 1969. *The Ideal of the University*. Boston: Beacon Press.

Wollan, Malia, and Tamar Lewin. 2009. "Students Protest Tuition Increases." *New York Times*, November 20.
Woodhouse, Howard. 2009. *Selling Out: Academic Freedom and the Corporate Market*. Montreal: McGill-Queen's University Press.
Wright, Simon, and Colin Cortbus. 2014. "Watch Dodgy Firms Offer Ready-Written Essays to Help Cheating Students Get a Degree." *The Mirror*, June 28.
York University. 2012. "York University Factbook." At <yorku.ca/factbook/factbook.asp?Year=2011+-+2012>.
Young, Terence. 2012. "Facts on Prescription Drug Deaths and the Drug Industry." *DCA Watch*. At <dcawatch.com/facts-on-prescription-drug-deaths-and-the-drug-industry/>.

INDEX

academic capitalism, 26–31, 39, 143, 151, 176
academic capitalists, 28, 30, 32, 148, 158
academic dishonesty, 83–4, 165–6
academic freedom, 4, 10, 17, 25–6, 32, 64, 66, 107, 118–9, 123–6, 136–7, 148, 155, 169, 172n6, 175–6, 178, 187
academic labour (see also employment; teaching, universities), 4–5, 11, 25, 42, 44–5, 49–52, 59–60, 68–9, 72, 176–7, 180–1, 192
    casualization of academic labour, 4–5, 44, 50, 53, 56, 60, 65–6, 68–9, 173, 176–7, 180–1
    contract faculty, 10–11, 26, 28, 46, 49–72, 73n2, 73n4, 73n5, 73n6, 73n7, 74n8, 118, 175, 180–1, 191n1
    contract faculty in Ontario universities, 49–59, 71–2, 180
    hiring, 25–6, 37, 45, 50–61, 63, 65–6, 71–2, 106, 108, 111, 118, 135–7, 181
    job security, 49, 53, 57, 64–6, 69–71, 180, 187
    labour "flexibility", 60, 71, 181
    salaries, 15, 25–6, 48, 50, 59, 61–2, 69–70, 72n1, 107, 109, 180, 184
    teaching-stream positions, 47–8, 57, 59, 68, 180
    tenured/tenure track faculty, 26, 28, 48–65, 68–9, 71–2, 73n2, 135, 138n2, 180–1, 186
    transformation of, 52, 59–60, 70
    unions/unionization, 29, 42n2, 49, 55, 65, 68, 107, 180–1, 184
Acadia University, 14
access to higher education, 14, 21–2, 24–5, 47, 75, 87, 90, 93, 97, 100–2, 104, 121
    universal access, 21–2, 25, 87
access to information (ATI) requests (see also FIPPA), 53–5, 71, 119, 125
administrators, higher education, 11, 17–19, 26–8, 30, 35, 37, 44, 48–9, 53–5, 59–62, 64–5, 69, 71, 73n2, 73n5, 78, 91–2, 95, 105, 105n3, 106–12, 116–26, 129, 136, 138n1, 138n2, 148–9, 151, 175–6, 178–9, 181, 187–8, 193
    administrative growth, 48, 108–10, 122, 138n1
    administrative salaries, 108–9, 112
    administrative secrecy, 53–5, 106, 108, 118, 124, 135, 137, 142
Algoma University, 133
American Association of University Professors (AAUP), 52, 66, 179
Association of Universities and Colleges of Canada (AUCC), 6, 40, 45, 47, 49, 57, 59, 61, 67, 73n1, 81, 91, 123, 134, 142, 146, 149–50, 171–2n1
Athabasca University, 23, 112

austerity, 2, 36–9, 41, 43n6, 50, 57, 108, 118, 183

biotechnology, 150, 159, 162–3, 171, 179
Bissell, Claude, 19, 110, 122
Brock University, 58, 133, 148–9, 172n4
business administration (see higher education, universities)
Business Council on National Issues (BCNI), 35, 38

Canada Research Chairs (CRC) program, 39, 143–4
Canadian Association of University Business Officers (CAUBO), 35, 48, 109, 133
Canadian Association of University Teachers (CAUT), 10, 24, 40–1, 51, 62, 72, 73n1, 85–6, 95, 98, 101–2, 106, 109, 112, 115, 118–9, 133, 136–7, 138n3, 143, 145, 160, 161, 188
Canadian Council of Chief Executives (CCCE), 35, 50, 115, 130, 148
Canadian Federation of Students (CFS), 93–5, 98, 101–2, 105n3, 133
Canadian Foundation for Innovation (CFI) (see also infrastructure, universities), 28, 39, 114, 131–3, 138n5, 142–3
Canadian Institutes of Health Research (CIHR), 143, 145, 170
Canadian Manufacturers' Association (CMA), 16, 22, 35
Carleton University, 50, 56, 58, 92, 115, 137, 172n4
Centres of Excellence for Commercialization and Research (CECR), 143–4
Chomsky, Noam, 13–14, 16, 90, 185, 187, 189
class size, 26, 46, 67, 71, 119, 121
CLASSÉ (see also student movements), 1, 183–4
climate change, 9, 145, 162, 171, 184–5, 190–1

collective bargaining, 64, 107, 181
commodification, 1, 10, 17, 27, 34, 82–3, 187, 193
completion times, 102–3, 119
compulsory fees, 86, 88
Concordia University, 82, 115
Conservative Party
  of Alberta, 119
  of Canada, 37, 40–1, 78, 125, 127, 137, 138n4, 140, 143–6, 170
  of Manitoba, 87
  of Newfoundland, 88
  of Ontario, 36, 39, 87, 120
contract faculty (see academic labour)
Corporate-Higher Education Forum (CHEF), 35, 38, 43n4, 114, 141, 155
corporate-university partnerships, 4, 35, 38–9, 42n3, 48, 92, 108, 111, 118–9, 130–7, 140–3, 145, 150, 155, 159–62, 175–6, 178–9
corporatization, 2–5, 9–12, 26–42, 173–7
  the corporate university, 3, 5, 16, 20–1, 26–7, 42, 50, 60, 72, 106, 122–3, 128, 158, 170, 174, 178, 192
  resistance to corporatization, professors, 182, 185–90
  resistance to corporatization, students, 1–2, 182–6, 190–1
Council of Ontario Universities, 52, 67, 127, 133
curriculum, 4, 15, 17, 19, 23–5, 27, 33–4, 46, 62, 107, 118, 122, 125–6, 128, 132, 135–7, 153, 193
  curriculum reform, 9, 11, 24–5, 78, 125–31, 192–3

Dalhousie University, 15, 63, 73n7, 80, 92, 112, 115
deferred maintenance, 37, 133
Dewey, John, 77
donor agreements, 4, 130, 134–7, 176

economic (national) competitiveness, 9,

22, 32, 34, 141, 190
economic/corporate elites, 14–16, 21–2,
    35, 38, 113–4, 124
economic growth, 9, 22–3, 25, 32–3, 190
employment (see also academic labour;
    job training), 6–7, 20, 22, 25, 27,
    50, 75, 78, 190
  precarious employment, 6, 10, 55,
    61, 64–5, 69–72
  student employment, 102–3, 105n1,
    159
  unemployment, 2, 9, 103, 183, 190
  of university faculty, 10, 50–5, 57,
    60–3, 65–7, 70, 72, 111, 180–1
  of university graduates, 6–7, 89, 97,
    119–20, 123, 127–8, 130
enrolment, 6, 12n1, 24, 26, 38, 41, 64,
    71–2, 81, 92–3, 95, 98, 100–2, 108,
    118, 121, 127, 131
entrepreneurs/entrepreneurialism, 27,
    30–2, 47, 143, 150, 154, 172n4,
    192

faculty (see academic labour)
fossil fuel industry, 41, 125, 137, 144–6,
    160, 162, 184–5
Freedom of Information and Protection
    of Privacy Act, Ontario (FIPPA),
    54–5, 71, 137
funding, universities
  capital funding (see also infrastruc-
    ture, universities), 130–4
  corporate funding, 11, 24, 28–9, 35,
    38–41, 43n5, 78, 111, 123, 126,
    129, 146, 153, 164–6, 169, 171n1,
    176, 178–9, 193
  fundraising, 18, 41, 108–11, 122,
    131, 134, 158
  operating revenues, 24, 38–9, 41,
    43n6, 85, 120, 129, 133–4, 138n5
  public funding, 10–11, 24–5, 36–42,
    85, 87, 92–8, 125, 129, 131–4,
    142–6, 150, 165, 170–1, 173, 188
  public funding cuts, 2, 11, 27, 31,
    35–9, 42, 43n6, 69, 78–9, 87,

89–92, 94, 107–8, 116, 188, 192–3
  research funding (see also research,
    universities), 19, 26, 28, 41, 48,
    139, 141–7, 153, 155–9, 161–2,
    165–7, 170–1, 171n1, 178–9
  underfunding, 9, 36, 38, 41

General Agreement on Trade in Services
    (GATS), 6, 34–5
"golden age" of Canadian higher educa-
    tion, 21–6, 37, 107, 114
governance, universities, 2, 4–5, 10–12,
    16, 18, 22, 24–7, 36–7, 42n2,
    47, 50, 53, 62, 71, 106–7, 113–4,
    116–9, 129, 134, 137, 173–8, 180,
    193
  boards of governors, 16–18, 20, 25,
    106–7, 110, 112–6, 118, 124–5
  collegial governance, 4, 10–11, 18,
    25–6, 36, 53, 62, 68, 71, 107–8,
    117–9, 126, 175–6
  corporate governance models, 4, 37,
    42, 105–10, 116–9, 126, 129, 134,
    137, 173–4, 176–8, 193
  managerialism, 60, 106–8, 116–8,
    120, 137, 178, 192
  senates, 25, 106, 113, 118
  university-corporate board inter-
    locks, 113 –5
  university presidents/CEOs, 15,
    19–20, 26, 35, 41, 43n4, 49, 55,
    61, 66, 92, 110–15, 122, 124–5,
    138n2, 150, 174, 177
grades (grading), 82, 103, 122

Harper government (see also Conserva-
    tive Party of Canada), 40–1, 78,
    125, 127, 137, 138n4, 143–6, 170
health care, 34, 38, 94, 134, 183
higher education, universities
  business administration/schools, 16,
    81, 85, 128–9
  credentials, 5, 7, 81, 83, 93, 193
  in crisis, 12, 21–3, 36, 66, 169, 174,
    178

and decentralization in Canada, 10, 29, 87
degrees, 5–6, 24, 51, 62, 67, 73n8, 81–4, 89, 93, 96, 102–3, 105n2, 122, 128, 145
and "efficiency", 67, 71, 84, 94, 116–7, 177, 193
engineering, 16, 22–3, 78, 81, 111, 126, 128–32, 134, 140, 142–3, 145, 156, 159, 161
and the global economic crisis, 57, 94, 103
and globalization, 32–3, 191
graduates (see also employment), 26, 51, 62, 75, 77, 81, 93, 96–101, 103–4, 113, 119–20, 127, 129–30
health sciences, 131–3, 142–4, 156–7
humanities, 28, 40, 51, 55, 68, 72, 81, 125, 128, 130–2, 134, 143–4, 148
and inequality, 4, 7–8, 15, 19, 34, 52, 62–3 67, 73–4n8, 77, 93–4, 97, 101–2, 130, 134, 182–3, 185, 190
and "innovation", 132–3, 142
natural sciences, 23, 78, 131–2, 142–5
policy, 10–11, 21, 27, 29–30, 32, 37, 39, 41, 71, 78, 87–8, 97–9, 105, 113–4, 116, 124, 139–47, 171
professional programs, 16–17, 28, 51, 76–8, 85, 91, 101, 103–4, 128
as a public good (public service mission), 7–10, 14, 21, 25, 27–8, 32–3, 93, 137, 176, 186
and social activism 1–2, 9, 33, 64, 104, 106, 124, 182–5, 190
and social justice, 7–8, 19, 21, 93, 185, 190–1
and social movements, 1–2, 21–2, 25, 56, 106, 125, 174, 182–91
social sciences, 19, 24, 28, 40, 42n1, 51, 55–6, 81, 127, 131–4, 143–4, 148, 157
subversive function, 8, 13, 33, 176, 186–7, 191

and values, 2–4, 7–8, 10–11, 14, 18, 21, 26–7, 31–2, 34, 36, 64, 75–6, 80–1, 84, 116–7, 126, 130, 155, 160, 173, 175–6, 192
humanities (see higher education, universities)

Industry Canada, 132–3, 142
infrastructure, universities, 4, 15, 22, 49, 107, 126, 130–4, 142, 148–50, 179
institutional differentiation, 41, 47–8, 108, 126
institutional transformation, 4–5, 10, 12, 25–7, 42, 52, 59–60, 70, 75, 77, 79, 81, 84, 105, 107, 122, 125, 137, 141, 148, 158, 174–6, 180, 182
intellectual property (see also technology transfer), 11, 28, 34, 119, 135, 139–40, 142–3, 147–9, 152–4, 158–9, 171, 192
  licensing, 27–8, 120, 150–4, 159
  patents, 27–8, 119, 147, 150–4, 159, 167
  spin-off companies, 27, 143, 150, 152–4
intellectuals, 16, 31, 33–4, 64, 70, 110, 114, 182, 185–9
ivory tower, 9, 19–20, 110, 147, 181, 190

job (vocational) training, 8, 17, 19–20, 23–4, 35, 38–9, 75–8, 105n1, 113, 119, 126–7, 130, 173–4, 193

Kerr, Clark, 20
Knowledge Infrastructure Program (KIP) (see infrastructure, universities)

labour market, 38, 52, 60, 78, 94, 110, 127, 129–30, 181, 190
Lakehead University, 122, 149
Laurentian University, 58
liberal arts (see also higher education, universities), 4, 6, 17, 24–5, 28, 38, 52, 56, 73n5, 81, 126–30, 193
liberal education, 4, 8, 10, 17, 24–5, 38,

49, 75–8, 107, 126, 128
Liberal Party
   of British Columbia, 87
   of Canada, 37–40, 105n3, 142–3
   of Newfoundland, 88
   of Ontario, 87, 120
   of Quebec, 1, 87–8

marketing, universities, 28, 79, 91–2, 122–3, 137, 193
   branding, universities, 5, 91–2, 122–3, 125
McGill University, 14–15, 41, 85, 114–5, 172n6
McMaster University, 15, 66, 72, 92, 111–2, 134, 179
medicine (see also research, universities), 50, 85, 103, 111, 128, 134, 156, 159, 162–70, 172n6, 179–80
   doctors (physicians), 104, 163, 170, 179
   medical schools, 83, 85, 104, 126, 162–3, 170, 179
Memorial University, 88, 100, 112
Mills, C. Wright, 76–7, 185, 188
Mount Allison University, 111
Munk School of Global Affairs, 135–6

National Research Council (NRC), 16, 146
Natural Sciences and Engineering Research Council (NSERC), 140–1, 143–5
neoliberalism, 2, 32–5, 49, 60, 84, 114, 116, 128, 134, 147, 183–5, 189–90
New Democratic Party (NDP), 87
Nipissing University, 58, 72
Noble, David, 3, 8, 10, 17, 26, 34, 124

online/distance education, 5, 10, 23, 28, 71, 129, 193
Ontario Confederation of University Faculty Associations (OCUFA), 40, 45, 48, 52–4, 57, 67, 71–2, 95, 102, 105n2, 180
Organization for Economic Cooperation and Development (OECD), 6, 90, 96, 127, 146, 152

peer review, 25, 127, 147, 155, 162, 167–8, 170–1, 177
performance indicators (see also governance, universities), 107, 119–20, 178, 193
pharmaceutical industry (see also research, universities), 145, 156, 159, 161–71, 179–80
plagiarism (see academic dishonesty)
privatization, 4, 36, 89, 114–5, 147, 157, 183–4
professoriate, 27, 31, 53, 62, 107, 118, 126, 148
public sector, public sphere, 1–2, 4, 7, 11, 21–2, 25, 30, 34, 39, 43, 50, 81, 116, 182, 184–5

Queen's University, 14, 16, 58, 115, 172n3

ranking systems, universities, 107, 117, 120–1, 175, 193
research, universities (see also funding, universities)
   basic research, 141, 145, 147–8, 154, 170–1
   clinical trials, 163–4, 167–9, 172n5
   commercialization, 4, 8, 11, 28–31, 40, 42, 47, 111, 117, 119, 129, 132, 139, 141–55, 159, 162–4, 169, 171, 177, 192
   conflicts of interest, 119, 155, 160–2, 164–6, 178
   drug research, 145, 156, 159, 162–70, 172n5, 172n7
   ghost writing/ghost management (in biomedical research), 166–8, 179
   medical journals, 163–8, 170, 179
   medical research, 126, 140, 150, 162–70
   research bias, 139, 148, 160–2, 164–6, 168–9, 179
   research culture, 10, 30, 149, 153,

155, 158
research and development (R&D), 29, 146, 149, 154–5
research granting councils (see also CIHR, NSERC, SSHRC), 40, 140, 143–5
research grants, 27, 46–7, 120, 140, 143, 145–6, 178
research policy (federal), 139–47, 170–1
research secrecy, 26, 148, 155, 157–60, 177
retrenchment, 36, 38, 41, 107–8
Ryerson University, 58, 150

scholarships, 46, 96–7, 105n3, 113, 122, 128, 145
science and technology (S&T), 32, 102, 140, 143–4
Science Council of Canada, 140, 142
sciences (see higher education, universities)
"service university", 27, 140, 142, 193
sessional faculty (see academic labour)
Simon Fraser University, 92, 112, 172n3
"skills gap", 127–8
social sciences (see higher education, universities)
Social Sciences and Humanities Research Council (SSHRC), 125, 127–8, 140, 145, 159
Statistics Canada, 6, 48, 53, 62, 73n4, 81, 85, 88, 91, 102, 109, 127, 149, 152–4
students, 1–2, 4, 6–8, 11–12, 12n1, 14–15, 19–20, 24–6, 33, 35, 37–8, 40–2, 42n2, 43n3, 44–7, 49, 56–7, 59–69, 71–2, 75, 78–85, 87–105, 105n1, 105n3, 106–8, 117–31, 143, 153, 158–9, 174, 179, 182–5, 187–90
international students, 91–2, 128
students as consumers/customers, 4, 26, 72, 75, 78–84, 93, 99, 120, 122–3, 176

student learning, 10, 28, 34, 44–5, 48, 65–8, 71–2, 75–8, 81–4
student aid, 10, 24, 26, 88–9, 93, 95–99, 102, 104
provincial variation, 98–9
student debt, 38, 41, 69, 78, 84, 88, 95–105, 183
student movements (see also corporatization; higher education, universities), 1–2, 19–20, 33, 88, 90, 106, 182–5, 187, 190–1
Quebec student strikes, 1, 88, 183–4
student recruitment, 91–2, 121–3

tar sands, 119, 144
taxation, taxpayers, 37, 93–6, 101, 130, 135–6, 148, 151, 169, 179
education tax credits, 39, 96–9
teaching, universities (see also academic labour), 4–5, 9–12, 18, 28, 40–2, 44–9, 107, 117, 119, 122, 126, 133–4, 139, 142, 173–4, 180, 188
contract faculty teaching, 46, 50–2, 56–57, 59, 61–70, 72–3n6
unity of teaching and research, 44–9
technology transfer (see also intellectual property), 39, 120, 143, 149, 151–2, 154, 163, 192
technology transfer offices, 28, 149–52, 172n3
tenure, 25, 31, 42n2, 45, 64–6, 68–9, 71, 106, 111, 124, 126, 142, 186–7, 193
tenured/tenure track faculty (see academic labour)
Trent University, 56, 58, 71
tuition fees, 1–2, 4, 11, 26, 29, 38–41, 42n2, 75, 78–9, 81–2, 84–101, 105, 105n2, 111, 122, 128, 155, 182–4, 188
provincial variation, 87–9
tuition deregulation, 85, 87, 93, 101, 111
tuition freeze, 87–8, 95, 98

University of Alberta, 41, 112–3, 115,
    119, 129, 144
University of British Columbia, 112–3,
    115, 121, 134, 170, 185
University of Calgary, 47, 109, 112, 122,
    125, 144–5
University of California, 2, 20, 90, 182
University of Guelph, 58, 83, 112, 148,
    172n4
University of King's College, 15
University of Lethbridge, 112, 144
University of Manitoba, 47, 92, 109, 112,
    150, 159
University of Montreal, 41, 73n7, 108
University of Ontario Institute of Technology (UOIT), 58, 71, 133
University of Ottawa, 46, 58, 73n6, 79,
    109, 115, 124–5, 172n4
University of Prince Edward Island, 134,
    73n7
Université du Québec, 23, 109
University of Regina, 43n4, 82, 109, 115,
    122
University of Saskatchewan, 109, 112,
    124, 189
University of Sherbrooke, 73n7
University of Toronto (U of T), 15–16,
    19, 35, 41, 47, 56, 58, 80, 110–2,
    114–5, 122, 129, 133–5, 136, 153,
    172n6
University of Victoria, 14, 112, 172n3
University of Waterloo, 23, 58, 72, 115,
    136, 153
University of Western Ontario, 58, 73n6,
    82, 112, 133
University of Windsor, 58, 71, 92, 110, 149
University of Winnipeg, 62, 73n7, 115

Veblen, Thorstein, 2, 17–18, 76, 176

Wilfrid Laurier University, 59, 136

York University, 47, 49–50, 56–8, 73n6,
    80, 111–2, 115, 124–5, 134, 136,
    180